J. Banks

Letters on Iceland (1772)

J. Banks

Letters on Iceland (1772)

ISBN/EAN: 9783743335110

Manufactured in Europe, USA, Canada, Australia, Japa

Cover: Foto ©ninafisch / pixelio.de

Manufactured and distributed by brebook publishing software (www.brebook.com)

J. Banks

Letters on Iceland (1772)

Cdr. J. Sinkankas USN
June 1955

LETTERS

ON

ICELAND, &c.

ITE, J. BEATTY, F. HIGLY, and P. BYRNE.

M, DCC, LXXX.

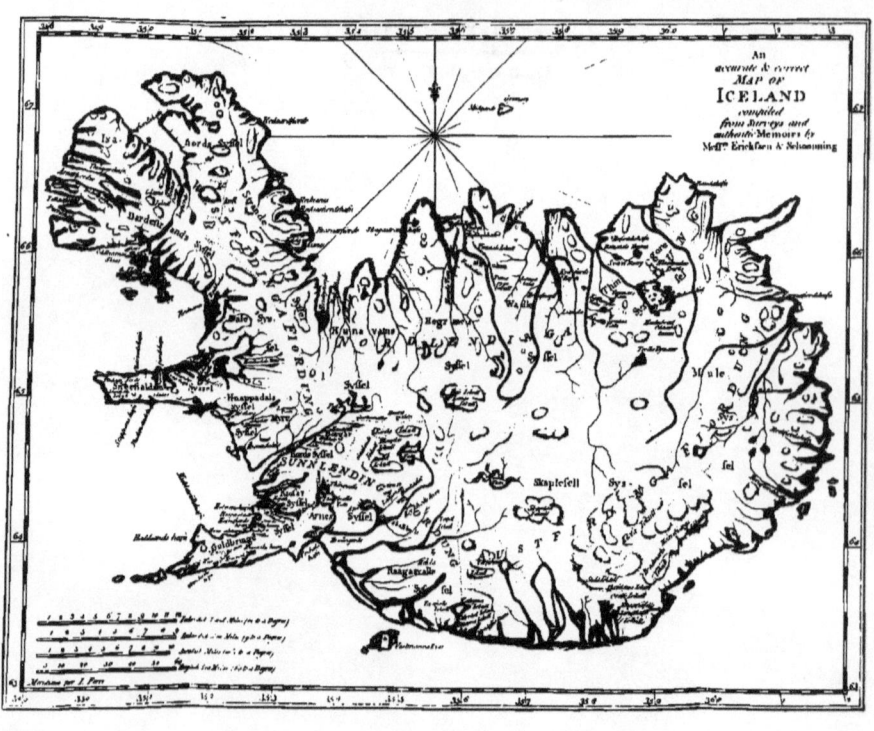

LETTERS
ON
ICELAND:
CONTAINING
OBSERVATIONS
ON THE

Civil, Literary, Ecclesiastical, and Natural History; Antiquities, Volcanos, Basaltes, Hot Springs; Customs, Dress, Manners of the Inhabitants, &c. &c.

MADE,

During a Voyage undertaken in the Year 1772,

By JOSEPH BANKS, Esq. F.R.S.

Assisted by

Dr. SOLANDER, F.R.S. Dr. J. LIND, F.R.S.
Dr. UNO VON TROIL,

And several other Literary and Ingenious GENTLEMEN.

Written by UNO VON TROIL, D.D.

First Chaplain to his Swedish Majesty, Almoner of the Swedish Orders of Knighthood, and Member of the Academy of Sciences at Stockholm.

TO WHICH ARE ADDED

The LETTERS of Dr. IHRE and Dr. BACH to the Author, concerning the Edda and the Elephantiasis of ICELAND:

ALSO,

Professor BERGMAN's Curious Observations and Chemical Examination of the Lava and other Substances produced on the Island.

With a new Map of the Island, and Representation of the remarkable Boiling Fountain called by the Inhabitants GEYSER.

DUBLIN:

PRINTED BY G. PERRIN,

For S. PRICE, W. and H. WHITESTONE, J. POTTS, T. WALKER, C. JENKIN, W. HALLHEAD, J. VALLANCE, L. WHITE, J. BEATTY, P. HIGLY, and P. BYRNE.

M,DCC,LXXX.

CONTENTS.

INTRODUCTION.

LETTER I.
On the Effects of Fire in Iceland.
page 1

LETTER II.
Of Iceland in general 18

LETTER III.
On the Constitution of the Country 36

LETTER IV.
Of the Arrival of the Norwegians, the Government and Laws in Iceland 59

LETTER V.
Concerning Ecclesiastical Affairs in Iceland. - - - 74

LETTER VI.
Of the Character and Manner of Life of the Icelanders - - 83

LETTER VII.
Of the Dreſs of the Icelanders page 94

LETTER VIII.
Of the Houſes and Buildings of the Icelanders - - - 99

LETTER IX.
Of the Food of the Icelanders - 103

LETTER X.
Of the Employment of the Icelanders, and their Chronology 113

LETTER XI.
Of the Diſeaſes of Iceland - 119

LETTER XII.
Of Fiſhing and Fowling, and the Breed of Cattle in Iceland - - 124

LETTER XIII.
Of the Trade of Iceland - 148

LETTER XIV.
Of Icelandic Literature - 153

LETTER XV.
Of Printing in Iceland   page 181

LETTER XVI.
Of the Remains of Antiquity in Iceland - - - 187

LETTER XVII.
Of Icelandic Poetry - 195

LETTER XVIII.
Of the Volcanos in Iceland - 220

LETTER XIX.
The Subject continued - 231

LETTER XX.
Of Mount Heckla - 239

LETTER XXI.
Of the hot spouting Water Springs in Iceland - - - 245

LETTER XXII.
Of the Pillars of Basalt; to which is subjoined Mr. Banks's curious account of the island of Staffa - 266

LETTER XXIII.
From Chev. IHRE to Dr. TROIL—*Concerning the Edda* - page 289

LETTER XXIV.
From Chev. BACH to Dr. TROIL—*Of the Icelandic Elephantiafis* - 319

LETTER XXV.
From Profeffor BERGMAN to Dr. TROIL.—*Of the Effects of Fire both at the Volcanos and the Hot Springs; and also of the Basaltes* - 338

INTRODUCTION.

THE accounts of Iceland, which have hitherto made their appearance in the English language, are of such nature, that it would betray ignorance or partiality to recommend them to the public as satisfactory and faithful.

The first writer of any known history of Iceland in the present century, was John Anderſſon, afterwards Burgomaſter of Hamburgh, who undertook a voyage to this not much-frequented iſland in a Greenland ſhip; but the anthenticity of his performance is far from being ſuch as may be relied on with confidence.

Niels Horrebow, a Daniſh aſtronomer, was ſent to Iceland by the court of Denmark, on purpoſe to contradict, Anderſſon's account; he publiſhed ſome obſervations on Iceland, but from a too great deſire to pleaſe his employers, he fell into the oppoſite error,

error, and paints all his objects with a glow of colouring, that does not exactly correspond with the truth.

In Richer's Continuation of Rollin's History is a history of Iceland, a most pitiful compilation, and full of the grossest errors that ever disgraced the historical page.

Under the authority of the Royal Society of Sciences at Copenhagen, Eggert Olafsen and Biarne Povelsen, two men of learning, natives of Iceland, and residing in the country, travelled all over that island, and gave, in two volumes in quarto, a faithful and ample account of all that deserves the attention of the learned and curious, illustrated by numerous engravings: but though the performance is accurate and circumstantial, yet it is unfortunately clogged with repetitions, and the facts are recounted in so tedious and uninteresting a manner, that it requires a most phlegmatic temper, and a large fund of patience, to go through the whole of this work, for it is filled with a long and dull recital of events, methodized in the most

moſt formal manner poſſible. It can therefore by no means be thought ſuperfluous, that Dr. Von Troil has favoured the literary world with his inteteresting Letters on Iceland; a work which on account of its varied matter, and the great learning diſplayed every where for the inſtruction of the curious reader, deſerves the warmeſt approbation of the public.

Men of talents and learning will, we flatter ourſelves, think highly of this preſent performance by Dr. Von Troil, though perhaps it may be ſometimes a little deficient in point of language.

The preſent tranſlation has been made from the laſt German edition, publiſhed by Meſſrs. Troil and Bergman, with numerous additions and corrections; and tho' it is not oſtentatiouſly recommended to the public for any elegance or accuracy of ſtyle, it may however be ſafely ſtated as a faithful tranſlation from the original, and a work of real merit and utility.

We leave it to the unprejudiced reader to form a judgment of this performance, which is replete with variety of matter, treated on in an inſtructive and ſatisfactory manner; and likewiſe on the great learning relative to natural hiſtory, hiſtorical, antiquarian, and philological ſubjects, which are every where blended in the context of the following letters; and we are of opinion, that in reſpect to theſe points, this work requires no apology for offering it to the impartial public.

As to its utility, it will not be unneceſſary to prefix a few obſervations on the importance of Icelandic literature.

The Engliſh language was originally ſo nearly related to that of Iceland, that we need only caſt our eyes on a gloſſary, to ſee the affinity of both languages, and the great light the one receives from the other.

The Normans and Danes, who were during a conſiderable time maſters of England, introduced into it many cuſtoms, cuftoms, laws, and manners, which would remain inexplicable; but the Icelanders being originally defcended from the fame Normans, and living on an ifland which has very little intercourfe with the reft of the world, have preferved their language, manners, and laws in their primitive fimplicity; nay, all the hiftorical accounts of the North are contained in the hiftorical fayings *(fagas)* of the Icelanders, which are very numerous, and would be of very important fervice in the inveftigation of the origin of the language, manners, and laws of England. Nor can it be advanced that this kind of ftudy could not be purfued amongft us for want of thefe hiftorical monuments of the Icelanders; fince by the known indefatigable zeal for the promotion of all branches of literature, and the moft difinterefted generofity of Jofeph Banks, Efq. P. R. S. one hundred and fixty-two Icelandic manufcripts have been prefented to and are depofited in the Britifh Mufeum.

The history of the northern nations, their divinities, religion, principles, and tenets, together with their poetry, present the philosophic reader with subjects worthy of his speculation; they at the same time account for many historical events, and for many a curious custom preserved by some one or other of the nations descended from the same root with these inhabitants of the north.

The subject of volcanos, and of the origin of certain kinds of stones and fossils, have of late attracted the attention of philosophers; but in my opinion, they are no where treated with so much candour, truth, and philosophical precision as in those remarks which the Chevalier Torbern Bergman sent to our author in form of a letter, and which he has here communicated to the public.

The whole island of Iceland is a chain of volcanos, the soil almost every where formed of decayed cinders, lava, and flags; and the numerous hot springs, especially that called *Geyser*, give full scope to the most curious

curious remarks on thefe fubjects, fince they are here obvious in fo many varied fhapes, and for that reafon become inftructive. Lava and fome other productions of nature have not been hitherto fubjected to chemical proceffes: profeffor Bergman therefore deferves the thanks of the public for his excellent letter, giving a very interefting account of his experiments on all the various foffils and natural productions of Iceland. The origin of bafaltic pillars, fuch as form the Giant's Caufeway in Ireland, the whole ifland of Staffa, and more efpecially Fingal's Cave, has of late been much fpoken of by travellers and learned mineralogifts. Some afcribe their regular configuration to cryftallization: others pretend the fubterraneous fire to be the caufe of their regular columnar fhape; but the ingenious Chevalier Torbern Bergman proves by the moft folid arguments, that the bafalt pillars are no lava, or any ways related to volcanic fubftances, and that their regular columnar fhape, he fuggefts, is owing to another,

ther cause, and by his reasoning renders it highly probable.

We are at the same time presented with a view of the *primitive earths*, that originally compound all earthy and stony bodies hitherto discovered on the surface of our globe; and their characters are here also set forth in the most easy and obvious manner by experiments.

This great and interesting circumstance alone would be sufficient to recommend the present performance to the perusal of chemists, mineralogists, and philosophers.

The letter of the Archiater Bach to Dr. Troil on the diseases of Iceland, contains the most curious and interesting observations for the use of medical gentlemen. In short, there is scarcely a class of readers who will not find instruction and entertainment in the ingenious performance of Dr. Uno Von Troil, the author of this book.

He is a Swede by birth, and descended of a noble family: his father, Samuel Von Troil, was archbishop of Upsal.

After

After having ſtudied divinity, the oriental and northern languages and antiquities, together with the various branches of natural philoſophy, he travelled, and viſited Germany, France, England, and Holland.

During his ſtay in England he was introduced to Mr. Banks, who was then returned from his voyage round the world, and preparing to go on a ſecond; but that not taking place, he was prompted to make a ſhort excurſion towards the Weſtern Iſlands and Iceland; and eaſily prevailed upon Dr. Von Troil to accompany him on this literary voyage.

After the return of Dr. Von Troil, he wrote letters to ſeveral learned men in his own country, eminent in the various profeſſions and branches of literature and ſcience, on the different matters he had obſerved in Iceland during his voyage; they were at firſt only intended to ſatisfy the ſolicitations and curioſity of his friends, who wiſhed to be made acquainted with whatever he had diſcovered worthy the notice of a

literary

literary man, and that might likewife bid fair to afford amufement.

The fenator Charles Count Schetfer, a man of a benevolent character, and who patronizes learning in all its branches, together with its profeffors, folicited our author to communicate them to the public: in compliance with which, they were publifhed at Upfal in 1777 in octavo; and the next year after they appeared at the fame place tranflated into German, very much enlarged with additions of the author and alfo of Chevalier Bergman.

Dr. Von Troil has for his talents, learning, and character been promoted in his native country to feveral places of honour and emolument, fo that he may now be confidered as the firft man in Sweden in point of eminence in the ecclefiaftical line, and in point of learning inferior to none: he has taken his degree of doctor of divinity, is principal chaplain to the king, prefident of the confiftory, rector of the great church of Stockholm, and prelate of all the Swedifh orders of knighthood.

Thefe

These cursory hints were thought necessary for ushering his Letters on Iceland into the literary world; the public will, no doubt, be curious to know the particular observations made by a learned man on an island that Mr. Banks, one of the first characters of this country, thought deserving a nearer inspection by a voyage he undertook at a great expense, accompanied by several learned and ingenious men.

For the information of those who wish to be acquainted with all the publications that have appeared, to treat either at large of Iceland, or examine some of its particular objects, we have here subjoined a very curious and complete catalogue of them.

CATALOGUE of Writers on ICELAND.

1. JOACHIM Leo wrote some verses on Iceland in the German language, full of errors. There are four editions of them. Arngrim Jonæ, in his Commentario de Islandia, quotes the edition of 1561.
2. Jacobi Ziegleri Scondia seu Descriptio Groenlandiæ, Islandiæ, Norvegiæ, & Sueciæ. Francofurti 1575.
3. Jonsbogen (i. e. Jonsbook, an old book of laws) Hoolum (in Iceland.) 1578. 8vo. and several editions subsequent to it.
4. Arngrim Jonæ brevis commentarius de Islandia. Hoolum 1592. 8vo. and Hafn. 1593. 8vo.
5. Fjusd. Crymogæa seu rerum Islandicarum libri tres Hamburg. 1609, 1610, 1614, 1618, 1620, and 1630.
6. Blefkenii Islandia s. populorum et mirabilium, quæ in ea insula reperiuntur, accurata descriptio. Ludg. Batav. 1607. 8vo.
7. Arngrim Jonæ Anatome Blefkeniana. Hoolum 1612. 8vo. and Hamburg 1613. 4to.
8. Dan Fabritius de Islandia & Groenlandia. Rostock 1616. 8vo.
9. Arngrim Jonæ epistola pro patria defensoria. Hamburg 1618. 4to. written in opposition to the preceding book.
10. Arngrim Jonæ Apotribe calumniæ. Hamburg. 1622.
11. De regno Daniæ & Norvegiæ insulisque adjacentibus, tractatus varii collecti a Stephano Stephanio. Ludg. Batav. 1629. 12mo. from whence the part concerning Iceland is taken out, and printed separately with the title.
12. Islandicæ gentis primordia & vetus republica. Lugd. Bat. 1629. 12mo.
13. Arngrim Jonæ Athanasia Gudbrandiana. Hamburg 1630.

14 Peder

14 Peder Clauſſon's Norriges og omliggende öars Beſk‑ rifvelſc. Kiöb. 1632. 4to. and Kiöb 1637. 8vo.
15 Arngrim Jonæ ſpecimen Iſlandiæ hiſt & magna ex parte chorographicum. Amſt. 1643.
16 La Peyrere Relation de l'Iſlande, in a letter to Mr. de la Motte Vayer, dated 18 Dec. 1644. Is inſerted in the Reccuil des Voyages au Nord, tom. I. Amſt. 1715. 8vo.
17 Wolfii Norrigia illuſtrata. Hafn. 1651. 8vo. and 4to.
18 Wolffii Norriges, Iſlands og Grönlands Beſkrifvelſc. Kiöbhafn. 1651. 4to.
19 Hieronym. Megiſeri Septentrio Nov‑antiquus, ſive die neue Nord‑welt Iſland, Groenland, &c. Leipz. 1653. 12mo.
20 Edda Iſlandorum A. C. 1215, per Snorronem Sturlæ iſlandice conſcripta, iſlandice, danice & latine edita, opera P. J. Reſenii. Hafn 1665. 4to.
together with
21 Philoſophia antiquiſſima Norvego‑danica dicta Voluſpa, quæ eſt pars Eddæ Sæmundi, primum publici juris facta a P. J. Reſenio. Hafn. 1665.
together with
22 Ethica Odini, pars Eddæ Sæmundi, vocata Haaramal, edita per P. J. Reſenium. Hafn 1665.
23 Theod. Thorlacci diſſ. chorographica hiſtorica de Iſlandia, præs. Ægid. Strauch. Wittent 1666 and 1670. 4to. item 1690. 4to.
24 Erici Bartholini experimenta Chriſtalli Iſlandici diſdiaclaſtici. Hafn. 1669. 4to.
25 Voluſpa. Kiöbenhavn. 1673. 4to.
26 Martiniere neue Reiſe in die nordiſchen Landſchaften. Hamb. 1675. 4to. Tranſlated from the Engliſh. There is likewiſe a French edition. Paris 1682.
27 Aræ Multiſtii Schedæ. Skalholt 1688. 4to. Oxford 1696. Kiöb. 1733. 4to.
28 Landnama Bok. Skalhot 1688. 4to. Is likewiſe publiſhed at Copenhagen, with a Latin tranſlation,

notes,

notes, and several indexes. Islands Landnama-Bok, h. e. Liber originum Islandiæ. Editio novissima, ex manuscriptis Magnæanis sumptibus perill. Suhmii. Havn. 1774. 4to.

29 Gahm de ratione anni solaris apud veteres Islandos. This memoir is printed at the end of Aræ Schedæ, in the Copenhagen edition.

30 Thordr Thorlaks Diss. de ultimo montis Hecklæ in Islandia incendio, Hafn. 1694.

31 Gahm de prima religionis in Islandia fundatione. Hafn. 1696.

32 Description du Nord. 1698. 12mo.

33 Niewe beschryvinge van Spitsbergen, Island, Groenland end de beygelegen Eylanden.

34 Einar Thorst. vita. Hafn. 1700.

35 Reise nach Norden, worinneu die sitten, Lebensarten and Aberglauben der Norweger———and Islander accurat beschrieben werden. Leipz. 1711. 12mo.

36 Blefkenii Historie van Lap-and Finland, hier is by gevoegt de beschryving van Is-en Groenland. Leuvarden 1716. 8vo.

37 Vetterften de Poesi Scaldorum Septentrionalium. Upsal. 1717. 8vo.

38 Relation om det foerskrekkelige Vandfall og exundation af Bierget Katlegiaa paa Island 1721. Copenhagen 1727. 4to.

39 Kort berættelse on berget Krabla paa Island, samt audre Dernefs intil grantsande Berg, Hwilka nyligen begynt at inspruta eld och brinna. This account of the burning of the mount Krabla was printed probably in the year 1727, at Stockholm, on four pages in 8vo.

40 Benedict Thorstenson essterrettning om den jordbrand som 1724 og folgende Aar i Bierget Krafla og de dar omkring liggende Herreder har grasseret. Kiöbenhafn 1726. 8vo.

41 Olavi O. Nording Diss. de Eddis Islandicis. Upsal. 1735. 4to. Mr. Oelrichs at Bremen has reprinted

this

this Diff. in his Opufculis Daniæ & Sueciæ litteratæ, tom. I. 1774.
42 Joh. Dav. Koehler prolufio de Scaldis feu poetis gentium arctoarum. Altdorf 1738. 4to.
43 Er. Jul. Biörner, Inledning til de Hiwerborna Goeters gamla Hafder far deles gotifka fprakets Forman och Sagornas Kanned om. feu, Introductio in Antiquitates Hyperboreo-Gothicas. Stockholm 1738. fol.
44 Ejufd. tractatus de Varegis heroibus Scandianis. Stockholm 1743. 4to.
45 Lackmannus de computatione annorum per hyemes prifcis gentibus hyperboreis ufitata. Kiel 1744. 4to.
46 De Yfverborna Atlingars Lara—Hyperboreorum Atlandiorum feu Suiogotorum et Nordmandorum Edda, hoc eft Atavia, feu fons gentilis illorum & Theologiæ & Philofophiæ. Iam demum verfione Suinonica donata accedente latina—ad MS. quod poffidet Bibliotheca Upfalienfis—opera Joh. Corffon. Upf. 1746. 4to. This edition of the Edda was not finifhed.
47 Iflanfka taxan. Hoolum 1746. 4to.
48 John Anderflon Nachrichten von Ifland, Groenanland, und der Straffe David. Hamb. 1746. It appeared likewife tranflated into the Danifh language Copenh. 1748. A French tranflation has likewife been publifhed by Mr. Sellius, 1751. 12mo. 2 vols.
49 Octroy foer det Iflandfke Societet. Kiöb. 1747. 8vo.
50 Avertiffement om Anderffons Tractat om Ifland. Kiöb. 1748. 8vo.
51 Joh. Thorkelffons tillgift til Anderffon om Ifland. Kiöb. 1748. 8vo.
52 Eggerhard Olavius Enarrationes hiftoricæ de Iflandiæ natura & conftitutione. Hafn. 1749. 8vo.
53 Ejufd. Diff. de ortu & progreffu circa ignem Iflandiæ fubterraneum. Hafn. 1749. 4to.

Biarni

54 Biarni Pauli Obfervationes de alga faccharifera maris Iflandici. Hafn. 1749. 8vo.
55 Arnae Oddef. vita, inferted in the Nova literaria. Hafn. anni 1750.
56 De Gamla Normanners Patriarkalifka Lara pa Swenfka och Lat. af Joh. Goorahffon. Stockholm 1750. 4to.
57 Olai Wormii Epiftolæ. Hafn. 1751. 2 vols. 8vo.
58 Tilforladeliga efterretningar om Ifland med ett nytt Landkort, og 2 Aars metereologifka Obfervationer af Niels Horrebow. Kiöb. 1750. 8vo. This performance is likewife tranflated into German 1752. 8vo. and into Englifh.
59 Specimen Iflandiæ non barbaræ, in nouvellis literariis Hafnienfibus 1752.
60 Nachrichten von Ifland, a fhort abftract of Horrebow's book inferted in a periodical paper called Beytragen zum Nutzen und Vergnugen. Greifswald 1753. 4to.
61 Erici tentamen de nominibus & cognominibus Septentrionalium. Hafn. 1753. 8vo.
62 Th. Nicolai de commeatu Iflandorum navali. 1753. 8vo.
63 Svein Solvefen Tyro Juris Iflandicus. Kiöb. 1754. 8vo.
64 Vidalins Bref til Jon Arnefen de jure patronatus Iflandorum, tranflated into Danifh, and publifhed by Magnus Ketilfon.
65 Differtatiuncula de montibus Iflandiæ cryftallinis, auct. Theodr Torkelli I. Vidalino, fcholæ Skalholtenfis eo tempore Rectore. Tranflated from the Latin MS. into German, and publifhed in the Hamburg Magazine, volume XIII. Nº I. and II. 1754. 8vo.
66 Difquifitiones duæ hifloricæ antiquariæ. Prior de veterum Septentrionalium, imprimis Iflandorum peregrinationibus; pofterior de Philippia feu amoris equini apud prifcos boreales caufis—per Joh. Erici. Lipf. 1755. 8vo. The firft is tranflated

into

into German, and inferted into Schlozer's Northern Hiftory. 1771. p. 556.
67 Fjuld. Specimen Obfervationum ad antiquitates Septentrional.
68 Ejufd. Commentarius de expofitione infantum ad veteres Septentrionales.
69 Introduction à l'Hiftoire de Dannemark, par Mr. Mallet, à Copenh. 1755. 4to. to which a tranflation of the Edda is prefixed. The fame is tranflated into Englifh, 2 vols. 8vo. and into German, Greifswald 1765. 4to.
70 Joh. Snorronis de Agriculturâ Iflandorum. Hafn. 1757. 8vo.
71 Hald Jacobfens efterretningar om de i Ifland ildfprudende Bierge. Kiöb. 1757. 8vo.
72 Ol. Eigilfon's Berettnelfe om de tyrkifke Soerovere i. Ifland. Kioeb. 1757. 8vo.
73 Nic. Pet. Sibbern idea hiftoriæ litterariæ Iflandorum in Dreyer's Monumenta anecdota. I Tom. Lubecæ 1760. 4to.
74 Balle oekonomifka Tanker ofwer Ifland til hoyere betankning. Kiöb. 1760, 1761. 2 vols. 8vo.
75 Joh. Finnæus tentamen hiftorico-philologicum circa Norvegiæ jus ecclefiafticum prifcum, and
76 Ejufd. Curæ pofteriores in hoc jus. Hafn. 1762 and 1765. 4to.
77 Thorften Nicol. de commeatu veterum Iflandorum reftituendo. Hafn. 1762. 8vo.
78 Joh. Arnefpn Inledning til den gamle og nya Iflandfke Rattegaang, udgiven af I. Erichfen. Kiöb. 1962. 4to.
79 Ioach. Stechau de fide hiftorica monumentor. Iflandic. Lund. 1763.
80 Five pieces of Runic poetry, tranflated from the Icelandic language. London 1763. 8vo.
81 M. Olafsen's foerfoeg til Landrafenets forbedring i Ifland. Kiöb. 1765. 8vo.
82 Ejufd. Anmarkningar till Jons boks Danfka ofwerfattelfe. Kiöb. 1765. 8vo.

83 Egil Thorhallfens forfwar for fin ofwerfattelfe. Kiöb. 1765. 8vo.
84 H. Finnfen efterettning om tilgragelferne vid Bierget Hekla udi Ifland i April og foljende manader. Kireb. 1767.
85 Olavii Syntagma de Baptifmo veterum. Hafn 1769. 4to.
86 Breve om Agerdyrknings muelighed i Ifland fra Hans Finnfen 1769 and 1772.
87 Joh. Peterfen om den faa Kallade Iflandfke fkiorbiugg. Soroe 1769. 8vo.
88 Erichfen om Iflands up Komft. Kioebenhbafn 1770. 4to.
89 Skuli Magnuffon um thann Iflenfka Garnfpuna. Kiöb. 8vo.
90 Ol. Olafsens Iflanfk Urtagaards bok. Kioeb. 1770. 8vo.
91 Thor Oddefons tanker om akurdyrkin paa Ifland. Kiöb. 1771. 8vo.
92 Iuel Norrlands Trompet.
93 Martefeld om Iflands Huufholding med fedhe vahre og Hamborgs Kiodrogning. Kiöb. 1771. 8vo.
94 Ol. Olfon um fifki-veidar og fifki-nettan. Kiöb. 1771. 12mo.
95 Upartifke tanker om det Iflandfke Handels-Kompagnie og dets farende Kiobmand. Kiöb. 1771.
96 Anmerkningar oever Compagniets Handel paa Ifland. Kiöb. 1771.
97 Lud. Harboe Tuende of handlingar om reformationen i Ifland.
98 Ejufd. Hiftory of the Iflandic tranflation of the Bible.
99 Finnei Johannæi, Fpifcopi Diocefeos Skalholtinæ in Iflandia. Hiftoria Lcclefiaftica Iflandiæ. T. I. II. III. Hafn. 1772 & 1775.
100 Ion Olffon om den Iflandfke Handel. Kiöb. 1772. 8vo.
101 Bref til Hr. Cancellie Radet Lagerbring rorande then Iflandfka Epda (by Chevalier Ihre). Stock. 1772. 8vo.

102 Relation d'un Voyage dans la Mer du Nord par de Kerguelen de Tremarec. Amfterdam 1772. 4to.
103 Eggert Olafsens og Biarne Povelfens Riefe igienem Ifland, 2 vols. Soroe 1772. 4to. It appeared likewife tranflated into German. Leipz. 1774. & 1775. 4to. 2 vols
104 Steph. Thorafens de homicidis fecundum leges Iflandorum antiquas. P. I. Hafn. 1773.
105 Kriftni Saga, S. Hiftoria Religionis Chriftianæ in Iflandiam introductæ, nec non: Thattr af Ifleif Bifkupi, f. narratio de Ifleifo Epifcopo—cum interpretatione latina, notis, &c. Hafn. 1773. 8vo.
106 Iflandifche Literatur und Gefchichete. Erfter Theil. Goettingen 1773. 8vo. The ingenious Prof. Schlozer at Gottingen is the author.
107 Iflandifche Zeitungen. Thefe newfpapers were publifhed in Iceland in the year 1775.
108 Bualagen. Hrappfej 1775.
109 Biörn a Skardzaa Annalar Hrappfej. 1774 and 1775. 4to. 2 vols. Thefe annals contain the hiftory from 1400 to 1645; and are publifhed with a Latin tranflation: Annales Biörnis a Skardfa. Ex manufcriptis inter fe collatis cum interpretatione Latina, variantibus lectionibus, notis & indice.
110 Kriftin-rettr hinn gamli—Jus Ecclefiafticum vetus f. Thorlacco-Kettilianum conftitutum, A. C. 1123, Iflandice & Latine, edit Grimus Joh. Thorkelin. Hafn. 1775.
111 Berattelfe om den Iflandfke farfkiotfeln, upfatt af Theod. Thoroddi. Thefe obfervations appeared tranflated into Swedifh by Mr. Barchaus, in the Journal of hufbandry 1776, the month of November. Stockh.
112 Vorlaufender Bericht und zugleich die Vorrede von der alten und raren Iflandifchen Edda, fo uber 700 Jahr und daruber in Norden bifher

uner-

unerklarbar verfteckt gelegen. Stettin 1776. 4to. Its author is Mr. Schimmelmann of Stettin, who likewife had printed in 1774; Abhandlung abgefaſſt in einem Schreiben an einen Gelehrten von der alten Iſlandiſchen Edda. 4to.

113 Sven Sölvefen Iſlandiſke Jus criminale. Kiöb. 1776. 8vo.

114 Iſlandiſche Merkwurdigkeiten, in a periodical paper called Mannichfaltigkeiten, firſt year fecond quarter. Berlin 1777. 8vo.

115 Sciagraphia Hiſtoriæ litterariæ Iſlandiæ, auctorum & fcriptorum tum editorum tum ineditorum indicem exibens, cuivis delineandæ periculum fecit Haldanus Einari, Ph. Mag. & Rector Scholæ Cathedr. Holenſis. Holmiæ 1777. 8vo.

116 Modern Hiſtory of the Polar Regions. The firſt part is to be met with in Richers's Modern Hiſtory or Continuation to Rollins's Antient Hiſtory, Vol. XXVII. Berlin 1778. 8vo.

117 Diſſ. inauguralis de Lichene Iſlandico, Præſ. Trommſdorff. Reſp. Reiſſe. Erfurth. 1778.

118 Die Iſlandiſche Edda. Das iſt: die geheime Gotteslehre der ælteſten Hyperboraer—im Jahr. 1070—1075, aus alten runiſthen Schriften edirt von Samund Froden, hiernæchſt im Jahr. 1664, durch Refen, und nun in die hochtentſche Sprache mit einem Verſuch zur rechten Erklarung uberſezt und edirt von J. Schimmelmann. Stettin. 1778. 4to.

119 Bref rærande en Refa til Iſland 1772. Upſala. 1777. 8vo. and tranſlated into German by Joh. George Pet. Moeller. Upſala and Leipz. 1779. 8vo. The work which is now here appears tranſlated into Engliſh.

120 Joh. Theod. Phil. Chriſt. Ebeling de Quaſſia & Lichene Iſlandico. Glaſgoæ. 1779. 8vo.

This Catalogue contains all the writers of any conſequence on Iceland, or on matters any way relative to, or concerning that country.

LETTERS on ICELAND.

*LETTER I.

To Professor BERGMAN.

On the Effects of Fire in Iceland.

SIR,

SINCE I am happily returned from a very pleasant summer's excursion through the western islands of Scotland, to Iceland and the Orkneys, it is with peculiar pleasure that I take this opportunity of assuring you of my esteem and friendship. It is probably not unknown to you, that Mr. Banks and Dr. Solander have been disagreeably disappointed when they were on the point of setting out on a new voyage round the world last summer. How-

---

* This letter was first published in the year 1773, in the Upsala newspapers, N° 3, 4, 6, and 8.

ever, in order to keep together and employ the draughtsmen and other persons whom they had engaged for their voyage to the South-Sea, they resolved upon another excursion. It was impossible to chuse a better one than that to Iceland; and you may easily conceive, Sir, that though I was ready to set out on my return to Sweden, I did not hesitate a moment in accepting their offer to accompany them. To say the truth, I was glad to visit a country where I could not alone hope to find many remains of our ancient language, but where I was certain to see nature in a new point of view.

I have not been disappointed in either of my expectations; and I could never have found a happier opportunity than that of making this voyage in the company of Mr. Banks and Dr. Solander, of whom it would be unnecessary to say one word more, as they are both known so well to you, and to the learned and ingenious throughout Europe.

I know, Sir, that every information will be welcome to you, which concerns

cerns thofe objects that attracted my attention there; and there is no one who would communicate this information to you with more pleafure than myfelf; but as it would require too much prolixity to mention every thing, I fhall only in this letter fpeak of the principal operations of fire in Iceland, a fubject which, I am convinced, is one of the moft important.

On our arrival in Iceland on the 28th of Auguft 1772, we directly faw a profpect before us, which though not pleafing, was uncommon and furprizing. Whatever prefented itfelf to our view bore the marks of devaftation; and our eyes, accuftomed to behold the pleafing coafts of England, now faw nothing but the veftiges of the operation of a fire, heaven knows how ancient!

The defcription of a country, where quite clofe to the fea you perceive almoft nothing but fharp cliff's vitrified by fire, and where the eye lofes itfelf in high rocky mountains covered with eternal fnow, cannot poffibly produce fuch emotions as at firft fight might

entirely

entirely prepoſſeſs the thinking ſpectator. It is true, beauty is pleaſing both to our eyes and our thoughts; but gigantic nature often makes the moſt laſting impreſſions.

We caſt anchor not far from Beſſeſtedr, the dwelling-place of the celebrated Stourleſon, where we found two tracts of lava, called *Gorde* and *Hualeyre-Hraun* (for what we and the Italians call Lava, is called in Iceland *Hraun*, from *Hrinna*, to flow) of which particularly the laſt was remarkable, ſince we found there beſides a whole field covered with lava, which muſt have been liquid in the higheſt degree, and whole mountains of turf. Chance had directed us exactly to a ſpot on which we could better, than on any other part of Iceland, conſider the operations of a fire which had laid waſte a ſtretch of ten or twelve miles.*

* The miles mentioned by Dr. Troil are always Swediſh, ten and a half of which are equal to a degree on one of the great circles of the globe; and therefore one Swediſh mile is nearly equal to ſix Engliſh ſtatute miles. Ten or twelve miles are 60 or 72 Engliſh miles.

We spent several days here, in examining every thing with so much the more pleasure, since we found ourselves, as it were, in a new world.

We had now seen almost all the effects of a volcano, except the crater, from which the fire had proceeded: in order therefore to examine this likewise, we undertook a journey of twelve days to mount Heckla itself; we travelled fifty or sixty miles * over an uninterrupted track of lava, and had at last the pleasure of being the first who ever reached the summit of this celebrated volcano. The cause that no one has been there before, is partly founded in superstition, and partly in the extreme difficulty of the ascent, before the last discharge of fire. There was not one in our company who did not wish to have his cloaths a little singed, only for the sake of seeing Heckla in a blaze; and we almost flattered ourselves with this hope, since the Bishop of Skalholt had informed us

* Three hundred or three hundred and sixty English miles.

by letter, in the night between the 5th and 6th of September, the day before our arrival, flames had proceeded from it; but now the mountain was more quiet than we wifhed. We however paffed our time very agreeably, from one o'clock in the night till two next day, in vifiting the mountain. We were even fo happy, that the clouds which covered the greateft part of it difperfed towards evening, and procured us the moft extenfive profpect imaginable. The mountain is fomething above five thoufand feet high, and feparates at the top into three points, of which that in the middle is the higheft. The moft inconfiderable part of the mountain confifts of lava, the reft are afhes, with hard, folid ftones thrown from the craters, together with fome pumice-ftones, of which we found only a fmall piece, with a little native fulphur. A defcription of the various kinds of ftones that are to be found here, would be too prolix, and partly unintelligible; and I fo much the more willingly omit it, as I hope to fatisfy your curiofity, as

foon

soon as the collection I made of them arrives in Sweden.

Amongst many other openings, four were peculiarly remarkable; the first, the lava of which had taken the form of chimney-stacks half broken down; another, from which water had streamed; a third, all the stones of which were red as brick; and lastly, one from which the lava had burst forth in a stream, which was divided at some distance into three arms. I have said before, that we were not so happy to see Heckla throw up fire; but there were sufficient traces of its burning inwardly; for on the upper half of it, covered over with four or five inches deep of snow, we frequently observed spots without any snow; and on the highest point, where Fahrenheit's thermometer was at 24° in the air, it rose to 153° when it was set down on the ground; and in some little holes it was so hot that we could no longer observe the heat with a small pocket thermometer. It is not known whether, since the year 1693, Heckla has been burning till 1766, when it began to throw up flames

flames on the firſt of April, and was burning for a long while, and deſtroyed the country many miles around. Laſt December ſome flames likewiſe proceeded from it; and the people in the neighbourhood believe it will begin to burn again very ſoon, as they pretend to have obſerved, that the rivers thereabouts are drying up. It is believed that this proceeds from the mountain's attracting the water, and is conſidered as a certain ſign of an impending eruption Beſides this, the mountains of Myvatn and Kattlegia are known in this century, on account of the violent inflammations of the former, between the years 1730 and 1740, and the latter in 1756.

But permit me, Sir, to omit a farther account of the volcano at this time *, in order to ſpeak of another effect of the fire, which is much finer, and as wonderful as the firſt, and ſo muſt be the more remarkable, as there is not in

---

* Dr. Troil treats more at large of the Icelandic volcanoes in his 18th and 19th letters; and in the 20th, he ſpeaks more particularly of mount Heckla.

any

any part of the known world any thing which refembles it; I mean the hot fprings of water which abound in Iceland †.

They have different degrees of warmth, and are on that account divided by the inhabitants themfelves into *laugar*, warm baths, and *huerer*, or jets d'eaux; the firft are found in feveral other parts of Europe, though I do not believe that they are even employed to the fame purpofes in any other place: that is to fay, the inhabitants do not bathe in them here merely for their health, but they are likewife the occafion for a fcene of gallantry. Poverty prevents here the lover from making prefents to his fair one, and nature prefents no flowers of which elfewhere garlands are made: it is therefore cuftomary, that inftead of all this, the fwain perfectly cleanfes one of thefe baths, which is afterwards honoured with the vifits of his bride. The other kind of fprings mentioned above deferves more attention. I

---

† The 21ft letter treats more fully of the hot fprings in Iceland.

have

have feen a great number of them; but will only fay fomething of three of the moſt remarkable. Near Laugervatn, a fmall lake of about a mile in circumference, which is about two days journey diſtant from Heckla, I faw the firſt hot jet d'eau; and I muſt confefs that it was one of the moſt beautiful fights I ever beheld. The morning was uncommonly clear, and the fun had already begun to gild the tops of the neighbouring mountains; it was fo perfect a calm, that the lake on which fome fwans were fwimming was as fmooth as a looking-glafs; and round about it arofe, in eight different places, the ſteam of the hot fprings, which loſt itfelf high in the air.

Water was fpouting from all thefe fprings; but one in particular continually threw up a column from 18 to 24 feet high, and from 6 to 8 feet diameter the water was extremely hot. A piece of mutton, and fome falmon trouts, we boiled in it; as likewife a ptarmigan, which was almoſt boiled to pieces in fix minutes, and taſted excellently. I wifh it was in my power,

Sir,

Sir, to give you such a description of this place as it deserves; but I fear mine would always remain inferior in point of expression. So much is certain, at least, nature never drew from any one a more chearful homage to her great Creator than I here paid him.

At Reikum was another spout of the same sort; the water of which, I was assured, rose to 60 or 70 feet perpendicular height some years ago; but a fall of earth having almost covered the whole opening, it now only spouted between 54 and 60 feet sideways. We found a great many petrefied leaves in this place, as likewise some native sulphur, of which too the water had a much stronger taste than any where else.

I have reserved the most remarkable water-spout for the end; the description of which will appear as incredible to you as it did to me, could I not assure you that it is all perfectly true, as I would not aver any thing but what I have seen myself. At Geyser, not far from Skallholt, one of the episcopal sees in Iceland, a most extraordinary

dinary large jet d'eau is to be seen, with which the celebrated water-works at Marley and St. Cloud, and at Gaffel, and Herrenhausen, near Hanover, can hardly be compared. One sees here, within the circumference of half a mile *, forty or fifty boiling springs together, which, I believe, all proceed from one and the same reservoir. In some the water is perfectly clear, in others thick and clayey; in some, where it passes through a fine ochre, it is tinged red as scarlet; and in others, where it flows over a paler clay, it is white as milk.

The water spouts up from all, from some continually, from others only at intervals. The largest spring, which is in the middle, engaged our attention particularly the whole day, which we spent here from six in the morning till seven at night. The aperture through which the water arose, and the depth of which I cannot determine, was nineteen feet in diameter; round the top of it is a bason, which,

* About three English miles.

together

together with the pipe, has the form of a cauldron; the margin of the bason is upwards of nine feet one inch higher than the conduit, and its diameter is of fifty-fix feet. Here the water does not fpout continually, but only by intervals feveral times a day; and as I was informed by the people in the neighbourhood, in bad rainy weather, higher than at other times.

On the day that we were there, the water fpouted at ten different times, from fix in the morning till eleven A. M. each time, to the height of between five and ten fathoms; till then the water had not rifen above the margin of the pipe, but now it began by degrees to fill the upper bafon, and at laft ran over. The people who were with us told us, that the water would foon fpout up much higher than it had till then done, and this appeared very credible to us. To determine its height therefore, with the utmoft accuracy, Dr. Lind, who had accompanied us on this voyage in the capacity of an aftronomer, fet up his quadrant.

Soon

Soon after four o'clock we obferved that the earth began to tremble in three different places, as likewife the top of a mountain, which was about three hundred fathoms diftant from the mouth of the fpring. We alfo frequently heard a fubterraneous noife like the difcharge of a cannon; and immediately after a column of water fpouted from the opening, which at a great height divided itfelf into feveral rays, and according to the obfervations made with the quadrant, was ninety-two feet high. Our great furprize at this uncommon force of the air and fire was yet increafed, when many ftones, which we had thrown into the aperture, were thrown up with the fpouting water. You can eafily conceive, Sir, with how much pleafure we fpent the day here; and indeed I am not much furprized, that a people fo much inclined to fuperftition as the Icelanders are, imagine this to be the entrance of hell; for this reafon they feldom pafs one of thefe openings without fpitting into it; and, as they fay, *uti fandens mun,* into the devil's mouth.

But

But I think it is time to finish my long letter, and I will only try your patience with one thing more, which likewise deserves to be better known. Natural historians always observed those large remarkable pillars, which the hand of nature has prepared in Iceland, and in some other places, with the greatest attention. The Giant's Causeway has, till now, been considered as the largest and most regular assemblage of these columns; but we have discovered one on our expedition through the western islands of Scotland, which infinitely surpasses it. The whole island of Staffa* consists almost entirely of these pillars, which are as regular as can be imagined; they seem to be of the same substance as the Irish ones, and have from three to seven sides; each pillar is surrounded by others, that join so closely

* See the account of Staffa, by Joseph Banks, Esq. inserted in Pennant's Tour in Scotland, and Voyage to the Hebrides, 1772, page 299, 309, and the fine representations of these basalts, executed after the accurate drawings executed by Mr. John Frederick Miller, employed by Mr. Banks, and communicated by the last mentioned gentleman, for the adorning of Mr. Pennant's Scots Tour.

to

to it, as to have a very fmall fpace between them, which is frequently filled up with a cryftallized incruftation. In moft places the pillars are perpendicular; in others they are a little inclined, and yet in others they have the configuration of the timber-work in the infide of a fhip. The higheft pillar was 55 feet one inch long; and each joint, from one to two feet. There is a cavern here which confifts entirely of thefe pillars; it is 367 feet long; 53,7 broad, and 117,6 high. There are three fathoms of water in it, fo that it is eafy to enter into it with a boat.

It is difficult to determine the queftion, how thefe pillars have been formed; but it is more than probable, nay almoft certain, that they are the remains of an ancient volcano, many indifputable tracts of which are found in many parts of Scotland. You muft not in this place apply to me the ftory Helvetius tells of a clergyman and a fine lady, who together obferved the fpots in the moon, which the former took for church fteeples, and the latter for

for a pair of happy lovers. I know that we frequently imagine to have really found what we moſt think of, or moſt wiſh for; but I ſincerely aſſure you, that I do not ſpeak of ſuch fires without the moſt deciſive opinions. I will, however, reſerve a further account of theſe extraordinary productions till my return home, when I flatter myſelf I ſhall be able to give you entire ſatisfaction.

LETTER II.

To the Royal Librarian Mr. G. JÖRWELL.

Of Iceland in general.

SIR, Utrecht, Jan. 22, 1773.

YOU are, no doubt, informed of the voyage Mr. Banks and Dr. Solander undertook laſt ſummer to Iceland, as well as of my having accompanied theſe gentlemen on that expedition. I need not tell you what reaſons determined me to become one of their company. You can eaſily conceive how many different circumſtances might have perſuaded a curious Swede to viſit a country remarkable in ſo many reſpects; I am perfectly ſatisfied with my voyage, and can eaſily convince you of it, by communicating to you ſome little account of what principally attracted our attention during its courſe.

We

We set sail from London on the 12th of July last in a ship, for which one hundred pounds sterling were paid every month. Besides Mr. Banks, Dr. Solander, and myself, we had on board an astronomer *, a lieutenant of the navy (a very worthy man, his name is Gore, and deserves to be mentioned, as he is, as far as we know, the first who has sailed three times round the world †) together with a lieutenant, three draughtsmen, and two writers, who, with the seamen and servants, made about forty people.

We first landed on the Isle of Wight, which is a little paradise, where we spent two days. Nature seems to have spared none of her favours in embellishing it; and I know no place in it which does not present a pleasing

---

* Dr. James Lind of Edinburgh, who is well known by many memoirs inserted in the Philosophical Transactions, and other ingenious publications.

† Captain Dampier did it a long time before Mr. Gore, viz. Cowley and Dampier, 1683, 1684; Dampier and Funnel, 1689, 1691; Woodes, Rogers, and Dampier, 1708, 1711. If lieutenant Gore and captain Charles Clerk return safe home from the voyage they are now engaged in, they both will have sailed four times round the world.

view to the obferver. The inhabitants refemble their ifland; they live in a little community among themfelves; they are not very rich, neither have they any beggars. They are generally cheerful,. cleanly, and obliging; and there are but few inftances among them of any one marrying a perfon who did not at that time refide or afterwards fettle on the ifland.

From thence we failed to Plymouth, where we faw the docks, magazines, and every thing belonging to them worthy of notice, and then proceeded towards St. George's channel.

We had intended to land on the Ifle of Man, as it is one of the few places where the Runic characters have been brought by the Danes, and the only one, except the north, where fome of our old Runic ftones are found; but at fea we cannot always act according to our pleafure; the wind obliged us to leave the Ifle of Man on our right, and to continue our courfe to the weftern iflands of Scotland.

It is exceedingly pleafant to fail among thefe iflands, though not very fafe, without a good wind and expert pilots:

for

for in the firft cafe you muft depend upon the ebb and flood; and in the fecond you are in continual danger on account of the great number of rocks.

The nature of the country is fuch, that I do not wonder at its having given birth to a Fingal, and an Offian. It is not the only place where we have feen heroes produced among the mountains; and what can be more calculated to form a poet, than wild romantic and enchanting fcenes of nature, which are here fo pleafingly blended.

It would be tedious to enumerate all the ifles we have vifited. The moft remarkable are Oranfay and Columfkill, on account of their antiquities; Scarba, for its known water-drain, (Vatta-drag); and Staffa, on account of its natural pillars, which hitherto have been little known, and furpafs whatever has been obferved before of the kind.

You know, Sir, that the inhabitants of thefe ifles, as well as in the Highlands of Scotland, have a language of their own, which they call Erfe, and which is a remnant of the Celtic. In this

this language Ossian wrote his admirable poems; and though the inhabitants cannot at present produce any thing comparable to them, yet I hope, on my return home, to give you proofs of their being able to write both with elegance and sentimental feelings. As it is very extraordinary that this language should have preserved itself here so long *, it will perhaps not be disagreeable to you to be

* The very little connection which the antient inhabitants of the Scots Highlands and of the Hebrides had with other nations (especially before the Union, which has in every respect been beneficial to them) is the true cause that the Erse language has so long been preserved among them. Besides these reasons there is another, which accounts almost for them all; the poverty of the soil and inclemency of climate admit of very little cultivation, so that these parts have very few natural productions which might tempt foreigners to visit them: some few gifts of nature are, no doubt, lodged in the bosom of the Scots hills; but hitherto indolence and want of industry in the natives have neglected these riches: within a few years only it is that commerce has begun to raise its head, which alone induces other nations to frequent this or any country. It is therefore not so very extraordinary, that in a mountainous country the remains of ancient nations, should be found, who long preserve their language. In the Caucasus are still existing the posterity of several nations who crossed these mountains in their attempt to conquer Asia and Europe; and within a small compass, more than five or six different languages are spoken.

more

more particularly acquainted of the limits within which it is confined. I will readily sketch them out to you, being able to do it with so much the more certainty, having received my information from Mr. Macpherson, the only man in England who has particularly studied this language.

It begins to be spoken on the eastern side at Nairn, and extends from thence through the whole country, and all the western isles. In the north its limits are at Cathnefs, where Erse is only spoken in four parishes out of ten; in the other six, better English is spoken than in any other part of Scotland. There is in Ireland another dialect of it, as well as in Wales and Britany; however, they are not so different, but a man born in either of these provinces, may make himself understood in the others. Had I been acquainted with the language of the Dalikarlians, I should have had an opportunity of examining how far that similarity is founded which, as it appeared to my ear, subsists between these two languages.

The country abounds with northern antiquities, such as castles, strongholds, burying-places, and monuments, (Bautasteinar); and the people, who are obliging and extremely hospitable, have a number of customs resembling those observed by our country-people, such as the celebration of the first of May*, and many others.

We now left these islands, and continuing our voyage arrived at last, on the 28th of August, at Iceland, where we cast anchor at Besseftedr, formerly the dwelling place of the famous Sturleson. We seemed here to be in another world; instead of the fine prospects with which we had fed our eyes, we now only saw the horrid remains of many

---

* It is called in Sweden *war Fruday*; *le jour de notre Dame*, our Lady's Day. The witches are supposed to take, in the night preceding that day, their flight to Blakulla, a famous mountain; but it was formerly believed in Germany, that the witches travelled to the Bloxberg or Brocken, a high mountain contiguous to the Hartz forest. In Sweden the spring comes on about this time, and of consequence the hard labour of ploughing, mowing and reaping follow one another from that time, and require the best exertion of the strength of the husbandmen, to which they prepare themselves on this day by frequent libations of their strong ale, and they usually say, *Maste man dricka marg i benen*; You must drink marrow in your bones.

devasdevaftations. Imagine to yourfelf a country, which from one end to the other prefents to your view only barren mountains, whofe fummits are covered with eternal fnow, and between them fields divided by vitrified cliffs, whofe high and fharp points feem to vie with each other, to deprive you of the fight of a little grafs which fcantily fprings up among them. Thefe fame dreary rocks likewife conceal the few fcattered habitations of the natives; and no where a fingle tree appears, which might afford fhelter to friendfhip and innocence. I fuppofe, Sir, this will not infpire you with any great inclination of becoming an inhabitant of Iceland; and indeed at firft fight of fuch a country one is tempted to believe that it is impoffible it fhould be inhabited by any human creature, if one did not fee the fea, near the fhores, every where covered with boats.

Though there is fcarcely any country fo little favoured by nature, and where fhe appears throughout in fo dreadful a form, yet Iceland contains about 60,000 people, who cannot properly

perly be called unhappy, though they are unacquainted with what in other places conſtitutes happineſs. I ſpent there above ſix weeks with the greateſt pleaſure, partly in ſtudying one of the moſt extraordinary ſituations of nature, and partly in collecting information from the natives, concerning their language, manners, &c. &c. As to the former, I have treated of it in a letter to profeſſor Bergman, which I doubt not he will communicate to you with pleaſure, if you deſire it. Of the latter I will here mention ſome particulars.

You know, Sir, that Iceland firſt began to be cultivated in the eleventh century by a Norwegian colony, among which were many Swedes. They remained perfectly free in this corner of the world for a long time; but were, however, at laſt obliged to ſubmit to the Norwegian kings, and afterwards became ſubject, together with Norway, to the kings of Denmark. They were at firſt governed by an admiral, who was ſent thither every year to make the neceſſary regulations;

lations; but that mode has been changed many years, and a governor * appointed, who conſtantly reſides in the country. This poſt is, at preſent, occupied by Mr. Larr Thodal, who has formerly been Daniſh plenipotentiary in the commiſſion for ſettling the limits between Sweden and Norway, and has ſpent ſeveral years at Stockholm.

The Icelanders are of a good honeſt diſpoſition; but they are, at the ſame time, ſo ſerious and ſullen, that I hardly remember to have ſeen any one of them laugh: they are by no means ſo ſtrong as might be ſuppoſed, and much leſs handſome. Their chief amuſement, in their leiſure hours, is to recount to one another the hiſtory of former times; ſo that to this day you do not meet with an Icelander who is not well acquainted with the hiſtory of his own country: they alſo play at cards.

Their houſes are built of lava, thatched with turf, and ſo ſmall, that you find hardly room to turn yourſelf in them. They have no floors; and

* Stiftſamtmann.

their windows, inftead of glafs, are compofed of thin membranes of certain animals. They make no ufe of chimneys, as they never light a fire, except to drefs their victuals, when they only lay the turf on the ground. You will not therefore think it ftrange, when I inform you, that we faw no houfes, except fhops and warehoufes; and on our journey to Heckla we were obliged to take up our lodgings in the churches.

Their food principally confifts of dried fifh, four butter, which they confider as a great dainty, milk mixed with water and whey, and a little meat. They receive fo little bread from the Danifh company, that there is hardly any peafant who eats it above three or four months in the year. They likewife boil groats, of a kind of mofs (Lichen Iflandicus) which has an agreeable tafte. The principal occupation of the men is fifhing, which they follow both winter and fummer. The women take care of the cattle, knit ftockings, &c. They likewife drefs, gut, and dry the fifhes brought
home

home by the men, and otherwife affift in preparing this ftaple commodity of the country.

Befides this, the company who yearly fend fifteen or twenty ſhips hither, and who poffefs a monopoly which is very burthenfome to the country, export from hence fome meat, edder-down, and fome falcons, which are fold in the country for feven, ten, and fifteen rix-dollars a-piece. Money is very rare, which is the reafon that all the trade is carried on by fiſhes and ells of coarfe unſhorn cloth, called here Wadmal; one ell of wadmal is worth two fiſhes; and forty-eight fiſhes are worth a rix-dollar in fpecie. With gold they were better acquainted at our departure, than on our arrival.

They are well provided with cattle, which are generally without horns; they have likewife ſheep, and very good horfes; both the laft are the whole winter in the fields: dogs and cats they have in abundance. Of wild and undomefticated animals they have only rats and foxes, and
fome

some bears*, which come every year from Greenland with the floating ice: these, however, are killed as soon as they appear, partly on account of the reward of ten dollars, which the king pays for every bear, and partly to prevent them from destroying their cattle. The present governor has introduced rein-deer into the island; but out of thirteen, ten died on their passage, the other three are alive with their young.

It is extraordinary that no wood grows successfully in Iceland; nay, there is scarcely a single tree to be found on the whole island, though there are certain proofs of wood having formerly grown there in great abundance. Corn cannot be cultivated here to any advantage; though I have met with cabbages, parsley, turnips, pease, &c. &c. in five or six gardens, which were the only ones in the whole island.

---

* The bears here mentioned are the white polar or arctic carnivorous bears, absolutely forming a species widely distinct from our brown and black bears; though the celebrated Linnæus only suspected them to be a new species, not having seen and examined any of these animals.

I must

I muſt now beg leave to add a few words about the Icelandic literature. Four or five centuries ago the Icelanders were celebrated on account of their poetry and knowledge in hiſtory. I could name many of their poets, who celebrated in ſongs the warlike deeds of the northern kings; and the famous Snorre Sturleſon is the man to whom even the Swedes are indebted for the firſt illuſtration of their hiſtory. We for this reaſon ſet ſo high a value upon the antient Icelandic records and writings, that they have almoſt all been drawn out of the country: ſo exceedingly ſcarce they are become, that, notwithſtanding the pains I took during the whole time of my ſtay there, I got a ſight of only four or five Icelandic manuſcripts. In the inland parts of the country, our old language has been preſerved almoſt quite pure; but on the coaſts, where the natives have an intercourſe with the Daniſh merchants, it has been ſomewhat altered. Some ſpeak the Daniſh language very well; but thoſe who did not, could ſooner make themſelves intelligible

telligible to us Swedes, than to the Danes. We likewise found three or four Runic inscriptions, but they were all modern, and consequently of no value. I have said before that the Icelanders took pleasure in listening to their old traditional sayings and stories; and this is almost the only thing that remains among them of the spirit of their ancestors; for they have at present but few poets; and their clergy know little besides some Latin, which they pick up in the schools established in the episcopal sees at Skallholt and Hoolum. Some of them, however, have studied at the university of Copenhagen; and I became acquainted with three men of great learning among them, who were particularly well versed in the northern antiquities. One of them is the bishop of Skallholt Finnur Jonson, who is compiling an ecclesiastical history of Iceland; the two others are the provost Gunnar Paulson, and Halfdan Ginarson, rector at Hoolum.

That there is a printing-office in Iceland cannot be unknown, as we are acquainted with the rare editions of Olof

Olof Tryggwaſſons, Landnama, Greenland, and Chriſtendoms Sagas, or Traditions, printed at Skallholt; but I did not expect to find the art of printing ſo antient here, as it was repreſented to be. A Swede, whoſe name was John Mathieſon, brought hither the firſt printing-preſs between the years 1520 and 1530; and publiſhed in the year 1531 the Breviarium Nidaroſienſe. I have collected as many Icelandic books as I have been able to diſcover; among the rareſt is the Icelandic bible, printed in folio at Hoolum in the year 1584. I hope likewiſe, that fifteen (till now unknown) traditional hiſtories or ſagas will be no unwelcome acquiſition.

You may judge, Sir, how agreeably I ſpent my time here in theſe occupations, which I applied to with ſo much the more pleaſure, as they all related to objects entirely new: added to which I was in ſociety with Mr. Banks and Dr. Solander; the latter of whom is a moſt worthy diſciple of our Linnæus, and unites a lively temper to the moſt excellent heart; and
the

the former is a young gentleman of an unbounded thirſt after knowledge, reſolute, and indefatigable in all his purſuits, frank, fond of ſocial converſation, and at the ſame time a friend of the fine arts and literature: in ſuch company you will confeſs it was impoſſible I ſhould have the leaſt reaſon for regretting the time ſpent in this voyage.

I had almoſt flattered myſelf with the hopes of ſeeing Mr. Banks and Dr. Solander in Sweden; but I learn that they will be detained in England for ſome time. I much fear Dr. Solander will be for ever loſt to his native country, as well on account of the univerſal eſteem in which he is held in England, as of his being preferred to a more beneficial place at the Britiſh Muſeum than that which he formerly poſſeſſed.

Their voyage to the South Seas will probably make its appearance in April or May next. They have already begun to engrave the collections of animals and plants they have made on their voyage, which will employ them

ſeveral

several years, as they must consist, I should apprehend, of near 2000 plates.

It would be writing a natural history were I to attempt to give a proper description of these admirable collections. They have alone above 3000 fishes and other animals preserved in spirits most of which are new: Linnæus might find among their plants, of which, they have several sets, (one of which I flatter myself, will find its way into Sweden) subjects for a new mantissa.

I propose, when I have seen Holland, to make a little excursion to Germany to see Mr. Michaelis, and soon afterwards return to my native country, where I shall have the honour of assuring you personally of the affectionate regard, &c. &c.

LETTER III.

To CHEVALIER IHRE.

On the physical Constitution of the Country.

Stockholm, June 20, 1773.

SIR,

THERE is no duty more agreeable to me, than that of obeying your commands, in transmitting to you some account of Iceland, its antiquities, and what else relates to it. As I have happily had an occasion of seeing the country myself, it may with justice be required of me, that I should willingly communicate to others the informations I have been able to procure; and it would give me peculiar pleasure if they enabled me satisfactorily to answer those questions which you kindly proposed to me.

Iceland

Iceland is juftly reckoned amongft the largeft iflands in the known world. It is fixty miles in length, and its breadth exceeds forty Swedifh miles *.

The moft ufeful among many maps of this country is that which has been made by Meffrs. Erickffen and Schoonning in the year 1771, though it might be further improved.

Beffeftedr, in the fouthern part of the ifland, not far from Hafnefiord, lies, according to Horrebow's account of Iceland, in 64 degrees 6 minutes of north latitude, and in 41 degrees of longitude, from the meridian of Stockholm; fo that it is almoft in the latitude of Hernòfand †.

The country does not afford a pleafing profpect to the eye of the traveller, though it prefents him with objects worthy of attention in many refpects: for befides innumerable ridges of mountains that crofs it in feveral directions, and fome of which, on

---

* About 360 Britifh fea-miles in length, and about 240 in breadth.

† A town in Sweden.

account of their height, are covered with continual ice and fnow, you only fee barren fields between them, entirely deftitute of wood, and covered with lava for the fpace of many miles. This is certainly as incapable of giving the eye pleafure, as it is unfit for any other ufe. On the other fide, however, it caufes the greateft furprize in the attentive fpectator, to fee fo many fpeaking proofs of the dreadful effects of volcanoes.

Though the coafts are better inhabited, the inland parts of the country do not lie wafte and neglected; and one finds every where, fometimes clofer together, and fometimes at greater diftances, farms with fome land belonging to them, which generally confifts of meadow-land, and fometimes of hills thick fpread with low fhrubs and bufhes, and which they honour with the appellation of Woods.

In the whole ifland there are no towns, nor even villages; nothing but fingle farms are to be feen, fome of which, however, confift of feveral dwelling-

dwelling-houses, destined for the owner of the farm and his tenants, *biâ leygu-mann*) who procure from the proprietor a house and pasture for as many cows, horses, and sheep as they chuse to agree for. On the estates of some peasants who are better circumstanced, there are even sometimes dwellings for labourers (*huusman*) who work for daily hire. All these farms belong either to the king, the church, or the peasants themselves *. I will mark the price of two of these farms, which were sold a little before our arrival, that you may judge of their value. The one farm, whereon ten cows, ten horses, and four hundred sheep might be kept, was sold for one hundred and twenty rix-dollars; and the other, which had sufficient pasture for twelve cows, eighteen head of young cattle, above a year old, that had not yet calved *(ungnot)*, eight oxen, fourteen

* In order to shew at once in what proportion the farms are distributed beetween the king, the church, and the farmers, I will here annex an abstract taken from the Icelandic Villarium, or Land-book of the year 1695, which came into my possession.

Abstract from the Icelandic Land-Book of 1695

Names of the syssels or districts	Number of farms	Of these farms to each syssel belong	To the king	To the bishop's see of Skalholt	To the bishop's see of Holum	Church glebe	Glebe of clergy	Glebe of superannuated clergy	For maintaining the poor	For maintaining hospitals	To farmers	Total sum
	718	304	345	640	140	45	16		184	47		4058
Arne.		4	202		32	14	3			1	91	347
Rangervalla.		6	32		64	6	7				153	268
Skaftefialds.		102	13		8	9	4	2		1	47	183
Mule.		45	4		81	23	12		5		187	357
Thingey.		51	1	49	55	14		2			134	306
Vaide.		82		61	33	13				1	133	323
Skagafiords.		40		196	14	10					104	366
Hunavatns.		83		39	46	14				1	145	329
Strande.		21	3		29	3	3				66	125
Isefiords.		21			64	10		1	2		161	259
Bardastrands.		6	4		38	4	3				132	187
Dale.		2			24	3	2				149	180
Hnappadals.		15			18	2					23	68
Snefialdsnas.		22			44	4				1	59	159
Borgarfiords.		10	3		6		4		1		216	344
Kiosar.		40	2			2	2				31	91
Julibringe.		90	6		14	3	1		1		11	126

horses, and three hundred sheep, for one hundred and sixty dollars.

In some few places they have small fenced spots near their houses in which they cultivate cabbage, parsley, spinach, turnips, patientia, potatoes, and some other roots and vegetables, together with flax and hemp. Fruit trees are looked for in vain, which is not to be wondered at, since storms and hurricanes are here very frequent. These have given rise to the name of *(Wedrakista)* Storm-coast, which has been given to some places in Iceland.

They have likewise prevented the growth of fir-trees, and Norway pitch-firs *, which governor Thodal had planted here, whose tops seemed to wither as soon as they were about two feet high, when they then ceased growing.

That wood has formerly grown in Iceland, can be proved from the Sagas or tradition stories of Landnama, Kialnesigna, Savarfdala, and Egill Skallagrimsonare. It is likewise proved by

---

* Pinus picea, Linn. and pinus abies, Linn.

pieces which are frequently dug up in marshes and fens, where not a single bush is to be seen at present. The substance, called by the natives *futurbrand*, is likewise a clear proof of it.

This futurbrand is evidently wood, not quite petrified, but indurated, which drops asunder as soon as it comes into the air, but keeps well in water, and never rots: it gives a bright though weak flame, and a great deal of heat, and yields a sourish though not unwholsome smell. The smiths prefer it to sea-coal, because it does not so soon waste the iron. The Icelanders make a powder of it, which they make use of to preserve their cloaths from moths; they likewise apply it externally against the cholick. I have seen tea-cups, plates &c. in Copenhagen made of futurbrand, which takes a fine polish. It is found in many parts of Iceland, generally in the mountains in horizontal beds; sometimes more than one is to be met with, as in the mountain of Lack in Bardestrand, where four strata
of

of futurbrand are found alternately with different kinds of ſtone.

I have brought a large piece of it with me to Sweden, in which there are evident marks of branches, the circles of the annual growth of the wood, leaves, and bark, in the ſurrounding clay; and there is ſome reaſon to believe, that theſe trees have been mixed in the thrown up lava in ſome eruption of fire or an earthquake.

I am almoſt inclined to believe that ſome ſtreams of lava, which at the depth of fifteen feet, according to obſervations that have beeen made, can advance twelve thouſand Swediſh ells, of two feet each, in eight hours, by a declivity of forty-five degrees, have ſwept away theſe trees, which ſeem to have been of a conſiderable ſize, and buried them; and this is ſo much the more probable, as the futurbrand frequently has the appearance of coal. But as I do not know whether this opinion has ever been advanced before, and having had no opportunity of making ſufficient obſervations upon this conjecture, and as there is even ſome reaſon

to

to suppose, that a tree would in so violent a fire directly be confumed to afhes, though the contrary may alfo be poffible, when it is in the fame inftant over-turned, covered, and in a moment fmothered; yet I will not even venture to offer this opinion as a probable conception.

There is ftill another probable fuppofition. The trees may have been overturned by an earthquake, and then covered beneath the hot afhes of a volcano, in the fame manner as happened at Herculanum, and other places, where whole towns have fhared the fame fate.

That there have been formerly confiderable woods in Iceland, can fcarcely be doubted; nay, there are at this time fome fmall fpots covered with trees, as at Hallarmftad, Hunfefeld, and Aa, and in feveral other places. However, there are no fir nor pine-trees; and the birch-trees now exifting never exceed the height of eight or twelve feet, and are not above three or four inches thick, which is partly owing to bad management, partly to the devaftations caufed by fire or hurricanes, and

and the Greenland floating ice: the laſt is the cauſe that at Stadar-hrauns, Eyry, and Kiolfield, whole ſpots of land are ſeen covered with withered birch-trees. But theſe being found inſufficient to ſupply the inhabitants with fuel, they likewiſe make uſe of turf, fern, juniper, and black crow-berry buſhes *(empetrum nigrum)*; in other places they burn the bones of cattle killed for butchers meat, and fiſhes moiſtened with train oil; alſo dried cow-dung that has been the whole winter in the meadow; and laſt of all floating wood. This floating wood is obtained in great abundance every year, particularly at Langanas on the north-weſt ſide, and every where on the northern coaſt of the country*. There are ſeveral different

* The immenſe quantity of wood floating down the Miſſiſſippi, the St Lawrence, and other Rivers of North America, are probably thoſe which are carried to the northern regions. From the gulph of Mexico a ſtrong current ſets acroſs the Atlantic in a ſouth-weſt to north-eaſt direction, or nearly, and carries many tropical fruits on the coaſt of Norway, the Ferois, and Iceland; which remarkable circumſtance has been noticed by

that

rent kinds of wood among it, the greatest part is Norway pitch-fir*; but besides this, one finds common fir, linder, willow ‡, cork-wood, and two

that curious obferver and delineator of nature George Edwards. But the wood coming down the Miffiffippi is remarked by Buffu, in his Travels through North America, vol i. pag. 19. The coaft of Greenland is benefited by drift-wood, in the fame manner as Iceland. See Crantz's Hift. of Greenland, vol. i. pag. 37. The northern coaft of Siberia is often covered with wood in a moft aftonifhing manner. See John George Emelin's Travels through Siberia, vol. ii. pag. 415. Nor is the coaft of Kamfchatka deftitute of floating-wood. See J. F. Miller's collection of Ruffian Tranfactions, vol. iii. pag. 67. The great rivers of Siberia, fuch as the Lena, Kolyma, Yenifea, and others, carry chiefly in fpring many wood trees along with their waters into the ocean, where it is often floating in various directions, fet by winds and currents, and checked by the immenfe maffes of ice, till, after many months and years, it is thrown up and left on the coaft, for the benefit of the inhabitants of thefe frigid regions, which are too cold for the growth of trees. Iceland receives its drift-wood by ftrong wefterly and northwefterly gales, varying with foutherly winds, which feems to confirm the opinion, that the drift-wood comes from North America: it confifts chiefly of pinus abies, picea, limbra, and larix, tilia europea, betula alba, and falix caprea, and fome unknown kinds of wood: and according to Catefby's Nat. Hift. of Carolina, great quantities of thefe enumerated woods are floating down the rivers of Virginia and Carolina; and another part feems to come round the North of Europe from the Siberian rivers.

* Pinus abies, Linn. ‡ Salix caprea, Linn.

forts

forts of red-wood, which are called *rauda grene* and *ftaffalejk* in Iceland, and on account of their colour and hardnefs are employed in various kinds of neat work. It comes moft probably from the northern parts of Tartary, and partly from Virginia and Carolina. As to what relates to agriculture, it may be difcovered by many paffages of the ancient Icelandic accounts, that corn formerly grew in Iceland. In later times feveral trials have been made with it, but they have been attended with little fuccefs.

Governor Thodal fowed a little barley in 1772, which grew very brifkly; but a fhort time before it was to be reaped, a violent ftorm fo utterly deftroyed it, that only a few grains were found fcattered about.

If we confider, befides thefe ftrong winds, or rather hurricanes, the frofts which frequently fet in during May and June, we fhall difcover a number of difficulties which check the rife and growth of agriculture in Iceland. If, notwithftanding thefe obftacles, it

can

can ever be brought to a thriving condition, it muſt certainly be under the preſent indefatigable governor, who has the welfare of the country much at heart, and, in conjunction with the government, ſtudies every poſſible means to promote it.

I conſider thoſe violent winds, and the Greenland floating-ice, which every year does great damage to the country, as the chief cauſe of the diminution of the growth of wood, as well as of the ill ſucceſs in the late attempts for introducing agriculture.

This ice comes on by degrees, alː ways with an eaſterly wind, and freǧ quently in ſuch quantities, as to fill up all the gulphs on the north-weſt ſide of the iſland, and even covers the ſea as far as the eye can reach; it alſo ſometimes drives to other ſhores. It generally comes in January, and goes away in March. Sometimes it only reaches the land in April, and, remaining there a long time, does an incredible deal of miſchief. It conſiſts partly of mountains of ice *(fiall-jakar)* which are ſometimes ſixty fathoms high

high above water, and announce their arrival by a great noise, and partly of field-ice *(hellu-is)* of the depth of one or even two fathoms. Of this last some parts soon melt, and other parts remain undissolved many months, often producing very dangerous effects to the country*.

The ice caused so violent a cold in 1753 and 1754, that horses and sheep dropped down dead on account of it, as well as for want of food; horses

* The immense masses of ice, which are so dreadful, affecting the climate of the country along the northern and northwest coast of Iceland, arrive commonly with a N W or N N W wind from Greenland. Field-ice is of two or three fathoms thickness, and is separated by the winds, and less dreaded than the rock or mountain ice, which is often seen fifty and more feet above water, and is at least nine times the same height below water: these immense masses of ice are frequently left in shoal water, fixed, as it were, to the ground; and in that state remain many months, nay years undissolved, chilling all the ambient part of the atmosphere for many miles round. When many such lofty and bulky ice-masses are floating together, the wood which is often drifting along between them, is so much chafed, and pressed with such violence together, that it takes fire; which circumstance has occasioned fabulous accounts of the ice being in flames: of the bulk of such ice-masses, see Forster's Observations made during a voyage round the world, pag. 69, 1773 and 1774.

D   were

were observed to feed upon dead cattle, and the sheep eat of each others wool. In the year 1755, towards the end of the month of May, in one night the ice was one inch and five lines thick. In the year 1756, on the 26th of June, snow fell to the depth of a yard, and continued falling through the whole months of July and August. In the year following it froze very hard towards the end of May and the beginning of June in the south part of the island, which occasioned a great scarcity of grass, in so much that the inhabitants had little or no fodder the ensuing winter for their cattle: these frosts are generally followed by a famine, many examples of which are to be found in the Icelandic chronicles*.

Besides

---

* The cold seems to have become more intense in Iceland since the time when these here-before-mentioned fir-trees were growing, and before the ocean was so very much covered with floating ice.

These facts seem to confirm very much the opinion of count Buffon in his Epoques de la Nature; in consequence of which he believes that the country towards the poles was formerly more habitable than it is at present: he is of opinion, that the skeletons of elephants found far north in Siberia, are almost irrefragable proofs

Besides these calamities, a number of bears yearly arrive with the ice, which commit great ravages, particularly among the sheep. The Icelanders attempt to destroy these intruders as soon as they get sight of them; and sometimes they assemble together, and drive them back to the ice, with which they often float off again. For want of fire-arms they are obliged to make use of spears on these occasions. The government itself takes every possible method to encourage the natives to destroy these animals, by paying a premium of ten dollars

proofs of the formerly milder temperature of the air; since they could scarcely be found in Siberia in such numbers unless they had existed there. Buffon Epoques de la Nature, p. 165, & seq. The Eastern shores of Greenland were formerly inhabited by a colony of Norwegians, and they had there a bishop's see, called Gardar, to which belonged farms, woods, pastures for cattle, granges, and tillage-land. See Crantz's History of Greenland, vol. 1. p. 245, which evidently proves the mildness of these now inhospitable regions. Ships sailed formerly to the Eastern coast; whereas for a great number of years past it has been inaccessible, on account of the immense masses of ice found there. Are Frode in Scheda de Iclandia, Oxon. 1716, cap. 2, p. 10, says, That at the first landing of the Norwegian colonists, Iceland was covered with woods and forests in the space between the shores and mountains.

for every bear that is killed, and by purchasing the skin of him who killed it. These skins are a prerogative of the king, and are not allowed to be sold to any other person.

It is as absurd to suppose that this floating ice consists principally of salt-petre, as that it might be employed in making gun-powder; and yet there are some persons who pretend to support this opinion, but they are certainly undeserving the trouble of refutation.

I must mention two other inconveniences to which Iceland is subject, the *Skrida* and *Snioflodi:* the name of the first imports large pieces of a mountain tumbling down, and destroying the lands and houses which lie at the foot of it. This happened in 1554, when the whole farm of Skidestedr in Vatndal was ruined, and thirteen people buried alive. The other word signifies the effects of a prodigious quantity of snow, which covers the tops of the mountains, rolling down in immense masses and doing a great deal of damage,

mage. There was an infance of this in the year 1699, during the night, when two farms, in the fyffel of Kiofar, were buried in the fnow, with all their inhabitants and cattle*.

The climate is not unwholfome, as the ufual heat is not extreme, nor the cold in general very rigorous. However, there are examples of the mercury in Fahrenheit's thermometer falling quite down in the bulb, which is 24 degrees under the freezing point; when at other times it has rofe to 104 degrees.

It cannot be determined with any degree of certainty how much the cold has increafed or decreafed prior to 1749, the year when Horrebow began his obfervations on the weather; which were afterwards continued by the provoft Gudlaug Thorgeirffon to the year 1769: fince which period obfervations have been made by Mr.

---

* Sniofled, or Snowflood, is a very expreffive word for this dreadful accident, which is not uncommon in all alpine countries, efpecially Switzerland. The Italians call fuch a rolling down of maffes of fnow, Lavine; the French, Lavaches; and the Germans, Lauihnen.

Eyolfs Jonson, who was formerly affiftant at the Round Tower at Copenhagen, and receives a falary as firſt obferver in Iceland*. His obfervatory is at Arnarhol near Reykarwick; and, what is remarkable, he makes ufe of a telefcope of his own conftruction, made of the black Iceland agate, inſtead of coloured glafs.

Lightning and thunder ſtorms are rare, and both in fummer and winter feldom happen any where elfe but in the neighbourhood of volcanoes. Northern lights frequently appear uncommonly ſtrong†. Sometimes a kind of the ignis fatuus is obferved *(Snoe-lios* and *brævas-eldur)* which attaches itfelf to men and beafts.

Amongſt other aerial phenomena, the lunar halo *(rofabaugu)* which

---

* This ingenious gentleman died in 1775, not many months fince the writing this letter.

† The northern lights appear in Iceland in all the different quarters of the compafs, efpecially on the foutherly horizon, where a dark fegment appears, from whence ſtrong columns of light dart forth. They are moſt frequently feen in dry weather, though there are inſtances of their appearance before, during and after a fhower of rain. The lights are often feen tinged with yellow, green, and purple. See Eggert Olafsen's & Biarne Faulten's Travels through Iceland, fec. 855.

prog-

prognosticates bad weather, likewise deserves a place here, as well as parhelions *(biasolar)* which appears sometimes from one to nine in number[*]. Fire-balls (called *Viga Knottur*) are likewise observed, and when they are oval are named *Wiigabrandur*; and last of all comets, or *Halestiernor*, which are often mentioned in their chronicles.

The ebb and flood here, which the Icelanders call *flod* and *fiara*, are perfectly the same as at any other places: they are stronger during the new and full moon than at other times, and strongest of all about the equinoxes.

As I am here speaking of the nature of the country, I cannot pass over in silence the earthquakes which often happen, particularly before volcanic eruptions. In September, in the year 1755, fifteen violent shocks were ob-

---

[*] The parhelions are observed in Iceland chiefly at the approach of the Greenland ice, when an intense degree of cold is produced, and the frozen vapours fill the air: there are many instances proving, that under such circumstances, the sun never appears without shewing one or several parhelions, and often a rainbow on the opposite side.

served

served within a few days; and it is not uncommon to see whole farms overturned by them, and large mountains burst asunder, as will be remarked hereafter, in the letter which treats of the conflagrations in Iceland.

In so mountainous a country, where there is no agriculture, and no commerce, except that carried on by bartering of the various commodities on the arrival of the Danish ships, no good roads can be expected: they therefore make use of neither carts nor sledges; and there are many places in which it is both difficult and dangerous even to ride on horseback, which have caused the names of *Ofoerur*, *Halsavegur*, *Hofdabrecka Illaxlif*, to be given to some roads. Their length is not reckoned by the number of miles, but that of *thingmanna-leid*, that is, as far as a man, who is travelling to a place where justice is administered, can go in one day, which is about three and a half Swedish, or four Icelandic miles*. Formerly houses were

---

* About twenty-one or twenty English miles.

built

built in some particular places for the use of travellers, which were called *Thiodbrautar-skaala*; but now the churches are every where made use of for this purpose.

When the Icelanders travel to sea-ports to exchange their fish, &c. they have twenty, thirty, and sometimes a greater number of horses with them, which carry a load of 300 or 400 pounds weight each; but they have always some spare horses along with them to relieve those that are fatigued; this cavalcade is called *Lest*; and the man who guides them is called *Lestamadur*: he rides on before, accompanied with a dog, that, by uttering a certain word, drives the strayed or straggling horses into the right road. They never carry any food for their horses, as pasture is plenty every where.

The number of the inhabitants is by no means adequate to the extent of the country. It has been much larger in former times; but besides what is called the *Digerdeath*, and other contagious diseases, among which the plague carried off great numbers from

1402

1402 to 1404, many places have been entirely depopulated by famine. In the years 1707 and 1708, the small-pox destroyed 16,000 persons; so that the number of inhabitants cannot exceed 60,000.

LETTER

LETTER IV.

To Chevalier Ihre.

Of the Arrival of the Norwegians, the Government, and Laws in Iceland.

Stockholm, June 13, 1774.

AS I have treated in my former letter of the nature of the country in Iceland, an enquiry how, and when it was firſt peopled, might not perhaps be diſagreeable to you.

We know little or nothing of the firſt inhabitants of Iceland, who poſſeſſed the country when the Norwegians firſt arrived there. We are informed by ſome, that they were Chriſtians, who, according to the moſt probable conjectures, arrived there from England and Ireland, and were called *Papa* by the Norwegians *. They pretend to

---

* The ancient Norwegians, who firſt landed in Iceland, found there inhabitants who were Chriſtians, and were called by the Norwegians *Papas*, which is conjectured to ſignify prieſts. This is confirmed by the preface of the Landnama Bok, or Book of Colonization,

to affirm with the greatest certainty, that this English colony settled there in the beginning of the fifth century; but I look upon it as the safest way not to enter at all upon an affair wrapped up in such obscurity. There is notwithstanding reason to suppose that the English and Irish were acquainted with this country under another name

tion, written by various authors, the first of whom was Are Frode, born 1068; and he expressly says, in the first chapter of the book, that Iceland was settled by the Norwegians in the time of Alfred king of England, and of Edward his son. The same preface mentions, that Beda speaks of Iceland, under the name of Thyle, more than a hundred years before the arrival of the Norwegians in Iceland; and that the Norwegians found there Irish books, bells, and crosiers, which proved that these people came from the West. And it is added, that the English books mention an intercourse of navigation between those lands about those times. King Alfred certainly mentions in his translation of Orosius, the utmost land to the N. W of Iceland, called Thila; and that it is known to few on account of its great distance. See Alfred's Orosius, p. 31. The Landnama Bok was published at Copenhagen, 1774, in 4to. The circumstance of the Irish books left in Iceland is likewise mentioned by the same Are Frode, in Ara Multiscii Schedis de Islandia. Oxoniæ, 1716, 8vo. cap. ii. pag. 10. who says, they chose not to live with the Heathens, and for that reason went away, leaving behind Irish books, bells, and crosiers.

long

long before the arrival of the Norwegians; for the celebrated Beda in his time pretty accurately defcribes it. But I will not dwell upon thefe ancient inhabitants of Iceland, but proceed to examine how the Norwegians came to fettle there. Of this we have feveral accounts in the Icelandic Sagas*. I fhall particularly follow Landnama Bok, which treats of the arrival of thefe new colonifts.

Naddoddr, a famous pirate, was driven by the winds on the coaft of Iceland, on his return from Norway to the Ferro Gales, in 861, and named the country *Snio-land* (Snow-land) on account of the great quantity of fnow with which he faw the mountains covered. He did not remain there long; but however extolled the country fo much after his return, that one Gardar Suafarfon, an enterprizing Swede, was encouraged by his account to

---

* The word Saga fignifies the ancient hiftorical monuments in Iceland; fome of them are the hiftorical relations, others are fabulous ftories in the ftyle of the Arabian Nights. The diftinction between them requires a nice critical judgment. As the words occurs often, we once for all explain it here.

go in search of it in 864. He failed quite round the island, and then called it *Gardarsholmur* (Gardar's Island). He remained the whole winter in Iceland, and in spring returned to Norway, where he described the new-discovered island as a pleasant, well-wooded country. This excited a desire in Floke, another Swede, and the greatest navigator of his time, to undertake a voyage thither. As the compass (in Icelandic *Leitharstein* *) was not then known, he took three ravens on board, to employ them on the discovery. By the way he visited his friends at Ferro; and after having sailed farther to the northward, he let fly one of his ravens, which returned to Ferro. Sometime after he dismissed the second, which returned

---

* The word *Leitharstein* is certainly equivalent to the English word Loadstone, and probably has the same origin. The Anglo Saxon word Lædan signifies to lead; and the magnet being the leader of the navigator, it is very evident that the loadstone is the leading stone of the ship. The history of the three ravens is most evidently copied from the history of the deluge in Genesis. However it proves an uncommon sagacity in the navigator, who made use of birds for the first discovery of land.

to

to the ſhip again, as he could find no land. The laſt trial proved more ſuccefsful, ſince the third raven took his flight to Iceland; ſoon after they diſcovered land, and in a few days really arrived there. Floke ſtayed here the whole winter with his company; and becauſe he found a great deal of floating ice on the north ſide, he gave the name of Iceland to the country, which it has ever ſince retained.

When they returned to Norway in the following ſpring, Floke and thoſe that had been with him, made a very different deſcription of the country. If on the one ſide Floke deſcribed it as a wretched place, Thorulfr (one of his companions in the voyage) on the other ſide ſo highly praiſed it, that he affirmed butter dropped from every plant, which gained him the nick-name of Thorulfr Smior, or Butter Thorulfr *.

* The expreſſion which Thorulfr made uſe of in deſcribing the fertility and richneſs of the country, characterizes the genius and manners of the age he lived in, and is therefore not to be over-looked in this account. Theſe minute ſtrokes paint the character and ſimplicity of the age, and, when compared with our manners, ſet them off in the faireſt point of view.

After

After what I have related, there are no traces of any voyage to Iceland, till Ingolfr and his friend Leifr undertook one in 874. They found on their arrival that the country had not been misrepresented; and resolved, after having spent the winter on the island, to settle there entirely for the future. Ingolfr returned to Norway, to provide whatever might be necessary to accomplish a new and comfortable establishment in an unfertilized and dreary country; and Leifr in the mean while went to assist in the war in England. After an interval of four years, they met again in Iceland, the one bringing with him a considerable number of people, with the necessary tools and implements for making the country habitable; and the other imported his acquired treasures. Since this period many people went there to settle, and in sixty years time the whole island was inhabited; and king Harold, who did not contribute a little towards it by his tyrannical treatment of the petty kings and lords in Normandy, was at last obliged to issue an order,

order, that no one fhould fail from Norway to Iceland, without paying four ounces of fine filver to the king, in order to put a ftop, in fome meafure, to thofe continual emigrations which weakened his kingdom.

Though the greateft part of the inhabitants came from Norway, there are however many Danes and Swedes among them. Of the latter I will only mention the following, from that edition of Landnama Bok, which was printed at Skallholt. Ingimundur, an earl in the Gothic empire, one of the defcendants of Bore, Gore's brother, p. 90; with his friends Jorundr, Ejvindr Sorkver, Afmundr, and Hvatefridleifr; and his flaves Fridmundr, Bodvar, Thorer Reffkegg, and Ulfkell, p. 90: Thordur, defcended by the father's fide in the fifth degree from Ragnar Lodbrock, p. 102: Thordur Knappur, natural fon of Biorns of Haga; and Nafar Helge, p. 104: Bruni Hin Hviti, fon of Hareks, earl of Upland, p. 104: Thormodur Hin Rami, p. 105; Biorn Rolfffon of the blood royal, p. 105:

Helgi Hin Magri, p. 107: Thorir Snepill, a fon of Joruns, daughter of the Lagman Thorgnys, p. 117; and Gardar Suafarfon. Befides thefe, Are Frode mentions one of the name of Olafr, who was of the fame family as king Harold; another of the name of Hrollangur, brother of Rolfs firft duke of Normandy, who drew his origin from the Swedifh king Gore, grandfather of Gylfe.

Torfæus mentions one Bodvar, a Swede, who fettled in Iceland, and was a defcendant of the princefs Goja, fifter of Gore: Floke, who gave to the ifland its prefent name of Iceland, was defcended from the fame family. Dalin, in his preface to the firft volume of his Swedifh hiftory, likewife mentions, out of Peringfkold and Bjorner, the following: Snobjorn, Bjorn Oftrane, Grim, Orm Wedorm, Bjorn, and Grimkill, with their mother Helga, daughter of Harold, Barder Snefallfas, Barder Wiking, Brimle, Hjelm, Gote, Skolder Svenfke, Glamer, Wafur Helge, and Slåttubjorn.

As

As often as a new colony arrived there, the principal perfon in the company appropriated to himfelf as large a part of the country as he was able to occupy, and gave up as much of it as he thought fit to his companions, whofe chief he was, bearing the title of Godi. But in a period when robberies and violence, by fea and land, were confidered as valour and merit, peace could not long fubfift between the neighbouring leaders. There are every where inftances to be met with in the Icelandic Sagas of battles between the new and original fettlers. To prevent thefe conflicts in future, a perfon was chofen in the year 928, with the title of Laug-faugumadur, and great power and dignity conferred upon him. This man was the fpeaker in all their public deliberations, pronounced fentence in difficult and intricate cafes, decided all difputes, and publifhed new laws after they had been received and approved of by the people at large; but he had no power to make laws without the approbation and confent of the reft.

He therefore assembled the chiefs whenever the circumstances seemed to require it; and after they had deliberated among themselves, he represented the opinion of the majority to the people, whose assent was necessary before it could be considered as a law. His authority among the chiefs and leaders was however inconsiderable, as he was chosen by them, and retained his place no longer than whilst he had the good fortune to preserve their confidence.

Their first form of government was consequently a mixture of aristocracy and democracy: but all the regulations made by it were insufficient to maintain order among so many chiefs, who, though all of the same rank, were differently inclined, and unequal in power. Nothing was therefore more frequent than rapine and violation of the laws. They openly made war against one another, examples of which are to be met with in the Sturlunga Saga, where, it is said, 20 vessels, carrying 1300 men, had a bloody engagement,

which

which so weakened the contending parties, that their whole power at last became an easy prey to a few arbitrary and enterprising men, who, as is too generally the case, wantonly abused it, to the oppression of their countrymen, and the disgrace of humanity *.

Notwithstanding all these intestine troubles they remained entirely free from the Norwegian yoke; though the kings of that country, since the time of Harold Harfagers, viewed this new and powerful republic with envious eyes, which, though now separated, owed its origin to them; but at last they experienced that fate, which is almost always inevitable, wherever liberty degenerates into licentiousness, and public spirit into selfish views; that is, they were obliged to submit to one chief. The greatest part of the inhabitants in 1261, put themselves under the protection of king Hakans, and promised to pay tribute

* The account of the origin of the Icelandic republic is a curious and interesting circumstance for the history of humanity; the same must be said of the intestine feuds which gave an opportunity to the Norwegian kings to establish their authority over this once free nation.

to him on certain conditions agreed upon between them, and the reft followed their example in 1264. Afterwards Iceland, together with Norway, became fubject to the crown of Denmark, which intrufted the care of it to a governor, who commonly went there only once a year to examine every thing, though, according to his inftructions, he ought to have refided there. As the country fuffered incredibly through the abfence of its commanders, it was refolved a few years ago, that the governor fhould refide there continually, and have his feat at Beffeftedr, one of the royal domains, where old Snorre Sturlefon formerly dwelt. He has under him a bailiff, two laymen, a fheriff, and twenty-one *Syffelmen* *. Formerly the country was

* The place of *Amtman* is here tranflated Bailiff and is to be taken in the fenfe in which the French receive the word *Bailif*, i. e. the head of a Bailiwick. The word *Lagmann* fignifies properly a Lawman; i. e. a perfon who adminifters juftice, and might be tranflated Judge or Juftice. The *Landvœgt* is the perfon who adminifters the executive power of juftice and the criminal law; and he may be compared to a fheriff. The *Syffelmen* are the magiftrates of the fmaller diftricts in Iceland (called the *Syffel*) who not only act as juftices of the peace, but alfo as receivers

was divided into quarters *(Fiordungar)* each having its own court of juftice, of which one was formed of their public affemblies, under the denomination of *Fiordungs-doeme**. But as the public fecurity feemed to require a fuperior court of judicature, to which the fuffering party might appeal; a *Fimtar-doeme* was eftablifhed foon after the introduction of the Chriftian religion, which tribunal confifted of the four above-mentioned courts, and fome clergymen.

receivers of the land-tax. The governor is called in Iceland *Stifts-amtmånn*, which is the fame as a bailiff of the epifcopal diocefe; i. e. the chief magiftrate of the ifland. This place was occupied in 1772 by Mr. Thodal, counfellor of juftice, who had been employed in the final adjuftment of the limits between Sweden and Norway; his falary amounts to 1500 rix-dollars. Travellers praife his abilities, patriotifm, and hofpitality. The bailiff at the time of our arrival in Iceland, was Mr. Olafr Stephanffon, a native of Iceland, whofe parts and abilities we admired, and whofe hofpitality we experienced: his falary is 400 rix-dollars; and the fame appointment is given to the fheriff *(Landvogt)* Mr. Skule Magnufen, who is faid to deferve well of his country by his patriotifm and eminent fervices.

* The words *Fiordungs-doeme* and *Fimtar-doeme* are ftill in part preferved in the language. For *Doomfday* is the day of judgment, from the Gothic word *Doom*, to judge, with which the Englifh word Doom correfponds.

At prefent all caufes are firſt decided at the *Hærads-thing*, or county court, from which the parties concerned may appeal to the *Al-thing*, or common court of juſtice, which is kept every year on the 8th of July at Thingvalla. Here there are two courts, the one before which the caufe in appeal is firſt brought, and confiſts entirely of *lagmen**; the other to which recourfe may be had for a new hearing the following year, and more accurate examination; and this is compoſed of the governor, who prefides, and twelve affeffors, who are the moſt refpectable men in the country, moſtly *lagmen* and *ſyſſelmen*. From this court the parties may again appeal to the fupreme court of judicature at Copenhagen, which is final.

The Norwegians, on their firſt arrival in Iceland, made their own laws: but thefe proving infufficient, when the number of people increafed, Ulflitor undertook, in the year 987, a voyage to Norway, and compoſed an ac-

---

* At the fame time and at the fame place the fpiritual court called *Preſta-ſtefna* is held, wherein the governor and biſhop prefide: the prieſts are the affeffors.

curate code of laws from the regulations established there. He made use of the *Gulothing* law on this occasion, and returned to his native country after an absence of three years.

In 1118, the *Gragas*, a famous ancient code of laws, was received there; and in 1280, that called the *Jonsbok* *, according to which sentence is still pronounced in some cases; but at present most matters are decided after the Danish law, and some more recent regulations.

* The *Jonsbok* was received in 1272, according to an Icelandic Chronicle, published by Langebeck in the second volume of the Scriptores Hist. Dan.

LETTER

LETTER V.

To CHEVALIER IHRE.

Concerning Ecclesiastical Affairs in Iceland.

Stockholm, June 22, 1772.

IT is known from Landnama Bok, and the Shedæ of Are, that the Norwegians found some traces of Christianity on their arrival in Iceland. There were also some few Christians among these new colonists, who, however, soon apostatized to the heathen religion, so that it became general there. It is not known whether any attempts had been made to introduce the Christian religion before the year 981, when a certain bishop Friedric arrived there from Saxony, and was obliged to return, after a stay of five years, without having made any great progress.

However, a church was built in 984, by Thorvard Bodvarson, and some persons

persons received baptism; but others, though they had no objection to the Christian doctrine, could not be prevailed upon to suffer themselves to be baptized, as they pretended it would be indecent to go naked into the water like little boys to receive baptism, which, according to the custom of those times, could only be done by submersion. Some, however, to shew their detestation of paganism, suffered themselves to be signed with the cross, which they called *Primsigning*. These were not considered either as Christians or Heathens; however, they were allowed to eat with the former, and to be buried close to the church-yard.

Olof Tryggvasson afterwards sent them Stefr Thorgilsson, and after him his chaplain Thangbrand, a German by birth; but they were both received with stones and abusive language, as they attempted to convert them, which happened to be at the very spot where the common court of justice was held: nor were they spared by the poets of the country, who, being bribed for the purpose, poured

forth

forth in their poetical productions the keenest invectives and satire upon these champions of the Christian religion.

However, the Icelanders obtained some knowledge of the Christian doctrine, which by degrees operated upon their minds. Some of them refused to contribute any more towards the idolatrous sacrifices, and wished to enjoy more circumstantial and certain instruction in the Christian religion; so that on the arrival of Giffur and Hyalti in the year 1000, the whole country was converted without bloodshed, though not without opposition. They also obtained a jus canonicum from bishop Grimkell, drawn up by himself, which was valid as a law till 1123, when it was again revised by bishops Thorlak and Ketill †.

After this time monks and convents abounded in the country. Many monks of the order of St. Benedict and St. Austin settled there, and the people paid a tribute to the Roman see,

* See Kristnis Saga, printed at Copenhagen, 1776, in 8vo. p. 57.
† The canon law was printed at Copenhagen, 1775, in 8vo.

as well as other European nations, which confifted in one *nagli*, ten of which were equal to one ell of two feet *.

That Rome did not lofe fight of Iceland, though ever fo diftant, can be proved by the bifhop of Skallholt, Arne Therlakfon, keeping his own agent, Sighvatr Lande, cannon of Drontheim, at the fecond council of Lyons, which was convened by Gregory I. in the year 1274; and that the Icelanders did not yield in zeal to their fellow Chriftians, appears by the willingnefs with which they contributed both men and money to the crufades, which were then in fafhion.

Amongft other faints, the bifhop of Hoolum, John Ogmundffon, and the bifhop of Skallholt, Thorlax Thorhallffon, were worfhipped: the laft died in 1193, and though he was not canonized by any pope, yet he found

* The value of all things is fettled in Iceland by ells of *wadmal*, which is a coarfe woollen ftuff of their own manufaéturing: the fee of Rome taxed every man in Iceland as high as the value of ten ells of *wadmal*.

worfhippers

worshippers in Iceland*, Denmark, Norway, England, Scotland, the Orkneys, the Ferro islands, and in Greenland, and even had a church dedicated to him in Constantinople. His Saga is full of miracles, said to have been wrought by him. It was unanimously agreed, that the 10th of January, the day on which he died, and the third of July, when he was elected bishop, should both be annually celebrated. His body was taken out of the grave on the 13th of August, 1198, and put into a coffin plated with gold and silver; and it was resolved to keep this day also as a festival. The protestant bishop Giffur Ejnarsson, afterwards, from a mistaken zeal, caused the precious ornaments with which the box was adorned to be broken off, and had it covered with brass gilt, which is still preserved in

---

* Bishop Finnsen in his Ecclesiastical History mentions, vol. 1. p. 228, note b. That bishop Thorlax had been likewise worshipped as a saint in Sweden, but there are no vestiges of this found in the old Swedish Calendaria. The tenth of January is consecrated to Paulus Eremita, and August the thirteenth to Hippolitus and Lociis Martii.

the church of Skallholt, as a piece of antiquity. In the year 1715, bifhop John Widalin ordered the pretended relique to be buried, and only a bit of his fkull is fhewn, which, however, if clofely examined, will be found to be neither more nor lefs than a piece of cocoa-fhell. Arcimboldus, fo famous in the north for his fale of indulgences, was much too attentive to his intereft to have negleƈted Iceland. In 1517, he had his own agent there, who was, however, more coldly received by bifhop Stephen Jonſſon than he expeƈted.

The Icelanders firft received their own bifhops in the year 1057 at Skallholt, and at Hoolum in 1107. They were originally under the jurifdiƈtion of the archbifhop of Bremen and Hamborough; but in the year 1103 or 4, they became fubordinate to Azerus *, firft archbifhop of Lund in Scania, and in 1152 to the bifhop of Drontheim. The Icelanders preferve the memory of their prelates both in their

* In the Icelandic annals he is commonly called *Auſſur*.

annual

annual regifters, and in their Sagas, which particularly deferve attention, fince the actions of many worthy men are found recorded therein. I fhall mention the deplorable end of one of their bifhops, John Jerechini *, by birth a Dane, who was provoft and electus of Wefteras, and was appointed archbifhop of Upfala, by king Ericus Pomeranus. In this exalted fituation he behaved fo ill, that he was obliged to fly to Denmark in 1419; from whence, according to the account of the Icelandic regifters, he made the beft of his way to England, and from thence took his paffage for Iceland, where he did not arrive till the year 1430. He was received by the inhabitants with open arms, and appointed to the fee of Skallholt, which had been vacant eleven years. Here he difcovered fo much pride and felfifhnefs, that fome of the principal perfons in the country entered into a confpiracy, and when he was celebrating mafs in

* The Icelandic annals call him Jon Geirreckifon.

the

the cathedral church on the thirteenth of August 1433, in commemoration of St. Thorlak, they took him by force from the altar, stripped him of all his episcopal ornaments, and putting him into a sack, with a large stone round his neck, threw him into the river Bruar, which flows past Skallholt, from whence his body was afterwards drawn, and buried in the cathedral church *.

King Christian III. began to introduce the Lutheran religion in the year 1540: but the zeal with which the bishops (who were then very powerful) opposed him, prevented him from succeeding till the year 1551.

Since that period, the church of Iceland has enjoyed a happy tranquillity, every seed of discord being suppressed in its rise, though some attempts were made to disseminate the evil.

Iceland is divided into 189 parishes, of which 127 belong to the see of Skallholt, and 62 to that of Hoolum.

---

* This account will serve to correct what is erroneous in Rhyzelii Epiicopoſcopia, where the typographical faults in Peringſköld's Monumenta Uplandica, vol. I. p. 155, have been copied. Vide Finn. Hiſt. Eccl. Iſlan. vol. II. n. 471.

All the ministers are native Icelanders, and receive a yearly salary of 400 or 500 rix-dollars from the king, exclusive of what they have from their congregation.

LETTER VI.

To CHEVALIER IHRE.

Of the Character and Manner of Life of the Icelanders.

Stockholm, Sept. 1, 1774.

IN a former letter I treated of the arrival of the Norwegians in Iceland, of their firſt form of government, and the changes they experienced through their own miſmanagement and the viciſſitudes of time: give me leave, Sir, to draw your attention to their character and way of life.

In like manner as their anceſtors only lived by war, piracy, the chace, and agriculture, ſo our new Icelandic coloniſts were ſtrangers to any fame but that acquired by the ſtrength of their arm, and knew no exerciſes but ſuch as a hardened body was able to ſupport.

To go to war, to plunder, burn and deftroy, and furmount every obftacle which oppofed their defigns, they deemed the fureft path to immortality; even their games gave them an opportunity of exercifing both their ftrength and agility of body.

Glimu-lift, or the art of wreftling, was general among them; though it is mentioned in their old hiftories, that their heroes fometimes made ufe of an artifice which was called *Laufe-tók*, and is the fame as what we call tripping up one's heels. *Skylmeft*, or the art of fencing, was ftill more common; for though they treated one another pretty roughly on thefe occafions, yet thofe rules of art were wanting which a weaker arm may at prefent apply to his advantage upon occafion.

The *manjafnadur* was held in the higheft efteem: a man, dextrous in that exercife, was held in the utmoft veneration by them, and was celebrated even in their fongs. This was a kind of fingle combat, to which a man might challenge any one who was defirous

firous to be recorded in the annals of fame. Life or death was alike indifferent to thefe gladiators; and it was deemed a noble art to underftand well how to fharpen the inftruments of death, as may be feen by *Rigfthulu*.

The fituation in which the Icelanders were, in regard to the kings of Norway, who always kept a watchful eye over them, and fought every opportunity to fubjugate them, obliged them to have recourfe to other ftates for a knowledge in government and literature. For this purpofe, they often failed to Norway, Denmark, Sweden, England, and Scotland. The travellers, at their return, were obliged to give an account to their chiefs of the ftate of thofe kingdoms through which they paffed. For this reafon hiftory, and what related to fcience, was held in high repute, as long as the republican form of government lafted; and the great nnmber of Sagas and hiftories which are to be met with in the country, if not all equally important, fhew at leaft the defire they had of being inftructed.

During this time Greenland was discovered by an Icelander, Eyrek Rauda, in 932; and America in 1001, by Bidrn Herjulfsſon and Leif Erichſſon.

To ſecure themſelves, therefore, againſt their powerful neighbours, they were obliged to enlarge their hiſtorical knowledge; they likewiſe took great pains in ſtudying perfectly their own laws, for the maintenance and protection of their internal ſecurity. Thus Iceland, at a time when ignorance and obſcurity pervaded the reſt of Europe, was enabled to produce a conſiderable number of poets and hiſtorians. When the Chriſtian religion was introduced there, more were found converſant in the law, than could have been expected, conſidering the extent of the country, and the number of its inhabitants. Fiſhing was followed among them; but they devoted their attention conſiderably more to agriculture*, which has ſince entirely ceaſed.

* Hans Finſſen, in his letter on the feaſibility of agriculture in Iceland, Copenhag. 1772, 8vo, demonſtrates this by a written document during the time of Snorre Sturleſon, pag. 64, which likewiſe appears from Landnama Bok, chap. 21.

Two things have principally contributed towards producing a great change both in their character and way of life, viz. the progress of the Christian religion under Olof Tryggwason, and the loss of their liberty under king Harold. For if religion, on one side, commanded them to desist from their ravages and warlike expeditions; the secular power, on the other, deprived them of the necessary forces for the execution of them; since this time, we find no farther traces of their heroic deeds, except those which are preserved in their histories. Our present Icelanders give the preference to fishing, and the care of their cattle, to war.

The Icelanders are middle-sized and well made, though not very strong; and the women are in general ill-featured. The men have left off the custom of wearing beards long ago, though you find them represented with them in Eggert Olafsen's travels through Iceland; a drawing which, perhaps, may represent an inhabitant of Sondmoer, in Norway, but by no means an Icelander *.

Vices are indeed much lefs common among them than in other parts, where riches and luxury have corrupted the morals of the people. Theft is feldom heard of; nor are they inclined to incontinence, though there are examples of perfons having been punifhed more than once on that account.

Though their poverty difables them from imitating the hofpitality of their anceftors in all refpects, yet the defire of doing it ftill exifts: they cheerfully give away the little they have to fpare, and exprefs the utmoft joy and fatisfaction if you are pleafed with their gift. When they want to fhew

---

* This, however, is fubject to fome exceptions: for the inhabitants of Omund Fiorden, and fome families on the north fide of the ifland, ftill wear beards; and in Fniofkadul lives a man named Benedict, known on account of his beard. Between 1740 and 1750 it happened, between the icy mountains of Sneefaelds Jokne, that two brethren dividing between themfelves the inheritance left them by their father, one of them, called Helge, gave his brother four rix-dollars for the exclufive right of wearing a beard, which right, in their family, was the fole prerogative of their late father.

them-

themselves particularly affectionate, they kiss one another on the mouth on their visits: they do the same to the husband and the wife, the mother and the daughter; they are uncommonly obliging and faithful, and extremely attached to government *. They are very zealous in their religion ‡, and it must be owned not entirely free from superstition. They have an inexpressible attachment for their native country, and are no where so happy. An Icelander, therefore,

* To prevent smuggling, there is a severe penalty for piloting a strange ship into harbour. When the philosophic travellers made the coast, they were under necessity to force an Icelander to stay on board, and to serve them as a pilot. And though appeased by good treatment and presents, he nevertheless carried the ship to an unsafe place, till the governor granted his leave to bring the ship to a safe anchorage. When the reason of this strange behaviour was asked, the Icelander answered, he would rather suffer himself to be cut in pieces, than to act against the regulations of his king. It is however told, that the inhabitants on the northern coast are not quite so docile, and therefore less obsequious.

‡ An Icelander never passes a river, or any other dangerous place, without previously taking off his hat, and imploring divine protection; and he is always thankful for the protection of God, when he has passed the danger in security.

rarely

rarely settles in Copenhagen, though ever so advantageous conditions should be offered him *.

* It seems that Providence wisely instilled into the human heart the love of that soil whereon a man is born, and probably with a view that those places, which are not favoured by nature with her choicest blessings, may not be left without inhabitants. It may be affirmed with some degree of certainty, that the love of ones native place increases in an inverse ratio of its having received favours from nature. A Frenchman seldom or never feels that longing desire for his home, which all Swedes are sensible of. A peasant of Scania (a rich country in a mild climate) eats his hasty-pudding (the favourite dish in Scania) with equal pleasure and enjoyment in whatever place it be; but a native of Elfredahl and Særna (places ill-favoured by nature) thinks his bread made of flour, mixed with the bark of trees in his own country, more preferable to the best dishes he eats in the low country. The chiefest wish of a Switzer is to die in his own country. When a Switzer in the French army sung a certain song to his countrymen in the last war, there arose in the breasts of all that heard him such a disease-like longing for their native country, that it became absolutely necessary to the French generals, to give the strictest injunctions, that this song should never be heard again in the camp. This will appear incredible to those who are acquainted with no other happiness than that which is produced by the enjoyment of luxury, affluence, and voluptuousness. It always recalls to the memory that fine passage in Seneca: "Ulysses ad Ithacæ
" suæ saxa sic properat, quemadmodum Agamemnon
" ad Mycenarem nobiles muros; nemo enim patriam
" amat, quia magna, sed quia sua."

On the other hand, one cannot afcribe any great induftry to them; they work on in the manner they are once ufed to, without thinking of ufeful improvements. Perhaps this defect lies more with the government, which being unacquainted with the nature of the country, did not make the neceffary difpofitions and regulations for creating and encouraging induftry. They are not cheerful in converfation, but fimple and credulous, and have no averfion to a bottle if they can find opportunity; but it may eafily be conceived, that this is not to be underftood of all without exception. When they meet together, their chief paftime confifts in reading their hiftory *(fauguleftur)*; the mafter of the houfe makes the beginning, and the reft continue in their turns when he is tired. Some of them know thefe ftories by heart, others have them in print, and thofe that have not, have them in writing. One of thefe paftimes is *rumuleftur*, confifting in the recitation of fome verfes, which fometimes are indifferently fung. They
befides

besides amuse themselves in their meetings with what they call *wike-waka*, where a man and woman take one another by the hand, and by turns sing stanzas, which are a kind of dialogue, and to which the company sometimes join in chorus. This however affords little amusement to a stranger, as they generally sing very bad, without observing time, or any other grace, particularly as they have not the least knowledge of the modern improvements in music *.

To their diversions likewise belongs that called *glaeder*, where one among them is disguised; *ringbrud*, where ten or twelve men join hands, and form a ring in dancing; and it is reckoned a great dexterity to break through the ring, without destroying their order; *glimu-list*, which has been mentioned before, and means wrestling; *hnattleikur*, or playing with bowls on the

* I observed two kinds of musical instruments in Iceland, one called *langspil*, with six brass strings; the other called *fidla*, with two strings made of horses hair: both are played by a bow. I likewise heard of another instrument called *symphon*, but I never could get a sight of it.

ice;

ice; *lyftridin*, or riding races for a wager, &c. &c.

They are famous at playing at chefs, and had formerly two forts of this game; one of which was called *jungfru fchach* (ladies chefs), and the other *riddare fchach** (knight's chefs): at prefent only the laft is cuftomary. They alfo amufe themfelves with *kotra* (a game at tables) they play on it *togtadilla* or *olofstafl*, when the men are ranged blindfold, without dice, according to an old fong which muft be faid by heart. Befides thefe games they have others called *Mylna Faringar-tafl*, and *Goda-tafl*. They alfo play fome games at cards, called *Alkort*, *Handkarrer*, *Tru-fpill*, and *Pamphile*; all thefe games are merely for amufement, fince they never play for money, which feems however to have been formerly cuftomary among them, fince in one of their old laws a fine is deftined for thofe who fhould play for money.

* Vide letter of Arnus Magnaus to Widalin, communicated to me in manufcript by Mr. Thoroan.

LET-

LETTER VII.

To CHEVALIER IHRE.

Of the Dreſs of the Icelanders.

Stockholm, Sept. 6, 1774.

THE Icelanders have made very few alterations, if any, in their dreſs in modern times. It is not elegant or ornamental, but yet neat, cleanly, and ſuited to the climate. The men all wear a linen ſhirt next to the ſkin, with a ſhort jacket, and wide pair of breeches over it. When they travel they wear another ſhort coat *(hempa)* over it. All this is made of coarſe black cloth *(wadmal)*; only the inhabitants on the north ſide of Arnarfiord wear white cloaths. On the head they wear large three cornered hats, and worſted ſtockings, and Icelandic ſhoes on their feet.

Some of them have ſhoes from Copenhagen, but as they are rather too dear

dear for them, they generally make their own shoes, sometimes of ox hide, but mostly of sheep's leather: the manner in which they make them is this; they cut a square piece of leather, rather wider than the length of the foot, this they sow up at the toes, and behind at the heel, and tie it on with leather thongs. These shoes are convenient enough where the country is level; but it would be very difficult for us, who are not used to them, to go with them amongst the rocks and stones, though the Icelanders do it with great ease. I shall speak of their fishing cloaths afterwards.

The women likewise are always dressed in black *wadmal:* they wear a bodice over their shifts, which are sewed up at the bosom; and above this a jacket laced before, with long narrow sleeves reaching down to the wrists. In the opening on the side of the sleeve they have buttons of chafed silver, with a plate fixed to each button, on which the lover, when he buys them, in order to present them to his mistress, takes care to have his
name

name and hers engraved. At the top of the jacket a little black collar is fixed *(ſtrutur)* of about three inches broad, of velvet or ſilk, and frequently trimmed with gold cord. The petticoat is likewiſe of *wadmal*, and reaches down to the ancles. Round the top of it is a girdle of ſilver, or ſome other metal, to which they faſten the apron *(ſwinte)*, which is alſo of *wadmal*, and ornamented at top with buttons of chafed ſilver. Over this dreſs they wear a *hempa*, or upper-dreſs, nearly reſembling that of the peaſants at Wingaker in Sweden, with this difference, that it is wider at bottom: this is cloſe at the neck and wriſts, and a hand's breadth ſhorter than the petticoat. It is adorned with a facing down to the very bottom, which looks like cut velvet, and is generally wove by the Icelandic women. On their fingers they wear gold, ſilver, or braſs rings. Their head-dreſs conſiſts of ſeveral cloths wrapped round the head, almoſt as high again as the face; it is tied faſt with a handkerchief, and ſerves more for warmth than

than ornament: girls are not allowed to wear this head-drefs before they are marriageable. At their weddings they are adorned in a very particular manner: the bride wears clofe to the face, round her head-drefs a crown of filver gilt. She has two chains round her neck, one of which hangs down very low before, and the other refts on her fhoulders. Befides thefe fhe wears a leffer chain, from which a little heart generally hangs, which may be opened to put balfam or fome other kind of perfume into it.

The drefs here defcribed is worn by all the Icelandic women, high and low, without exception; with this difference, that the poorer fort have it of coarfe *wadmal*, with ornaments of brafs; and thofe that are eafier in their circumftances of broad cloth, with filver ornaments gilt. I faw one of thefe dreffes, which belonged to the bailiff's wife, and was worth at leaft three hundred dollars. Perhaps it would not be difagreeable to perufe a lift of the different articles which compofe an Icelandic woman's drefs, one of which Mr. Banks bought, in order to take to England, with his other Icelandic collections.

	Rix Dol.	Shil. Dan.
Hempa (upper dress) -	4	0
Hœttve (travelling hat) -	5	0
Upphlutur (bodice) -	2	24
Svinta (apron) -	6	0
Treja (jacket) - -	4	3
Mallinda (girdle) -	6	0
Fat (petticoat) - -	8	0
Kjedja (chain) - -	4	0
Laufa prionar (bodkins ornamented with silver)	6	0
Koffur (fillet) - -	2	0
Erma knappar (sleeve-buttons)	1	24
Quen vetlingar (rough gloves)	0	46
Aubreida (a cloth to wrap their cloaths in)	4	0
	53	46

LET-

LETTER VIII.

To CHEVALIER IHRE.

Of the Houses and Buildings of the Icelanders.

Stockholm, Sept. 14. 1774.

THE houses of the Icelanders are not alike throughout the country. According to some descriptions, they are tolerable on the north side of the Island; but on that part of Iceland which I have seen, they were all extremely bad, excepting those of the governor at Besseftedr, the physicians at Seltiarnarnes, and the sheriffs at Wido, which were built of stone at the king's expense. In some parts the dwellings and other buildings of the Icelanders are made of drift-wood, in others they are raised of lava, almost in the same manner as the stonewalls we make for inclosures, with moss stuffed between the lava. In some houses the walls are wainscotted on the infide. The roof is covered with fods laid over rafting, or sometimes over ribs of whales, which is both more durable and more expenfive than wood. The timber-work refts on many beams laid length-ways. The walls are about three yards high, and the entrance fomewhat lower. The plan of one of thefe houfes is here annexed, to give a better idea of it.

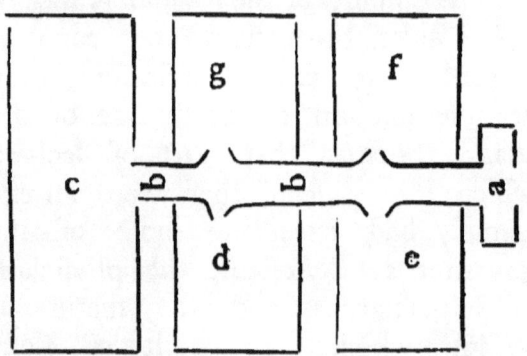

(a) is the door or entrance of the long lobby; (bbb) is about fix feet broad, and admits the light through fome holes in the roof, upon which a hoop, with a fkin ftretched over it, is laid. At the end of the lobby is a room (c) where the women do their work, and where the mafter of the houfe generally fleeps with his wife.

wife. The walls of this room are wainscotted; it has a cieling and floor, sometimes even small glass windows, but no fire place. On both sides of this long lobby are four rooms, two on each side, of which (d) is the kitchen, (e) the room made use of to eat in, (f) the dairy, and (g) the servants room: these rooms have neither cielings nor floors, and the walls are seldom or never lined. The windows are made of the chorion *(liknarbelgur)* and amnios of sheep *(vatzbelgur)*, or the membranes which surround the womb of the ewe. These are stretched over a hoop, and laid over an opening in the roof, upon which a wooden shutter is let down, if the weather be stormy. They have not even a chimney in the kitchens, and only lay their fuel between three stones, and the smoke issues from a square hole in the roof. Besides this house, they have a booth or shed to keep their fish in *(skæmma)*, sometimes another for their cloaths, &c. &c. and not far off the stable for their cattle. In the poorer sort of houses, they employ for
the

the windows the inner membrane of the ſtomach of animals, and which they call *ſkœna*; this is not ſo tranſparent as the before-mentioned membrane.

LETTER IX.

To Mrs. CARLSON.

Of the Food of the Icelanders.

Gothenburg, March 20.

THOUGH it cannot afford any great pleasure to examine the manner in which the Icelanders prepare their food, particularly after having so lately tasted at your table all the dainties of the four parts of the globe; I will, nevertheless, perform my promise in communicating to you a description of it. Methinks I see you sometimes disdaining their dishes; but, I assure you, an Icelander is not less happy for being unable to season his food with the productions of a distant climate: he is content with what nature affords him, satisfies the cravings of his stomach, and enjoys his health, whilst we frequently surfeit ourselves by feasting on delicacies, and loathe the most wholsome food.

The larders and pantries of the Icelanders are seldom so well stored as to contain every one of the articles at one time, which I am going to mention; some of them, however, they must be absolutely provided with, as their food entirely consists of the following articles.

Bread of several sorts, chiefly sour biscuit * from Copenhagen; but they have not much of this, as it is too dear for them; they content themselves therefore with providing it for weddings,

* In most northern countries the inhabitants live on rye bread; the flour taken to prepare it is seldom bolted, and it is commonly prepared with sour ferment or leven, which gives the bread an acidulated taste, disagreeable, and resisting the stomachs of weak persons, but palatable and wholesome to those of a strong constitution. The sour paste communicates an agreeable acidity to this bread; and as the northern climates, on account of their long winters, and the confinement of people in heated rooms full of noxious effluvia, as well on account of the chiefly salt-meat diet of the inhabitants, make the people inclined to the scurvy; this acidulated bread, the sour-crout, and in Russia their sour drink called *Guass*, afford such powerful antiseptics, that with the diet here described, the scurvy seldom or ever gains ground among the people. These sour biscuits, no doubt, are likewise made of rye-flour, or of rye and wheat mixed together, ground without bolting, and acidulated by fermentation with sour leven.

and

and other entertainments. Some, inftead of it, bake themfelves bread of flour of rye, though they likewife get fome from Copenhagen. The manner in which they bake it is thus: the flour is mixed with fome fermented whey *(fyra)*, and kneaded into dough, of which they make cakes one foot in breadth, and three inches thick; thefe are boiled in water or whey, and then dried on a hot ftone or an iron plate.

Flour of *Fiálgrás* (rock-grafs*), a oafk of which well cleaned and packed cofts a rix-dollar; it is firft wafhed, and then cut into fmall pieces by fome, though the greater number dry it by fire or the fun, then put it into a bag, in which it is well beaten, and laftly worked into flour by ftamping.

Flour of *Kornfyra* † is prepared in the fame manner, as well as the two other forts of wild corn *melur* §, by

* Lichen Iflandicus, Fl. Suec. 1085. Fl. Lappon, 145.
† Polygonum Biftorta.
§ 1) Arunda arenaria, 2) arundo foliorum lateribus convolutis.

feparating

separating it from the chaff, by pounding, and lastly grinding it.

Surt smoer (sour butter). The Icelanders seldom make use of fresh or salt butter, but let it grow sour before they eat it: in this manner it may be kept twenty years, and even longer; and the Icelanders look upon it as more wholsome and palatable than the butter used amongst us. It is reckoned better the older it grows, and one pound of it then is as much valued as two pounds of fresh butter.

Striug, or whey boiled to the consistence of sour milk, and preserved for the winter.

Fish of all kinds, both dried in the sun and in the air, and either salted or in winter frozen: those prepared in the last manner are preferred by many.

The flesh of bears, sheep, and birds, which is partly salted, partly hung or smoaked, and some preserved in casks, with sour fermented whey poured over it.

Misost, or whey boiled to cheese, which is very good. But the art of making other kinds of good cheese is lost, loft, though some tolerably palatable is sold in the east quarter of Iceland.

Beina-striug, bones and cartilages of beef and mutton, and likewise bones of cod, boiled in whey, till they are quite dissolved; they are then left to ferment, and are eat with milk.

Skyr, the curds from which the whey is squeezed, are preserved in casks, or other vessels; they are sometimes mixed with black crow-berries, *(empetrum baccis nigris)*, or juniper berries, and are likewise eat with new milk.

Syra is sour whey, kept in casks, and left to ferment, which, however, is not thought fit for use till it is a year old.

Blanda is a liquor made of water, to which a twelfth part of *syra* is added. In winter it is mixed with the juice of thyme, and of the black crow-berries, or the *empetrum nigrum*.

They likewise eat many vegetables *, some of which grow wild, and others

are

---

* The following catalogue of plants used for food in Iceland is taken from the journey of Eggert Olaf-sen; Rumex

are cultivated; as also shell-fish * and mushrooms †.

The Icelanders in general eat three meals a day, at seven in the morning, at two in the afternoon, and at nine in the evening.

Rumex acetosa, in the Icelandic language called *Sura*,
- - - digynus, - - - - - *Olafs Sura*.
- - - patientia, - - - - *Heimis-mole*.
Taraxacum, - - - - - - - - - *Aetti-fifill*.
Carex LIN. pinguicula, *Lifia-gras*, used against the dysentery.
Trifolium pratense flore albo.
Potentilla argentea, *Mura*.
Plantago maritima, LIN. foliis linearibus, *Kattartunga*.
Angelica archangelica, *Huónn*; *Ætte-huónn*.
Lichen Islandicus, *Fialla-graus*.
- - - Lichenoides, *Klounngur*.
- - - Coraloides, *Kræda*.
- - - Niveus, *Mariu-gras*.
- - - Leprosus, *Geitna-skof*.
Arundo Arenaria, *Melur*.
- - - foliorum lateribus convolutis.
Cochlearia, *Skarfa-kaal*.
Plantago angustifolia, *Selgrese*.
Epilobium tetragonum, *Purpura-blomslur*.
Polygonum bistorta, *Kornsura*.
Sisymbrium, Lin. *Kattar-balsam*.

* Ventrosa crassa, *Kuskel skelkuskel*.
Domiporta, *Kudungur, kufungur, kongur*.
Mytulus, *Kräklingur*.
- - - Major, *Ada*.

† Agaricus caulescens, pileo albo, *Ætte-sveps*.
- - - supra pileo plano, *Ætte-svepr*.
- - - subconvexo, *Reyde-kula*.
- - - of an unknown sort, *Bleikula*.

In the morning and evening they commonly eat curds mixed with new milk, and sometimes with juniper berries, and those of *empetrum nigrum*. In some parts they also have pottage of *fialgras*, which, I assure you, is very palatable; *vállidrafli*, or curdled milk, boiled till it becomes of a red colour; *seiddmijolk*, or new milk, boiled a long while. At dinner, their food consists of dried fish, with plenty of sour butter. They also sometimes eat fresh fish, and, when possible, a little bread and cheese with them. It is reported by some, that they do not eat any fish till it is quite rotten; this report, perhaps, proceeds from their being fond of it when a little tainted: they, however, frequently eat fish which is quite fresh, though in the same manner as the rest of their food, often without salt.

On Sunday, and in harvest-time, they have broth made of meat, which is often boiled in *syra*, instead of water; and in winter they eat hung or dried meat.

Their

Their common beveridge is milk, either warm from the cow, or cold, and sometimes boiled: they likewise make butter-milk, with or without water. On the coasts they generally drink *blanda**, and sour milk; which is sold, after it is skimmed, at two-fifths of a rix-dollar a cask: some likewise send for beer from Copenhagen, and some others brew their own. A few of the principal inhabitants also have claret and coffee. The common people sometimes drink a kind of tea, which they make from the leaves of Holta-sollyg† and Spudwell ‡.

This is the usual manner of life in Iceland. In all countries the living of the poor differs essentially from that of the rich; and if an Iceland gentleman can afford to eat meat, butter, shark, and whale, the peasants are obliged to content themselves with fish, blanda, milk,

---

* In the Elfdalln of Wermeland in Sweden, the common beveridge of the country people is milk, mixed with water, and called by them *Blanda*.

† Dryas octopetala.

‡ Veronica officinales.

pottage

pottage of rock-grafs, and *beina-ſtriug*. Though the Icelanders cannot in general be faid to be in want of neceſſary aliment, yet the country has feveral times been vifited by great famines: thefe, however, have been chiefly owing to the Greenland floating-ice, which, when it comes in great quantities, prevents the grafs from growing, and puts an entire ſtop to their fifhing.

I need not acquaint you, that we were not neceſſitated to fubmit to their manner of life during our ſtay in Iceland. Inſtead of *blanda* we drink port, and feveral other forts of good wine; and a French cook prepared for us fome favoury diſhes, and excellent puddings.

However, as we wiſhed to try every thing, we prevailed upon the phyſician, Biarne Paulfen, who had invited us to dinner, to entertain us after the Icelandic manner. We did not forget the good Swediſh cuſtom of taking a glafs of brandy before dinner, which was here genuine; we had only once Daniſh diſtilled corn-brandy, which

was

was served up with biscuit, cheese, and sour butter. In the middle of the table was placed a dish with dried fish cut small; the other dishes were a piece of good roast mutton, broth with *syra*, and a dish of salmon-trouts, &c. &c. We eat with a very good appetite; but the sour butter and dried fish were not often applied to: on the whole, we eat a greater quantity of bread than the Icelanders generally do.

So elegant an entertainment could not be without a desert; and for this purpose some flesh of whale and shark *(hafkal)* was served. This is either boiled or dried in the air, looks very much like rusty bacon, and had so disagreeable a taste, that the small quantity we took of it, drove us from the table long before our intention. Most probably you already thank me for my entertainment, and are happy to see the end of my letter.

LETTER

LETTER X.

To CHEVALIER IHRE.

Of the Employment of the Icelanders, and their Chronology.

Stockholm, Sept. 6, 1774.

THE Icelanders principally attend to fishing, and the care of their cattle.

On the coasts the men employ their time in fishing, both summer and winter; on their return home, when they have drawn and cleaned their fish, they give them to their wives, whose care it is to dry them. In the winter, when the inclemency of the weather prevents them from fishing, they are obliged to take care of their cattle, and spin wool. In summer they mow the grafs, dig turf, provide fuel, go in search of sheep and goats that were gone astray, and kill cattle. They likewise fill their *wadmal*, or coarse cloth; for which purpose they make

make ufe of urine, which they alfo employ in wafhing and bucking, inftead of foap and pot-afhes. The men likewife prepare leather, for which they ufe *maid-urt* (fpiraca ulmaria) inflead of birch-rind. Some few work in gold and filver, and others are inftructed in mechanics, in which they are tolerable proficients.

As a proof of this, I need only mention a fledge which a peafant contrived fome years ago in the form of a fhip with fails, and large enough to contain four or five perfons, that would fail, in the winter feafon, in an even country. Unluckily, two of his fons, in failing home from church, overturned, and broke the whole carriage to pieces.

On the weft fide of the country they make veffels of floating wood, large enough to contain from three to twelve tons, and make their charge according to the fize of the veffel, from four to fix dollars.

The women prepare the fifh, take care of the cattle, manage the milk and the wool, few, fpin, and gather eggs and down. When they work in
the

the evening, they ufe, inftead of an hour-glafs, a lamp, with a wick made of *fiva* (epilobium) dipt in train-oil, which is fo contrived as to burn four, fix, or eight hours.

Their work is in fome meafure determined by their *bya-lag*, or by-laws * of their villages, in which the quan-

* " By-laws are faid to be orders made in court-leets or court-barons, by common affent, for the good of thofe that make them, farther than the public law binds." *Atterbury.* See *Johnfon's Dict.* Though this may probably be the prefent meaning of the word *By-law*, it is not, however, the original meaning of the word; for it is derived from the old Saxon word *by* or *bye*, fignifying a town, from the Gothic word *bo*, to inhabit; and agreeable to this are many Englifh names of towns, viz. *Afh-by*, *Whit-by*, &c. &c. *By-law*, therefore, fignified formerly laws made by townfhips, and by diftricts belonging to a town, or to a leet, which amounted fometimes to a third part of a fhire. Thefe laws were made by common affent, and for the good of thofe that made them, which is, or ought to be, the chief aim of all laws, and they extend farther than the public law binds; becaufe the law of the land muft be general, and cannot provide for all particular cafes of fingle towns and diftricts. The fpecial regulations and reftrictions, therefore made by the common affent of the towns-people, for the common good of that particular town, beyond the law of the land, are *by-laws*, laws of the *bye* or *town*. The Icelandic word *bya-lag*, fignifies laws of villages or townfhips; and it confirms the fignification we have given to the Englifh word *by-law*.

tity of work they are bound to perform in a day is prescribed to them: they seldom do so much work now, so that it is called only *medelman's värk*, or the work of a man of middling strength. According to this prescription, a man is to mow as much hay in one day, as grows on thirty fathoms square of manured soil, or forty fathoms square of land not manured, or he is obliged to dig 700 pieces of turf eight feet long and three broad. If so much snow falls as to reach to the horses bellies, which they call *quedsnio*, he is to clear away daily the snow for a hundred sheep. A woman is to rake together as much hay as three men can mow, or to weave three yards of *wadmal* a-day.

The wages of a man are fixed at four dollars, and twelve yards of *wadmal*; and those of a woman at two dollars, and five yards of *wadmal*. When men are sent a fishing out of the country, there is allowed to each man, by the *bya-lag*, from the 25th of September to the 14th of May, six pounds of butter, and eighteen pounds of dried
fish

fish every week. This may appear to be too great an allowance; but it muſt be remembered, that they have nothing beſides to live upon. When they are at home and can get milk, &c. &c. every man receives only five pounds of dried fiſh, and three quarters of a pound of butter a-week.

As the diviſion of time among the Icelanders is not determined according to the courſe of the ſun, but by their work, this is perhaps the moſt proper place to ſay ſomething of it. Though they have, like us, four different ſeaſons, they only count two; the ſummer, which begins the Thurſday before the 16th of April; and the winter, which commences on the Friday before the 18th of October. During the firſt ſeaſon they perform their ſummer-work, and in the latter attend to their winter amuſements. Theſe two ſeaſons are afterwards divided into twelve months, as with us, which have their common names; but in antient records, and among the lower claſs of people, are called, 1. *Midſvctrar.* 2. *Föſtugangs m.* 3. *Iafndaegra m.* 4. *Sumar*

Sumar m. 5. *Fardaga m.* 6. *Nöttleyſu m.* 7. *Midſumar m.* 8. *Heyanna m.* 9. *Adratta m.* 10. *Slaatrunar m.* 11. *Ridtidar m.* 12. *Skammdeigis m.* Day and night are not divided into a certain number of hours, but into the following diviſions: *Otta* is with them three o'clock in the morning; *Midur morgon,* or *Herdis riſmal,* five o'clock; *Dagmal,* half paſt eight; *Haadeye,* eleven; *Nonn,* three in the afternoon; *Midur afton,* ſix in the morning; *Nattmall,* eight; and *Midnatt,* twelve o'clock at night.

When they want to know what o'clock it is, they attend to the courſe of the ſun, and the flux and reflux of the ſea; but generally they make uſe of an art to diſcover the ſun by their fingers. Watches are very rare among them; every peaſant, however, has an hour-glaſs.

LETTER XI.

To Chevalier Bach.

Of the Difeafes in Iceland.

Stockholm, Oct. 1, 1776.

YOU require, Sir, that I fhould give you fome account of the difeafes common in Iceland. I will obey your commands, though it is more the province of a phyfician to undertake the fubject, as it requires fo much exactnefs and penetration.

As I have been fo happy as to be unacquainted with any difeafe from my own experience, I have as little endeavoured to gain any knowledge by reading fuch books as treat of them; you will therefore pardon me if my account is not very perfect.

The climate of the country, and the purity of the air, contribute very much to make the Icelanders ftrong and healthy, though their food and way of life frequently produce the
con-

contrary effect. Young children, for example, are not fuckled more than two or three days, and afterwards brought up with cows milk, which, in times of dearth, is mixed with flour and water.

I remember to have heard, that this is alfo cuftomary in fome parts of Finland; but a different manner of living may render that unwholefome in Iceland, which is lefs dangerous in another place: and I think I may fafely venture to affirm, that the food and mode of living in Iceland do not at all contribute to the ftrength of the inhabitants. One feldom meets with any of them above 50 or 60 years of age, and the greater part are attacked in their middle age by many grievous complaints.

It is remarkable that among the female fex, who there, as almoft every where elfe, live to a greater age than the men, thofe particularly attain to an advanced life who have had many children. There are a great many of this clafs, as the women are commonly very fruitful; and it is no rare thing to meet with
a mo-

a mother who has had twelve or fifteen children.

Among the difeafes that are moft prevalent, the fcurvy *(Skyrbuigur)* is the moft common. In fome, it makes its appearance in the fame manner as with us, but in others it produces the moft dreadful fymptoms, and is then called *liktraad*, or leprofy, which, however, differs from that horrid difeafe fo common in the Eaft. Its firft appearances are, fwellings in the hands and feet, and fometimes alfo in other parts of the body: the fkin becomes fhining and of a bluifh caft, the hair falls off, the fight, tafte, fmell, and feeling are weakened, and often quite loft; biles appear on the arms, legs, and face; refpiration becomes difficult, and the breath fœtid; aching pains are felt in all the joints, a breaking-out fpreads over the whole body, and is at laft converted into wounds, which generally terminate in death.

The Icelanders make ufe of antifcorbutic decoctions, likewife baths, with turnips boiled in them; but
chiefly

chiefly mercurial remedies, by means of which the difeafe may be removed in its beginning. This difeafe is not contagious, but very obftinate; and it is remarkable, that two generations may be entirely free from it, when it fhall appear in the third. It does not always prove mortal, though many are tormented with it twenty or thirty years.

The gout *(torvàrk)* moft men have in their hands who go out a-fifhing, probably becaufe they are obliged to handle and manage the wet fifhing-tackle in cold weather.

The St. Anthony's fire, in Icelandic *a ama*, is pretty common. They make ufe of earth-worms *(anamadkur)* to cure it, which they bind alive on the wounded part; and when they become dry, others are applied till the difeafe is removed.

The jaundice, in Icelandic *guulfot*; the fever, *kvefsot*; the pleurify, *tak*, which is fometimes infectious, and then is called *landfarfot,* or an infectious difeafe, is frequently got by cold; lownefs of fpirits, *careinoma infantum*, in Icelandic *krabbe, a atumein*, the fpleen, spleen, and obstructions, are very common. In later years the rickets made their appearance; and the venereal disease was not known among them till the year 1753.

Besides the antiscorbutic plants, which are to be found in plenty in Iceland, they have a number of hot baths, which are of great benefit in the cure of these diseases.

There is an apothecary's shop established on the island, and four hospitals for the poor and leprous, the care of which is committed to their most skilful physicians, with proper assistants.

LETTER XII.

To Chevalier Ihre.

Of Fishing and Fowling, and the Breed of Cattle in Iceland.

Stockholm, Oct. 3, 1774.

THE inhabitants who live near the coasts employ themselves almost all the year in fishing; and even those who live in the inland parts of the country come to the sea-shore at certain seasons of the year. Every master of a family has a particular fishing-dress, and is obliged to furnish one to his servant as soon as he puts out to sea. They are made of sheep or calves skins, which, in manufacturing, are frequently rubbed over with train-oil. They consist of the following articles: *Leistrabrakur* are breeches and stockings all in a piece, which come up pretty high above the hips, and are laced on very tight; *stackur*, a wide jacket

jacket faſtened round the neck and the middle of the waiſt; *taatillar*, or coarſe fulled ſtockings, or ſtiff worſted; and *ſjoſkor*, or water-ſhoes, of thick leather.

Their boats are commonly ſmall, and only contain from one to four men, with theſe they fiſh near the ſhore; but with their larger boats, which are made to contain from twelve to ſixteen men, and are provided with ſails, they frequently venture from four to eight miles from the ſhore.

In theſe veſſels they always carry a man extraordinary, whom they call *formann*. He ſits at the helm; and the others, who are called *haaſeters*, obey his commands. At his call they all aſſemble at an appointed time near the veſſel, provided with knives, fiſhing-lines, and other proper tackle: they make uſe of ſhells, and ſometimes the fleſh of quadrupeds and birds for bait.

As ſoon as the boat is off the ſhore, they all take off their hats and caps, pray for good ſucceſs, and recommend themſelves to the divine protection by

a prayer

a prayer and hymn, which they call *vararſaungur*, and then ſtand out to ſea. As ſoon as they are come to a place where they expect a good draught, two of them ſit down at the helm, to prevent the boat's being moved out of its place by the current, and to take care that the fiſhing-lines are not entangled. In this manner they continue fiſhing the whole day; and when the boat will not contain any more fiſh, they cut off the heads of all the fiſh they have caught, which they throw into the ſea, together with their entrails. This not only enables them to carry a greater number of fiſh aſhore, but alſo invites many inſects to the place, which affords good bait.

At their return, all the fiſh are brought aſhore, and divided into equal ſhares: one ſhare belongs to the owner of the boat, though he ſhould not be out at ſea with them, and this is called *ſkipleiga (ſhipſhire)*; another is given to him who ſat at the helm; a third to him who governed the ſails; in a word, every fiſher gets a ſhare. But this equal diviſion vifion is only made with the fmaller fifh; for if any one in the boat is fo fortunate as to catch a turbot or other valuable fifh, it is immediately cut into pieces, and the three beft given to him who caught it.

As foon as they have thus fhared them, every one cuts off the heads of his fifh, draws them, and after cutting them up from top to bottom on the fide of the belly, take out the backbone from that part where it is fixed to the head, down to the third joint below the heart. If the weather be fuch as to give them hopes of drying their fifh next day, they lay them with the flefhy fide facing one another; but if the weather is unfavourable, they lay the pieces on a heap with the fkinny fide uppermoft, and this they call *lagga i kafe*; 'if they lie too long in this pofition (one above another) they fpoil, and are then fold to the merchants at a lower price, under the denomination of *kafad fifk*. When the weather is fair, thefe pieces are fpread feparately on ftones, or on the fhore, and are frequently turned by

the

the women, till they are entirely dry; this often requires a fortnight's time, and sometimes more. The fish prepared in this manner are called *flat-fiſkur* (flat-fiſh).

In ſome parts they do not dry the fiſh on ſtones or on the ſhore; but after they have ripped them up, place them in rows on ſtones which are laid croſs-wiſe in a houſe built for that purpoſe; theſe huts are called *hiallur* in Iceland, and ſomewhat reſemble the ſheds in which ſmiths ſhoe horſes. Theſe fiſh are called *hengi-fiſkur*, or hung fiſh.

The fiſh they principally catch is cod, of which they have ſeveral different ſorts, under the names of *thyrſk-liugur, upſe, iſk, langr, kerla*, &c. &c. Beſides theſe they have ſoles, flounders, herrings, ſalmon, ſalmon-trout, trouts, and ſeveral others. Of the trouts it has been obſerved, that when they come up the rivers and brooks, and approach the hot ſprings, they are fond of ſtaying in the lukewarm water, where they grow ſo fat as to be ſcarcely eatable.

It

It is unneceſſary to ſay, that the ſeas, as well as the rivers and lakes, abound with fiſh: I will therefore only mention the whale, of which there are ſeveral ſorts, divided by the natives into two claſſes, thoſe with and thoſe without tuſks.

The firſt are again divided into *ſkidis fiſkur*, ſmooth-bellied, and *reydar fiſkur*, or wrinkle-bellied. Among the *ſkidis fiſkur*, who have whalebone inſtead of teeth, the *ſlettbakr*, whoſe back is flat, is the largeſt; and ſome have been caught one hundred yards in length. The *hnufuba kr* has a hump on his back, and is next in ſize, being from ſeventy to eighty yards long. Of all the known whales, the *ſteipercidur*, which belongs to the claſs of the *reydar fiſkur*, is thought to be the largeſt, as there are ſome one hundred and twenty yards in length. Then follow the *hrafn reydur* and the *andarnefia*; they are all conſidered as very dainty food; and the Icelanders ſay, the fleſh has the taſte of beef.

The whales which have teeth inftead of whalebone, are alfo divided into two claffes, thofe that are eatable and thofe that are not. To the firft clafs belong the *bnyfen, bnydingur, bundfifkur*, and *kaahyrningur:* to the laft, to which the name of *illwhale* (bad whales) is given, are reckoned the *rodkammingur* and *naabvalur*. Thefe are forbidden as food by fome ancient regulations, and particularly by the church laws. The Icelanders believe, that the firft fort are very fond of human flefh, and therefore avoid fifhing in fuch places where they appear.

The other kinds of whales are fometimes ftruck with harpoons, and fometimes caught with nets. The Icelanders, however, feldom venture to attack the larger ones, as their boats are fmall, and they unprovided with inftruments proper for that purpofe. They ftand in fo great dread of fome of them, that when out at fea, they are afraid to mention even their names, and carry dung, brimftone, juniper-wood, and fome other articles of the fame nature in their boats, in order to terrify and prevent their too near approach.

Not-

Notwithstanding, it now and then happens that they catch some of the largest sort, which is done when the fish approach too near the shore at high water, and are unable to return as fast as the water ebbs, where they are killed with stones and lances. In this manner they had caught a large whale the year before our arrival at Hafnefiord.

To their fishery likewise may be reckoned the catching of *liadogs*, which is very considerable in some parts. They have four sorts of them, *roftungur, vade-felur, blaudu-feller*, and *gran-felur*. They are fattest in winter, and yield three or four pounds of fat, of which each pound produces seven quarts of oil: in summer, on the contrary, they are very lean. Their flesh is eaten, and their fat sold at five yards a pound. The skin is sold by weight, at the rate of sixty yards for twenty pounds.

Though the situation of Iceland renders it extremely proper for fishing, the fishery has decreased very much lately; which is partly owing to the many foreign ships which yearly come to fish in those parts, and partly to the want of men, as the number of people has decreased greatly. But I believe the chief cause is the monopoly of the trading company, which very much oppresses the country.

If the people had more encouragement, there would be more emulation and diligence amongst them than at present; for they are obliged to sell a *vaett*, or five pounds of dried fish to the company, at the rate of five-sixths of a dollar, which they sell in Hamborough, where the greatest part of what is caught in Iceland is usually sent, for five banco-dollars.

Next to fishing the principal support of the Icelanders is the breeding of cattle.

Their beeves are not large, but very fat and good. It has been reported by some, though without foundation, that there are none among them with horns: it is true however that they seldom have any.

They keep their large cattle at home in their yards the greater part of of the year, though fome have places appropriated to them in the mountains, which they call *fatr*, where they fend their cattle during the fummer, till the hay harveft is over. They have a herdfman to attend them, and two women to milk them, and make butter and cheefe. It is common to meet with oxen running wild about the mountains, which are however drove home in autumn, as every one knows his own by a particular mark put upon them.

The principal food of the cattle is hay, and they reckon a ftack of hay for a cow's winter provifion; one ftack confifts of thirty cocks of hay grown on manured land, and forty cocks grown on unmanured land. When there is a fcarcity of fodder, they feed them in fome parts with *fteenbitr*, a kind of fifh, which, together with the heads and bones of cod, is beaten fmall, and mixed with one quarter of chopped hay. The cattle are fond of it, and yield a good deal of milk after it; but yet it is faid to have a bad taste: they only make use of this food in time of need.

Their cows yield four quarts of milk a day, though they have some that give from eight to fourteen in four-and-twenty hours. A cow that yields six quarts is reckoned a good one and must not stand dry above three weeks before she calves.

A young calf is fed with milk for ten days or a fortnight, afterwards the milk is mixed with water and chopped hay, and at last they give it whey instead of milk.

The usual price of a cow, as well as of a horse, is one hundred and twenty yards, thirty of which makes a dollar. However, sometimes the better sort of horses are sold for eight or ten dollars. They have yet less trouble with their horses than their cows; for though some saddle horses are kept in stables during winter, the greater number of them are obliged to provide for their own subsistence, and when they cannot find this on land, they go in search of sea-weeds

on

on the coasts: but when a great quantity of snow has fallen, the natives are obliged to clear it away for them.

There is no breed of cattle so much attended to in Iceland as that of sheep. As these can easily find subsistence there, the Icelanders look upon it as less troublesome and less expensive to breed them; and there are many peasants who have between three and four hundred sheep. Before the epidemical disease, which raged among the sheep from 1740 to 1750, it was not uncommon to see flocks of one thousand or twelve hundred, the sole property of one person.

I will not venture to examine, whether it would be more advantageous to husbandry to keep more cows than sheep; but as the inhabitants seem to be more inclined to breeding of sheep, it would be well if such regulations were made as might enable them to cultivate it with more advantage.

This has really been thought of by government; for about twenty years ago they sent baron Hastfer, a Swede

Swede by birth, to Iceland for that very purpofe. He made feveral regulations, and invented and prepared a kind of powder, as a cure for the difeafes among fheep, which is very much made ufe of there, as well as in Denmark and Norway. They fpeak of him every where in Iceland, as of a man who had great knowledge in this branch of hufbandry, and a fincere defire to redrefs all defects.

I know not if the report was well founded which was fpread all over the country, that the trading company endeavoured to obftruct him in the execution of this defign: fo much however is certain, that the country has reaped little or no benefit from baron Haftfer's depofitions.

The Icelandic fheep differ from ours in feveral particulars; they have ftraight ears ftanding upright, a fmall tail, and it is common to meet with fheep that have four or five horns: in fome places they are kept in ftables during winter, but they are generally left to feek their food themfelves in the fields.

It

It is remarkable that they are fond of hiding themfelves in caves (of which there are a great many in Iceland) in ftormy, tempeftuous weather. But when they cannot find any retreat during a heavy fall of fnow, they place themfelves all in a heap, with their heads to the middle, and bent towards the ground, which not only prevents them from being fo eafily buried under the fnow, but facilitates the owner finding them again. In this fituation they can remain feveral days; and there have been examples of their having been forced by hunger to gnaw off each other's wool; which forming into balls in their ftomachs, prefently deftroys them. They are however generally foon fought for and difengaged. There are no wild fheep, as has been pretended by fome, for they all have their owners, who keep an exact account of them; and when they are driven to the mountains, they are fcarcely ever without a fhepherd to attend upon them.

Their food is grafs and herbs, and the fcurvy-grafs *(cochlearia)* in particular

ticular makes them so fat, that they yield more than twenty pounds of fat. They reckon one cask of dunged hay, and two not dunged, for a sheep's winter provision. When there is a bad crop, they are obliged to put up with fish bones chopped, as well as the other cattle.

Good sheep give from two to six quarts of milk a day, of which both butter and cheese is made; it has likewise a good taste when boiled.

The principal profit they have from their sheep arises from the wool; this is not shorn off as among us, but remains on till the end of May, when it loosens of itself, and is stripped off at once like a skin, and is then called *Ullafæl*. The whole body is by this time covered again with new wool, which is quite short and fine, and of better quality than the Swedish. It continues to grow the whole summer, and becomes coarser and stiffer towards autumn; it is likewise smooth and glossy, somewhat resembling camel's hair, but more shaggy. This covering enables the sheep to support
the

the rigours of winter; but after they have loft their wool, if the fpring proves a wet one, they take care to fow a piece of coarfe cloth round the ftomach of the weakeft, and thofe that have leaft wool.

A good fheep, againft which no exceptions can be made, muft, according to their by-laws, at leaft afford four pounds of wool, and it is not uncommon for them to produce more.

It is not unufual for an ewe to have two lambs at a time, and fometimes even three; they then take away one lamb from the mother, and give it to another who has loft hers. When the lambs are too weak to follow the mother, they are kept at home and fed upon milk, which is done by means of a quill and a wet piece of fkin.

The price of fix ewes, from two to four years old, together with their lambs and wool, is four dollars in autumn, according to the land-tax: a weather of four years old is fold for one dollar; but it is the cuftom for a merchant to pay only five marks. If any body fells a lamb ready killed, it is valued according

ing to the quantity of fat which it has, at the rate of two marks for every pound. The flefh alone, without the head, feet, entrails, fat, fkin, and wool, is valued at twenty yards, and the by-laws fix the price of a pound of dried mutton at half a yard. The fkin is fold by weight, after the rate of thirty fifh for ten pounds.

They have goats in fome places, but they are few in number; and, upon enquiry, I found the reafon to be that they do not thrive in a country where there is no wood.

Befides thefe animals they have three kinds of dogs in Iceland, *fiar hundar*, or *lumbar*, fhag dogs; and *dyrhandar* and *dverghundar*. As alfo, tame and wild cats, which laft are called *urdarkettir*; rats, white and brown foxes, fome of which eat grafs, and are on that account called *gras tofur*. To root out thefe animals, the king has fet a premium of a rix-dollar upon every ten fox fkins that are fold to a merchant. The natives have likewife made an agreement, that whofoever deftroys a fox's hole, together with the fox, the

fhe

she fox, and their young, is to receive one rix-dollar, which the neighbours collect among themselves.

Rein-deers were not known here formerly; but by Governor Thodal's order, thirteen heads were sent from Norway in 1770, by Mr. Perenson, merchant: ten of which died before they reached Iceland, for want of proper care: the three remaining ones, thrive extremely well, and had calved three times before we came there: they do not want for food, as the country abounds with mofs.

After having treated of their fishery, and the breed of their cattle, I think this a very proper place to say something of their birds, which, particularly in regard to those of the aquatic kind, are very important to them.

They are found in great abundance every where on the coast; but the greatest number by far are caught in the few places where they breed. The eggs the Icelanders make use of themselves, as likewise of the flesh, which is eaten by a great many of them; but

with

with the feathers and down they carry on a very confiderable trade.

It would be unneceffary to mention all the different forts of birds, efpecially as there is fcarcely any country where fo many kinds, and fuch great numbers of them, are to be met with as in Iceland. Among the great abundance of geefe, water-fowls, ducks, &c. &c. I will however fay fomething of the fwan and the eider-bird.

It is known that the fwan belongs to the clafs of birds of paffage; their numbers increafe very much towards winter, though there is no fcarcity of them at any time, as the greater part of the young breed conftantly remain there. In fpring we may often fee an hundred of them in a flock, and frequently many more; and it is then thought that part of them advance yet further to the north, and makes but a very fhort ftay in Iceland. During fummer they refort to the lakes; but when winter approaches, and they begin to freeze, they remove to the fea fhores. Their eggs are gathered in the beginning of fpring, which are large, and faid to be very palatable.

palatable. In Auguſt, when they loſe their feathers, they are hunted on the lakes, where they are to be found at that time, with dogs trained to catch them alive. They are ſaid to ſing very harmoniouſly in the cold dark winter nights; but though it was in the month of September when I was upon the iſland, I never once enjoyed the pleaſure of a ſingle ſong. An old ſwan has a fiſhy taſte, but the young ones are reckoned among the beſt eatable fowls.

· The eider-bird is yet more uſeful to the natives, who conſider it as a kind of treaſure; and it is ſeldom heard that a prudent houſe-keeper ſhoots or kills any of them.

The eider birds generally build their neſts on little iſlands not far from the ſhore, and ſometimes even near the dwellings of the natives, who treat them with ſo much kindneſs and circumſpection, as to make them quite tame. In the beginning of June they lay five or ſix eggs, and it is not unuſual to find from ten to ſixteen eggs in one neſt together, with two females, who agree
remarkably

remarkably well together. The whole time of laying continues fix or feven weeks, and they are fond of laying three times in different places: in the two firft, both the eggs and down are taken away, but in the laft place this is feldom done. Thofe to whom one of thefe places belong, vifit it at leaft once a week.

When they come to the neft, they firft carefully remove the female, and then take away the fuperfluous down and eggs, after which they replace the female on the remaining ones, when fhe begins to lay afrefh, and covers her eggs with new down which fhe has plucked from herfelf: when fhe has no more down left, the male comes to her affiftance, and covers the eggs with his down, which is white, and eafily diftinguifhed from the female's; where it is left till the young ones are hatched, who in an hour afterwards quit the neft together with the mother, when it is once more plundered.

The beft down and the moft eggs are got during the firft of their laying;
and

and it has in general been obferved, that they lay the greateſt number of eggs in rainy weather. As long as the female ſits, the male is on the watch near the ſhore; but as ſoon as the young are hatched, he leaves them. But the mother remains with them a conſiderable time after; and it is curious to ſee how ſhe leads them out of the neſt as ſoon as they creep out of the eggs, and goes before them to the ſhore, whilſt they trip after her: when ſhe comes to the water ſide, ſhe takes them on her back, and ſwims with them for the ſpace of a few yards, when ſhe dives, and the young ones, who are left floating on the water, are obliged to take care of themſelves. One ſeldom ſees theſe birds on land afterwards, for they generally live in the damp rocks in the ſea, and feed on inſects and ſea-weeds.

One female, during the whole time of laying, generally gives half a pound of down, which is however reduced to one half after it is cleanſed. The down is divided into *thang duun* (ſea-weed down) and *gras-duun* (graſs down).

down). The laſt ſort is thought to be the beſt, and is cleanſed in the following manner; ſome yarn is ſtreaked in a ſquare compartment round a hoop, on which the down is laid. A pointed piece of wood is then moved backwards and forwards on the lower ſide of the yarn thus ſtreaked, which cauſes the coarſer feathers to fall through, while the fine down remains on the yarn.

Down plucked from dead eider-birds is of little worth, becauſe it has then loſt the greateſt part of its elaſticity; for this reaſon it is of little value in Iceland. The other ſort is ſold at forty-five fiſh a pound when cleanſed, and at ſixteen fiſh when not cleanſed. There are generally exported every year on the company's account 1500 or 2000 pounds of down cleanſed and not cleanſed, excluſive of what is privately exported by foreigners. In the year 1750, the Iceland company ſold as much in quantity of this article, as amounted to 3745 banco-dollars, beſides what was ſent directly to Gluckſtadt.

Among

Among the land birds that are eatable, ptarmigans are not to be forgotten, and are caught in great numbers. Falcons alfo abound in the ifland, of which there are three forts : they are purchafed by the royal falconers, who give fifteen dollars a piece for the white, ten for thofe that are darker, and feven for the grey.

LETTER XIII.

To CHEVALIER IHRE.

Of the Trade in Iceland.

Stockholm, Nov. 12. 1774.

THE Iceland trade has been subject to many revolutions. Till the year 1408 the Norwegians were almost the only nation who sailed to Iceland, and brought all the fish the Icelanders did not consume or export in their own ships. The English afterwards had this trade till the Reformation, when it fell into the hands of the Germans, and was peculiarly advantageous to the Hamburghers. But Christian the Fourth, who had the improvement of the whole Danish trade very much at heart, likewise directed his attention towards Iceland. He prohibited the trade of the Hans-towns thither in the year 1602, and bestowed it on Copenhagen, Malmo, and

and some other towns at that time subject to the crown of Denmark.

The Iceland company at Copenhagen was, however, not established till the year 1620, after the king had once more prohibited the trade of the Hans-towns to Iceland in 1619. This company continued till the year 1662, when it was suppressed by a special order. What contributed to this was the great damage done in Iceland by some pirates in 1627, who carried away great numbers of its inhabitants; the greater part of whom were, however, redeemed by the king nine years after. The king resented this so much the more, as the Iceland company had not only undertaken to provide the country with all necessary articles, but likewise to protect it. This circumstance produced a disagreeable effect to the company, which was, that those who had shares in the stocks of 1000 dollars, only received 500; and those who had shares of 200 dollars, received not the least consideration. The company paid a certain sum to the king for every haven, and two rix-dollars to the governor

governor for every ship. It was likewise obliged to contribute something to the king's magazines on the Westmanns Islands.

The trade of every haven was afterwards disposed of to the highest bidder once in every six years; but since 1734 it has been in the possession of a trading company, who have a grant of it, for which they pay a duty of 6000 dollars a year to the king. They send from 24 to 30 ships thither every year, loaded with corn, bread, wine, iron, and wood, &c. &c. and they export in return from 22 havens, fish, flesh, butter, blubber, skins, wool, and woollen manufactures, which they exchange against the merchandize they have brought thither according to a tax published in the year 1702. It is difficult to determine whether the company gains much by this trade or not; so much at least is certain, that the Icelanders lose by it; for the Dutch, disregarding or evading the tax, import much better goods than the company. For this reason the Icelanders sell a considerable quantity of fish to them

them privately, though several Dutch ships have been confiscated on account of carrying on a smuggling trade. The agents of the Iceland company are aware of this, by the small stock that remains for their purchase, with which they are much dissatisfied.

There is a market kept every year at Hraundals-retter, to which those resort who live up the country: they exchange butter, cloth, and sheep, for fish, blubber, and other articles of that kind. At Reikavik there is a woollen manufactory, where ten or twenty workmen are employed: one likewise meets with a few looms here and there; and many more might be established amongst the peasants, if encouragement was given them.

Danish money is current in the country, but the whole stock of ready money cannot amount to many thousand dollars. Their accounts are not all kept in money, but according to yards and fishes: forty-eight fishes, each fish reckoned at two pounds, make one rixdollar, and twenty-four yards make one likewise. You may buy a horse for a hundred

hundred and fifty fifh, and a farm for fix thoufand yards. A *vatt* is 100 *l.* and *faering* 10 *l.* They reckon a hundred and fixty-three quarts to a tun, and five to a *kuttur.* The Icelandic ell is as big as the Hamborough ell, three of which make a fathom.

LET-

LETTER XIV.

To CHEVALIER IHRE.

Of the Icelandic Literature.

Stockholm, Dec. 4, 1774.

THE history of antient times shews us that our ancestors did not despise arts and sciences, though they peculiarly distinguished themselves by valour and heroic deeds. Their religion, mixed with fables, was, however, reduced to some rule; and their system of morality, though not the purest and best; yet inculcated certain virtues, which were in vain sought for among the more enlightened Greeks and Romans. The long voyages they made without knowing the use of the compass, is a proof of their having been much better acquainted with astronomy and geography, than could have been expected. Physic, and particularly surgery, must have

have been held in high esteem among so warlike a nation, though I question very much whether any person could now submit to the manner of curing an external hurt, such as was practised among the ancients. Their invention exhibits itself in riddles, history, and poetry; and how highly these were valued among them, may be proved by many examples, of which I shall only mention Egil's poem, in praise of Erick Blodoxe king of Norway, by which he saved his life; and Hiarne's epitaph on king Forde, on account of which he is said to have been made king of Denmark.

Though it cannot be entirely ascertained, that Odin brought the Runic characters to the north; yet it is proved almost beyond a doubt, that they were known among us in the fifth and sixth centuries. The art of writing was also known here, if not certain, at least as early as among the Franks and Germans; the former had no letters before they began to make use of the Latin ones in the sixth century, and the latter were likewise unacquainted
with

with them before the time of Charlemain.

Their taste for riddles, stories, and poetry, the Icelanders also brought along with them from their native country, to the island where they are now settled; and whilst these traces of science diminished in Norway, on account of the troubles which shook the whole north during several centuries, they not only preserved themselves in Iceland, which was not exposed to so many disturbances, but the care of their safety likewise excited the inhabitants to apply themselves to the study of history, 'that they might by it be informed of the designs of their powerful neighbours, and take the best and most necessary measures to oppose those who only wished for an opportunity of subjecting them to their yoke.

It is true they had no schools or public seminaries for the instruction of youth in the sciences, before the introduction of the Christian religion; but it was, however, not altogether neglected, for they took great pains, besides inuring the bodies of their young men to

feats

feats of strength and agility, and teaching them such exercises as enabled them to defend themselves and their countrymen, to instruct them also in history, religion, and law. Thence we find in their ancient chronicles frequent mention of persons who had made considerable progress in these sciences, and even before they received the Christian religion there were a number in the country well versed in the laws.

In their frequent voyages, before the use of the compass *(Leitarstain)* was known to them, they discovered new countries, when driven out of their course, which were however deserted almost as soon as discovered: however, some, if not all of them, have been discovered in later times.

Thus Bjorn Herjulfson, in a voyage he made to see his father in Greenland, was driven by a strong north-wind upon a flat woody country, from whence he afterwards reached his father, after a long and troublesome voyage, without thinking any more of his new discovery. After the death of his father,

ther, he again returned to Norway; where the account of his voyage raifed an inclination in Leifer to go in fearch of this country. He therefore fet fail with 35 men, and at firft landed on a mountainous country covered with fnow, without the leaft appearance of verdure; from whence he continued his voyage, and came to another country which was flat and woody; this he named Markland. He fet fail again with a north-eaft wind, and in two days time arrived at an ifland which lay north of the continent. He now entered weftward into a ftraight where his fhip ftruck on the fand at low water: he then had it drawn afhore with cables, and having built a houfe, remained there the whole winter: here they did not experience the leaft cold, and the grafs grew only a little reddifh in winter. The days were not of fo unequal a length as in Iceland; and the fun appeared above the horizon on the fhorteft day, both when they breakfafted and at fupper-time. The vine and wheat both grew wild, and this occafioned their giving the name of
Vineland

Vineland to the country. This gives us room to conjecture that he advanced pretty far towards the south of America. They afterwards carried on a trade with the natives of the country, whom they called Skralingar, for a long time, which, however, ceased at last, and the country, and even its name, are now totally forgotten.

Poetry formerly flourished very much in Iceland, Egil Skalla Grimson, Cormak Ogmundson, Glum Geirson, Thorleif, Jarlar Skald, Sighvatr, Thordson, Gunlaug Ormstunga, and Skad Ralfn, are celebrated as great poets. The art of writing was not, however, much in use till after the year 1000. It is true the Runic characters were known in the country before that period, and most probably brought thither from Norway. Though we have no reason to believe they were cut upon stones, as was practised among us (no Runic stones having been found there, whose age reaches to the times of Paganism); they used, however, to scratch them on bucklers, and sometimes on their cielings

and

and walls: and the *Laxdaela Saga* makes mention of one Olof of Hiardarhult, who had a large houfe built, on the beams and rafters of which remarkable ftories are faid to have been marked, in the fame manner as Thorkil Hake cut an account of his own deeds on his bedftead and chair. That Runic characters were made ufe of before the introduction of the Chriftian religion, may be proved by Olof Tryggwaffon's Saga, where he makes mention of a man, whofe name was Oddni, who, being dumb, made known, by means of Runic characters, that he had been infulted by Ivar, his father's gueft.

After the reception of the Chriftian religion in the year 1000, the fciences took another form. The Latin characters were immediately adopted; as the Runic alphabet, which only confifts of fixteen letters, was found infufficient. The firft Icelandic bifhop, Ifleif, founded a fchool at Skalholt; and foon after they founded four other fchools, in which the youth were inftructed in the Latin tongue, divinity,

and

and some parts of theoretic philosophy. Jonas Ogmundsson, first bishop of Hoolum, sent to Gothland in the year 1120 for one Gisle Finson to superintend the school at Hoolum. Arngrim Jonson, on this occasion, mentions a remarkable circumstance in his *Crymogaea*, p. 108. of the architect Thorodr, who, as he was employed in building the cathedral church at Hoolum, paid so much attention to the grammatical lessons given to the school-boys, as to make a considerable progress in them himself. The same author also mentions, that the bishop, who was a learned and zealous man, having one day surprized one of the scholars in reading Ovid's letters, and book *De Arte Amandi*, was so incensed thereat as to strike the book out of his hand. At a time when no great knowledge of the Latin language could be expected even in Sweden, an Icelander however was found of sufficient capacity and learning to instruct the young people to read and understand the Latin Poets. But notwithstanding the sciences were there only in their infancy,

infancy, thofe who defired to make greater progrefs in them, ftudied in foreign univerfities. Giflur Ifleifson ftudied at Erfurt; and many refort to Paris, as Samundr Sigfuffon did, from whence they were called *Parifklarkar* (Paris writers). Many, however, whofe names are become celebrated, have only ftudied in Iceland: as a proof of which, I will only mention the two moft famous Icelandic writers Are Frode and Snorre Sturlefon. It may therefore be affirmed that Iceland, from the introduction of the Chriftian religion there till the year 1264, when it became fubject to Norway, was one of the few countries in Europe, and the only one in the north, where the fciences were cultivated and held in efteem. This period of time has alfo produced more learned men than at any other period fince. We need only read their ancient chronicles, to be convinced that they had great knowledge in morality, philofophy, natural hiftory, and aftronomy. They had tolerably clear ideas of divinity, and ufed to read the Fathers: but their
L   poetical

poetical and hiſtorical productions, in particular, have bid defiance to time, even when ignorance was again beginning to reſume her empire. It would be an eaſy matter to mention a number of poets who diſtinguiſhed themſelves, not only in Iceland and the Orkneys, but likewiſe at the Swediſh, Daniſh, Norwegian, and Engliſh courts as the *ſkaldartal* (or liſt of poets) contains no leſs than 240: but it will be ſuperfluous to mention here any more than the three principal ones, viz. Snorre Sturleſon, who was beheaded in the year 1241, in the 63d year of his age, at Reikholt in Iceland; Olafr Huitaſkald, who died in 1259; and Sturla Thordſon, who made his exit in 1284. Some extracts of the works of theſe authors are inſerted in ſome printed and manuſcript chronicles.

Of much greater importance are their ſayings or hiſtories, the utility and authenticity of which have cauſed ſo many diſputes: for if they have been conſidered by ſome as ſure and irreverſible ſupporters of the hiſtory of of our forefathers, they have been looked upon by others as abſurd inventions and falſhoods, which belong to the ſame claſs as the hiſtory of the knight Finke, Fortunatus, the horned Siegfried, and other old women's tales. This laſt opinion is no leſs unreaſonable, than an exceſs of veneration paid to them would be inconſiderate and raſh. When they are conſulted with circumſpection and judgment, they are undoubtedly of great uſe, ſo much the more, as they are the only remaining monuments of the ancient northern hiſtory; and indeed ſome of them are written with great judgment and perſpicuity.

The Aræ Frodes Schedæ were written ſince 1122, and are the moſt ancient Icelandic accounts extant. The writings of Sturleſon, Gunlaug, Odde, and ſeveral others, are all of them works that will never be loſt or hurt by time; and I do not find any thing in them which ſhould induce us to deny them the ſame credit that we ſo implicitly give to the writings of Tacitus and Livy.

No one can doubt, that even thofe authors in the compilation of their hiftories, which have been confidered as patterns of language, have made ufe of the information of other writers. Nor have our Icelandic hiftorians been remifs in this; for Sturlefon himfelf quotes Are Thiodolfr, the *langfedgatal*, or genealogical table, and fome ancient fongs in which their kings were celebrated; from which indeed he compiled his accounts.

The Icelanders were remarkably ftudious in preferving the memory of their anceftors; and it was the moft agreeable occupation in their meetings and affemblies, to repeat thofe hiftories and poems for which their great men had been renowned, as was the practice among the Greeks. Add to this, the contents and compofition of the writings themfelves, which plainly prove, that the authors have not been inclined to relate marvellous ftories; and it would be unjuft to refufe them that reliance on their veracity, which we without hefitation beftow flow on other writers of the fame clafs.

The greateft part of their works were compofed in the 11th, 12th, 13th, and 14th centuries; and fome of them have even appeared in print. I have a lift of thefe hiftories in my poffeffion; and though they are by no means of the fame degree of merit, it will perhaps not be difagreeable to you to have a copy of it, as it is not only a proof of their love of fcience, but likewife of their application.

As a frefh inftance of their accuracy and affiduity in ftudy, I muft likewife mention their chronicles, in which they recorded whatever happened of importance both in Iceland and abroad. Thefe annals are in general confidered as more authentic than their fayings. Semundr and Are Frode were the firft who introduced them, and they have fince been continued down to our days. The following are confidered as the beft.

1. *Flateyar Annal*, which reaches to the year 1395, and of which

2. *Vatnsfiardar Annal* is a supplement which extends to 1660.
3. *Skallholt.*
4. *Hola.*
5. *Odda.*
6. *Biürns a Skardzaa* to 1645, of which
7. *Hefts Annal*, which goes down to the year 1718, is a supplement. *Hrafnagils Annal* begins where the laſt leaves off, and continues to 1754.
8. *Odds Ejrikſonar a fitium* to 1680.
9. Annales Regii, which go to the year 1341.
10. *Hirdſtöra.*
11. *Laugmanna.*
12. *Biſkupa.*
13. Annales antiqui.
14. Annales vetuſtiores go to the concluſion of the 13th century. *Bjarne Halldorſon*'s annal, as I have been informed, begins about the middle of the 7th century, and reaches quite down to 1772.

But even here the ſciences have been ſubject to the ſame revolutions, which they have experienced every where elſe.

else. The lustre in which they had maintained themselves so long, was succeeded by the most profound obscurity. To give a clearer idea of this, I shall borrow the expressions of the learned bishop of Skallholt, Dr. Finneus, on this occasion, who compares the state of the sciences in Iceland to the four stages of human life, in his well-written Hist. Eccl. Islandiæ. Their infancy extended to the year 1056, when the introduction of the Christian religion produced the first dawn of light. They were in their youth till 1110, when schools were first established, and the education and instruction of youth began to be more attended to than before. Their manly age lasted till about the middle of the 14th century, when Iceland produced the greatest number of learned men. Old age appeared towards the end of this same 14th century, when the sciences gradually decreased, and were almost entirely extinct, no work of any merit appearing. History now drooped her head, their poetry had no relish, and all other sciences were enveloped in darkness. The schools began to decay, and in many places they had none at all. It was very uncommon for any one to understand Latin, and few priests could read their breviary and rituals fluently.

But this was not alone the case in Iceland, the greater part of Europe experienced the same change. For the dawn of a brighter day, which had begun to spread from Greece over Italy and the southern part of Europe, after the taking of Constantinople by the Turks in 1453, had not yet penetrated to the north. Whatever bore the name of learning was not only despised; but so gross was their ignorance, that men of the highest rank, both spiritual and temporal, were incapable of writing their names. We cannot wonder at this in Iceland, when the history of the church affords so many examples of bishops who were present at councils, at the conclusion of which they caused to be written under the acts, *quoniam Dominus N. Episcopus scribere nescit, ideo ejus loco subscribsit N. N.* We were also informed, that the

ignorance

ignorance of this age was so great, that scarce any Swedish king before Gustavus I. knew how to write his name. In the annals of *Konungaoch Hofdinga styrelse* (supposed to be written by bishop Brynolf Carlsson, who died at Skara in 1430) it is said, no more ought to be required of a sovereign, than to know how to read, understand, and explain his letters.

The Reformation produced here, as in most places, a new dawn of knowledge. Some time before a printing press had been brought to Iceland, bishop Gissur proposed to open a new school in the convent of Videy, which had been seized by the crown; but as this had been designed for a dwelling-place to the king's receivers of the customs, Christian III. commanded, in the year 1552, that a school-house should be built near each of the cathedral churches; that at Skallholt for forty scholars, and that at Hoolum for thirty-four; but they have since been reduced, the one to thirty-four, and the other to twenty-four scholars. Each of these schools was to be provided

vided with a rector and an affiftant teacher; and the king appropriated as much land to thefe foundations, as was fufficient to afford tolerable falaries to the teachers, and board, books, and cloathing to the fcholars gratis, fo long as they remained at fchool.

Great pains have fince been taken to appoint men of known abilities as teachers to thefe fchools; and young men are fo well inftructed there, that few of the clergy ftudy any where elfe. Many Icelanders, however, ftudy at Copenhagen; and in the year 1773, there were no lefs than fifty-four at that univerfity, where excellent regulations have been made for the fupport of poor ftudents. Some likewife ftudy in foreign univerfities; and between 1760 and 1770 a native of Iceland, Paul Widalin by name, died at Leipfic, who was univerfally beloved and efteemed there. A Mr. Thorolti, who has been above three years at Upfala, has likewife on all occafions fhewn himfelf a man of great merit.

We fhould therefore form a very wrong judgment of Iceland, to imagine

gine it abforbed in total ignorance and obfcurity: on the contrary, I can affirm, that I have found more knowledge among the lower clafs than is to be met with in moft other places. You will feldom find a peafant who, befides being well-inftructed in the principles of religion, is not alfo acquainted with the hiftory of his country, which proceeds from the frequent reading of their traditional hiftories *(fagas)* wherein confifts their principal amufement: nor is it uncommon to find perfons among them who can repeat the poems of Kolbein, Grimfon, Sigurd, Gifles, Gudmund, and Bergthors by heart, all of them poets who flourifhed in later times; and among whom Vigfus Jonffon has particularly diftinguifhed himfelf by his wit, though fometimes at the expenfe of decency. The clergymen fpeak Latin well; and I have found better librararies in many parts of Iceland than could have been expected.

A learned fociety was erected here, which is fpoken of in the preface of the above mentioned Speculum

lum Regale under the name of Societas invifibilis; and I was intimately acquainted with the rector Halfdan Ejnarfon, and the late fyffelman Bjarne Haldorfon, who who were both members of that fociety, though I believe it does not exift at prefent. I could mention feveral whofe learning and tafte did honour to their country, but I fhall only name thofe who have acquired moft fame in the literary world.

Among thefe the bifhop of Skallholt, Dr. Finnur Jonfon, deferves the firft place; who, befides many learned writings on the antiquities of Iceland, fome of which have been publifhed, has lately prefented the public with an ecclefiaftical hiftory, in three volumes quarto, replete with information, criticifm, and erudition. I was happy in becoming more intimately acquainted with this worthy prelate, who has been bifhop ever fince 1754, and found no lefs inftruction than pleafure in his company. You may eafily conceive how much I wifhed, at taking leave of him, that his advanced age would permit him to put a finifhing stroke

ſtroke to his other works. We have ſome reaſon to hope for this at preſent, as one of his ſons, the learned Mr. John Finſſon, has lately been appointed his father's aſſiſtant and provoſt.

To this number alſo belong Halfdan Ejnarſon, rector of the ſchool of Hoolum, who has publiſhed the Speculum Regale, and is now employed in writing Hiſtoria Literaria Iſlandiæ. The provoſt and miniſter of Hiardarholt, Gunnar Paulſen, is juſtly celebrated on account of his great knowledge in ancient poetry. Bjarne Jonſon, rector of Skallholt, compoſes very good Latin verſes, and has a diſſertation of *Gangdagar* ready for the preſs. Bjarne Paulſen, in company with Eggert Olofsen, made a journey through Iceland to collect manuſcripts and curioſities at the expenſe of the ſociety of ſciences. The lagman Soen Solveſen has publiſhed ſeveral law-works; as has likewiſe the vice-lagman Jon Olſſon, and the provoſts Vigfus Jonſen and Gudlaug Thorgeirſon, beſides ſeveral others.

The profeſſor and counſellor of ſtate, Erichſen, who is not ſettled in Iceland, is likewife known on account of many differtations on antiquities, and is a ufeful member of the Collegii Magnæani. Arnas Magnäus, Torfeus, and feveral other Icelanders, have alfo particularly diftinguifhed themfelves for literature in this and the former century. I fhall give a fuller account of them in another letter, wherein I propofe to treat of the Icelandic antiquities in particular, where I fhall alfo mention thofe who have peculiarly diftinguifhed themfelves in that branch of literature.

The language in Iceland is the fame as that formerly fpoken in Sweden, Denmark, and Norway, and has preferved itfelf fo pure, that any Icelander underftands the moft ancient traditional hiftory, as eafily as we do letters written in the time of Charles IX. The general change, which took place in the northern language during and after the time of Erick of Pomerania, did not extend to Iceland, though fome trifling alterations were afterwards made in it in the fifteenth century, by the introduction of religion and their

trade

trade with the Danes, English, and Germans. Near the coast some Danish is understood, and some even speak it; nor is it uncommon for a peasant to say, *salve domine, bonus dies, bonus vesper, gratias, proficiat, dominus tecum, vale.* Notwithstanding, I cannot agree with Sperling in considering the language as being more Danish than Icelandic, since not a single word of Danish is understood in the interior parts of the country. The great pleasure they find in reading their traditional histories, has contributed not a little to preserve the language in its purity.

You have yourself treated of its origin in the preface to your Swedish-Gothic Dictionary; and one may form the best judgment of the language from Olof Tryggwasson's and some other historical traditions (Sagas) which have been written in the 11th, 12th, and 13th centuries, when it was in its greatest purity. But as these works are not in every person's hands, I will here insert a copy of the Lord's Prayer as a sample, both as it was expressed

preſſed and printed in 1585, and in 1746, which will clearly point out the ſmall change which the language has undergone during a ſpace of near 200 years.

1585.

Fader vor thu ſem ert a himnum. Helgjſt nafn thitt. Tilkome thitt riike. Verde thinn vilie ſo a jordu ſem a himne. Gief oſs i dag vort dagligt braud. Og fyrerlat oſs vorar ſkullder, ſo em vier fyrerlautum vorum ſkulldunautum. Og inlied oſs ecki i i freiſtne. Helldr frelſa thu oſs af illu, thuait thitt er riikit, maattur og dyrd um allder allda. Amenn.

1746.

Fader vor thu ſem ert a himnum, helgesſt thitt nafn, tilkomme thitt rike, verde thin vilie, ſo a jordu ſem a himne. Gief thu oſs i dag vort daglegt braud, og fyrer gief oſs vorar ſkullder, ſo ſem vier fyrergiefum vorum ſkulldunautum, og innleid oſs ecke i frieſtne, helldur frelſa thu oſs fra illu, thuaid thitt er riiked og maattur og dyrd um allder allda. Amen.

In regard to the pronunciation, they have four different dialects. Those who dwell on the east side of the country, drawl out their words in pronouncing them, which is not done in other places. On the western side they have many words which are peculiar to that part of the island; and in Snefialds Jokul the *aa* is pronounced as *ai*. In the southern part of Iceland *o* is pronounced short before *r* in certain words, as for example in *hvoriger*, *moraudt*, and others, though they are commonly long in other parts. In the northern part of Iceland the words are quite of different genders, as *skur*, which is usually feminine, but there is masculine; and *klara*, masculine, which is there feminine. In South Iceland I have observed the following pronunciation:

A is pronounced au in tha
Aa — au — aara
Ll — dl — gamall
Au — ö — thau
U — ü — upp
Ae — ei — vaere
Ja — iau — hia

O	oü	moder
Gu	guö	Gud
Y	i	fyrer
Aef	acp	kiaefda

Their alphabet confists of the fame letters as ours, except the (th), which character we have loft, together with the pronunciation; the Englifh have yet preferved it, though foreigners find it difficult to pronounce.

We have an Icelandic grammar of Runolph Jonfon, printed in 4to at Copenhagen in 1651: it was alfo printed in Hickefii Elementa linguarum feptentrionalium, Oxford 1688, and again in his Thefaurus, Oxford 1703. But the manufcript of Jonas Magnufen's Grammatica Iflandica, which you, Sir, poffefs, is more complete, and deferves to be publifhed, as likewife Eggert Olfen's Orthographia Iflandica. The moft ancient Icelandic dictionary we have is the Wormii Specimen Lexici Runici, compiled by Magnus Olafsen, which was publifhed in folio, at Copenhagen, in 1650.

After-

Afterwards Gudmundi Andreae Lexicon Iflandicum was publifhed by Refenius at Copenhagen, in quarto, in the year 1683. This was followed by Verelii Index linguae vet. Scyto-Scandicae, which Rudbeck caufed to be printed in folio, at Upfala, 1691, and by two Lexica Latina Iflandica, both publifhed in quarto at Copenhagen, the one in 1734, and the other in 1738; to thefe Rugman's Monofyllaba Iflandica Lat. Explicata, Upfala, 1676, in octavo, may be added. In the library at Upfala was a copy of a manufcript Lexicon Ifl. Lat. which I have brought with me from Iceland. In the Antiquity Archives is likewife a very ample work of Gudmundr Olafsen, which has been augmented and reduced to order by Mr. Affeffor Gagnerus, which will however moft probably never be printed for want of a publifher. It is to be lamented that Runolph Jonfon never was able to publifh his Lexicon Iflandicum, though a privilege was granted him for that purpofe in May 1650: we may however foon expect to have fomething more perfect on this subject, as the Collegium Magnaeanum in Copenhagen have promised to continue the important indexes, with which they have supplied the *Kristniss* and *Gunlaug Ormstunga* Sagas.

LETTER

LETTER XV.

To CHEVALIER IHRE,

Of Printing in Iceland.

Stockholm, Sept. 12, 1774.

I HAVE said in my last letter that the art of printing was introduced in Iceland a short time before the Reformation. But as many may be surprized that books were printed there so early, I shall endeavour to treat more at large in this of the different printing-offices in Iceland.

One of the most famous, but at the same time most illiterate and turbulent bishops in Iceland, was John Arefon, bishop of Hoolum. He made use of many arts, and particularly of his zeal for the Roman Catholic religion to undermine the king's power, and hinder the progress of the reformation. His plots however succeeded so ill, that he was beheaded in 1550. As this man was extremely ignorant, and had not the least knowledge of the Latin language, which was however made use of in letters of excommunication, and other ordinances, he commissioned a friend to procure him a person well versed in Latin, who might at the same time establish a printing-office. For this purpose John Mathiesson, a native of Sweden, was recommended to him, and he arrived in Iceland between 1527 and 1530.

I cannot determine with certainty whether he was in orders at his arrival in Iceland; however I am inclined to believe it, from the appellation of Sira being given him after his arrival, which is a term applicable to the clergy. The bishop immediately appointed him to the prebendary of Bridebolstad and Vesturhopi, which situation he enjoyed till his death in 1567, when at a very advanced age. Besides several other children he left a son whose name was John, who was a printer there in the time of bishop Guthrandr: he was succeeded in the printing-office by his son Brandur.

John

John Bradtfon, fon of the latter, died in an advanced age in 1681, as provoſt of Hytarnas. His fon John Johnfon, a clergyman, died in the fame place in 1732. This whole family is now reduced to poverty.

The printing-office was immediately eſtabliſhed; and in 1531 John Mathieſſon printed the firſt book in Iceland, which was the Breviarium Nidarofienfe. There was likewife an edition of this book printed at Dronthiem, the editor of which was archbiſhop Erick Walkendorf, which is now very fcarce. I do not remember to have feen this edition mentioned any where, except in the 28th number of the Daniſh Magazine, where a copy of it is faid to be in the library of Mr. Klevenfeldt. But in regard to the Icelandic edition, it is generally believed, that not a fingle copy of it remains, fince the only one I ever heard of was in Arnas Magnaei's library, which was confumed in the fire at Copenhagen in 1728.

Befides the Breviarium Nidarofienfe, he printed the *Handbok Præſta* (an Eccleſiaſtical fiaftical Manual) Luther's Catechifm, and other books of the fame fort. Printing however did not go on very well till 1574, when the bifhop Guthrandr Thorlakfon ordered new types to be brought thither; whereupon, amongſt other books, the Icelandic bible appeared in print in folio, in the year 1584. The printing-office was at this period fo well provided with types, that two preffes were employed, exclufive of thofe at Hoolum, where feveral books were printed and publifhed about that time. The Icelandic code of laws was printed in 1578, at Nupufell, twelve miles from Hoolum, as likewife the Viti Theodori Summaria in 1589.

The printing-office at Hoolum was taken from Thord Thorlakfon, in 1685, and transferred to Skallholt; where one-and-forty different books were printed: the firſt of which was *Paradyſar Lykell*, likewife *Forfadra Bok* in 1686; and the laſt, *Boenabok Sira Thordar Bardarſonar Med Vika Saung Olearii. ult. af Sira Steines*

Steines in 1697. But in the beginning of this century, the printing-office was again removed to Hoolum, after bifhop Bjorn Thorleifson had bought it, together with the privileges granted to it, for five hundred dollars; and the firſt book publifhed on the revival of printing at this place, was the Paraphrafis Medit. Dr. John Gerhardi, 1703. Since this time fome hiſtorical books, among which I will mention the life of Guftavus Landkrona, publifhed at Hoolum in 8vo, 1756, tranſlated from the Swedifh into the Icelandic language, have always been publifhed here; the greateſt part of them however are religious books. A new privileged printing-office has likewife lately been eſtablifhed at Hrappfey, by Olafr Olffen, where feveral valuable books have already been printed.

A liſt of Icelandic books might perhaps not be improper in this place; but as I am unable to furnifh you with a complete one, I did not think it worth while to fend you a catalogue

of

of about three hundred that I am acquainted with; of which number however I am happy to have upwards of one hundred now in my library.

LETTER

LETTER XVI.

To CHEVALIER IHRE.

Of the Remains of Antiquity in Iceland.

Stockholm, Dec. 21, 1774.

Dear Sir,

HOW infinitely happy should I be, were I able to satisfy your curiosity in respect to the great number of remarkable and ancient monuments with which Iceland is supposed to abound; but this is out of my power; all the information I can give you amounts to no more than that the country is so destitute of them, that it is in vain to go in search of any antiquities deserving the least notice. There are however some ruins of an old castle near Videdal, which was formerly about two hundred perches in circumference: the remains on the north side are about twenty
fathoms

fathoms in height, though they are very low toward the south. Near the parsonage Skaggestad, at Laugernas, are likewise some ruins of a lesser castle, but it is not known by whom, or when it was built. In other places are remains of Heathen Temples, viz. at Midfiord, Godale, Vidvik, and others: at Hegranas is a kind of ancient place of execution; there are also several burying-places from the times of Paganism, among which I shall only mention Thorleif Jarlaskalds, situate on a small island in the Oxaraa. Some old swords and helmets have likewise been found, but they have not cleared up any part of history. On the heaths of Thingmans and Threkyllis are two great stones standing upright, which most probably have been erected as monuments to the memory of some deceased persons, according to Odin's regulation. This custom, which was long practised in the North, has from thence been brought to Iceland; though it was not usual in Sweden till a long time after to put any inscription on the
monu-

monument. I have been told, that some years ago, forty small figures of brass were found in the ground near Flatey, representing animals and other objects; but unfortunately they fell into the hands of people who did not know their value, consequently they have been all lost.

There are no other monuments remaining of Sturlefon, besides his writings, but a mount over-grown with grass at Reikholt, which is said to have been raised from the ruins of his house; *Sturlunga Reitur*, the burying-place of his family; and at a little distance from them, *Snorra Laug*, one of the finest baths in Iceland. This bath, which is large enough to contain 50 persons at one time, is mured in with a wall of basalt, and concreto thermarum; it has a smooth level bottom, and is surrounded with benches. In Sturlefon's time a long covered passage led from thence to the dwelling-house, so that the bathers retire from the bath without being exposed to the cold. The spring is at forty paces distance, and is called
Scribla,

Scribla, and the water from it is conveyed to the bath through a conduit made of ſtones. At the end of this conduit is a hole in a rock, which is ſhut with a ſpigot and faucet, and through which you let in as much warm water as you think fit; this, when too hot, may eaſily be cooled by water from an adjoining brook.

Theſe are almoſt the only ancient monuments Iceland affords, and all, as you will readily allow, are of very little importance. There are no ancient manuſcripts, Icelandic ſagas, or hiſtorical traditions or accounts, to be met with, the iſland having been entirely ſtripped of them, owing to the zeal and induſtry of the antiquarians and others who formerly reſorted in numbers to this country, for the ſole end of collecting them.

The honour of having firſt begun to collect them belongs to Sweden: the firſt who undertook it was Jonas Rugman, who went to Iceland in 1661, at the expenſe of the court of Sweden, where he obtained a number of manuſcripts, which laid the foundation for the collection of Icelandic original records,

that

that are contained in the Swediſh archives of antiquities. Encouraged by his example, Thormundr Thorviſon likewiſe went to Iceland, furniſhed with an order from king Frederic the Third, of the 27th of May 1662, to the biſhops Bryniolf, Svenſſon, and Giſle Thorlakſon, to aſſiſt him in collecting Icelandic manuſcripts.

After the eſtabliſhment of the college it was propoſed to ſend Peter Salan to Iceland; but this did not take place, though they gained their point ſome time after, in 1680, by means of Gudmundr Olſon, who prevailed upon his brother Helge Olſon to leave Iceland and come to Sweden, whither he brought a conſiderable number of manuſcripts. Great additions were afterwards made to theſe collections by Arngrim Johnſon, Jonas Wigfuſen, Lopt Joſephen, Gudmund Gudmunderſon, and Thorvaldr Brockman, who were all employed as tranſlators by the college of antiquities. Jonas Eghardſen, Magnus Benedictſen, Iſleif Thorleiſſen, Ejnar Ejnarſen, Arnas Hakanſen, Francis Jacobſen, and
Thord

Thord Thorlakson have also very much enriched the collection, both when the college of antiquities was at Upsala, and when it was afterwards transferred to Stockholm.

The attention of the Danish court was at last excited: king Christian the Fifth, in 1685, dispatched Thomas Bartholin to Iceland with an order to the bailiff Heidemann, to assist him in collecting Icelandic antiquities: he forbad at the same time, in the strictest manner, any manuscripts, histories, or any other accounts relating to Iceland, to be sold to foreigners, or carried out of the country.

Stockholm, as well as Copenhagen, became therefore possest of a considerable number of Icelandic writings; but the latter court not satisfied with what they had already obtained, dispatched Arnas Magnäus and Paul Widalin to Iceland in 1712; where they sought for whatever might remain there with such extreme care, that it is almost impossible to get sight of any manuscript history in the whole country; and notwithstanding the pains I have

have taken, I could only obtain an imperfect copy of the Sturlunga Saga, which I purchafed.

It is in vain, therefore, that one now enquires for ancient Icelandic chronicles in Iceland; for befides the fine collection in the Swedifh archives of antiquities, there is a very admirable collection of them in the library of the academy at Copenhagen, which was a gift of Arnas Magnäus; befides feveral fmall collections of lefs importance in the hands of private perfons.

I have already mentioned the Icelandic hiftories which have been publifhed: fome of them have been printed in Iceland, among which thofe printed at Skallholt are very rare; but the greateft part have been publifhed in Sweden, though fometimes from very imperfect manufcripts. Olof Rudbeck the elder, Verelius, the two Peringfkolds, Renhielm, Biorner, Salan, and Brokman, have however acquired a great deal of merit by the care and diligence which they
beftowed

bestowed upon them. None of these editions however can be compared, in point of elegance and criticism, to those published in Copenhagen, by the Magnäanian College, the continuation of which is expected with great impatience by the literary world.

LET-

LETTER XVII.

To Baron Axel Lejonhufwud,

Of the Icelandic Poetry.

Stockholm, Dec. 12, 1775.

IT is with the utmoſt pleaſure that I prepare to obey your commands, in communicating to you a ſhort account of the Icelandic poetry; I only lament that my circumſcribed knowledge on a ſubject which is ſurrounded with ſo many obſcurities, will not permit me to make my account as perfect as I could wiſh, and as the importance of the ſubject requires; I regret this inability ſo much the more, as I am to ſubmit my thoughts to the eye of ſo great a connoiſſeur; but if even my obſervations ſhould not be very important, I will conſole myſelf for it, as they will, however, be a proof of my readineſs to comply with your wiſhes.

Though the opinion of some men of learning, that writing in verse has been earlier practised in Europe than writing in prose, may appear extraordinary at first, yet it seems more probable upon nearer examination. The poets among the Greeks and Romans were more ancient than their historians and most celebrated orators. The time when prose first began to be written among these nations, may be ascertained with tolerable accuracy; but it is almost impossible to determine the age of poetry among them, as it is far more ancient than the siege of Troy and the Olympic games. In the same manner we know that the first work in prose among the Romans was the speech of Appius Caegius, to the senate and Roman people in the 125th Olympaid; in which he advises them to refuse the conditions of peace offered by Pyrrhus, when it is certain that poetry had been known and cultivated among them long before.

This need not be wondered at, when we recollect that long before the knowledge

ledge of letters could have become general in Europe, many actions might, however, have been thought worthy to be configned to pofterity. How great an affiftance muft it have been to the memory, when the remembrance of an event, deftined to be refcued from oblivion, was preferved in words, compofed according to a certain meafure, where it might be determined, even by the ear alone, if any word had been omitted or altered. The laws of the ancient Germans were written in verfe, and the ftanzas in which they were compofed were generally fung. The French monarch, induced by the favourable reception given to every poetical work, caufed the Bible to be tranflated into verfe in the ninth century: from the fame motive Ottfried, a Benedictine monk in Alface, tranflated the four Evangelifts into German verfe about the fame period.

Thus we fee that poetry is extremely ancient among all nations; and in Sweden it may be confidered as a legacy of Odin, who first brought it thither. In ancient times there was no king or chief, or any other man of note, who had not his own skald or poet, who was obliged to be present on all important occasions, to remark whatever was worthy of attention, and to relate it in songs. He was present at battles in the *Skolaborg*, or in the midst of the bravest warriors, that he might behold with his own eyes those actions which were to be recorded: at their banquets he was obliged to animate the guests with happy inventions and poetical encomiums on their deceased heroes. These poets were every where held in high esteem; they were constantly admitted to the king's presence, and frequently were both his generals and ministers. They were called *skaldr*, which Chevalier Ihre derives from *skial*, reason or prudence, from whence the expression of *skislamán*, wise men. They were likewise called *spekingr*, from *speke*, wisdom, from whence the English word to Speak, derives its origin.

To

To the songs of these poets we owe the first accounts of the Swedish history, and cannot therefore deprive them of the honour Tacitus bestows on them in calling them Antiquissimum annalium genus. Our ancient traditions are likewise filled with these songs, which we cannot alter or reject as worthless, though they are, for the most part, unintelligible to us. The cause of this is, first, that the Skalds purposely composed their songs with so much art, that they were not only unintelligible to the vulgar, of which we find examples in Geila Sturfonar, Viga Glum, and Greltis's Sagas; but they were not even understood by the greatest poets, of which Gretter's history gives us a proof.

They were, secondly, accustomed to transpose the order of the words in their songs in so strange a manner, as necessarily augmented the obscurity. I will only mention one example of this from Renhjelm, where the words, to follow in their natural order, ought to have been

been ranged according to the number placed over them:

  1 2 8 9
Hilmir vann at holmi
  5 7 6
Hialm-skoth roihni blothi
  3 14 15 13
Huat ofduldu theff hoeldar
  4 10 11 12
Hoerd oc auftur i goerthom
  18 20 17 19
Rogs bra Recka laegir
  16 22 21
Riikur valkera lijki
  23 24 27
Herftefnir let hrofnum
  25 26 28
Hold flaemingia goldit.

They had, thirdly, a particular poetical language *(Skaldfkaparmal)* which was very copious, but could not be made ufe of in common life. This language probably made one of the principal parts of their ftudies in thofe times, as they were not infen-
fible

sible of its beauty and elegance. Thus for example, there are upwards of fifty sononymes of the word *bülja*, billow or wave. And Chevalier Ihre quotes Lopt Guttormson's Lyodalykil (a love-song) in which there are many different appellations, which all express the word woman. I shall borrow a few lines of this poem, which are mentioned in the Edda among the *kringaheiti*, and which prove how far these poets went in their Antonomasias.

  Heingi eg hamri kringdan
  Hang a riupu tangar.
  Grimnis sylgs a galga
  Gynnung bruar linna.

The natural disposition of these words is this: *Eg heingi hamri kringdan linna gynnung a hang riupu bruar tangar, a Grimnis sylgs galga*; which means, I hang the round beaten gaping snake on the end of the bridge of the mountain bird, at the gallows of Odin's Shield. To find the sense of these words, Mr. Ihre observes, that by the gallows of Odin's Shield is meant the
         arm,

arm, on which it is ufual to hang on the fhield. By the word *ripa* is underftood a falcon, for a Skald has the permiffion of putting one genus for another. The bridge of the falcon is the hand, on which the falconer places him, and its end or tong (tongue) is the finger. The gaping round beaten fnake means a ring; and confequently this long ftory means no more than, I put a ring on my finger.

Fourthly, to make themfelves ftill more intelligible, when two words had the fame found, the Skalds were allowed the liberty of putting the periphrafis of the one for the other: for example, the word *hof* fignifies a horfe's hoof or foot; but the fame word likewife means decency, moderation, underftanding; and to exprefs this the horfe's hoof was frequently made ufe of. But the principal difficulty in the explanation of this ancient poetry proceeds from the extreme incorrectnefs of the manufcripts of our Sagas, particularly of the poetry, which cannot be read correctly without great attention. Thefe are the caufes why the greater

part

part of the verses in their Sagas, published either in Iceland itself or in Sweden, cannot be understood; only very few are capable of comprehending them; that it is however possible, is proved by the new editions of Kristnis Saga, Landnamabok, and several others. The provost Gunnar Paulsen in Iceland is particularly distinguished for his great knowledge in this branch of literature.

The difficulties we meet with in ascertaining the true sense of these ancient poems, is likewise the cause of the contempt with which we consider these few remains of the genius of the ancients. I will readily acknowledge that they have no poem which could be proposed as a pattern of wit and elegance; yet it cannot be denied, but that very sublime thoughts and expressions, and sometimes very beautiful comparisons, are to be met with in them: and it is impossible to read the dying Lodbrok's Biarkamal, Eigils, Hofud, Laufn, and Ejvindrs, Haconarma, without pleasure, besides several others.

They

They chofe for the fubject of their poetry whatever happened in common life; however they principally occupied themfelves in compofing fongs in praife of the actions of their great men; in which they are accufed of not being over fcrupulous in beftowing their flatteries. We have feveral poems exifting on various fubjects, among which there is a tolerable epic one on Charles and Grim, befides another on Hialmar. They have likewife fome fatirical pieces, which they ufed to call *nidvifor*, and the undertaking of the author was named *yrkia nid*; but there are no traces of their having had the leaft idea of theatrical performances.

From what has been faid, it may be imagined that there is no language which allows a poet fo much liberty as the Icelandic; and indeed there is no language fo rich in poetical expreffions as this: it muft not however be thought that it is confined by certain rules : on the contrary, I believe there is no profody fo copious as the Icelandic, as, according to the

the Edda, they had no less than 136 different sorts of versifications (in Icelandic *battur*) each of which had its particular rules. However it will be extremely difficult, nay almost impossible, to say any thing certain on this subject, before we have a true explanation of that part which treats of it in the third volume of the Edda.

The Edda is one of the most celebrated remains of antiquity, and yet it has hitherto been very imperfectly known. It has generally been considered as the mythology of the ancients, and the *Voluspa* and *Havamal* have been forced upon it, as two of its volumes, though they do not in the least belong to it. But Chevalier Ihre has thrown more light on this affair: in his printed letter to Mr. Lagerbring, he has attentively examined the manuscript of the Edda, in the library at Upsala, and clearly proves that it is nothing more than an introduction to Icelandic poetry, consisting of three parts: the first, *daemisagor*, is an extract from the Historia mythica veterum: the second, *kenningar*,

kenningar, is a mere Ærarium poeticum; and the third, *liods greiner*, contains the Icelandic profody, &c. &c. The fo-called *dæmifagorne*, are for the moſt part tranſlated into the Swediſh language by Goranfon, but the tranſlation is very incorrect. Refenius has likewife publiſhed them, together with the *Kenningarne* in Latin. But the third part, which deferves no lefs attention, has not yet appeared in print; and it is much to be wiſhed that Chevalier Ihre would give it to the public, as there are fo few befides himſelf capable of doing it juſtice.

The various conjectures which have been formed concerning the true author of the Edda, have been no lefs erroneous than thofe relating to the fubject of the book itſelf. It has generally been thought that Samundr Sigfufon, who died in 1133, wrote a very ample work, entitled the Edda, which treated of many important fubjects, and was in a manner a magazine of all human knowledge; of which however fcarce one third

third has ever been preserved, and tranſmitted to us in the preſent Edda. But Chevalier Ihre aſſerts, that the Edda we now are in poſſeſſion of, has not been extracted from any one more ancient, but that it has originally been compoſed by Snorre Sturleſon.

The difficulties and objections which have been made againſt this opinion by the learned Arnas Magnäus, and afterwards by profeſſor Schloſern, can eaſily be removed; for moſt probably Sturleſon's Edda has been continued by the monk Gunlaug, as Bjorn of Skardſaa ſuppoſes, or rather by Olafr Hvitaſkald. It is not therefore ſurprizing, that ſomething in praiſe of Sturleſon ſhould be inſerted; and it may eaſily be explained from hence, why the author called Waldemar king of Denmark, his maſter.

It is difficult to determine the true nature of the ancient Icelandic poetry; however to give you ſome idea of it, I will ſay ſomething of the verſification moſt frequently uſed among them,

and

and which was called *drottquade* (king's fong).

It was divided into ftanzas, each of which confifted of four couplets, and each of thefe couplets was again compofed of two hemifticks, of which every one contained fix fyllables: and it was not allowed to augment this number, except in cafes of the greateft neceffity. Thefe fyllables confift of three or four feet, according to the different forts of verfification, and fometimes of more, in proportion to the fhortnefs of the fyllables. Befides this, the Icelandic poetry requires two other things, viz. words with the fame initial letters, and words of the fame found. This affonance is called *hending*, and is either more or lefs; in the firft cafe it is called *adalhending*, and in the fecond, *fkotthending*. This you may clearly fee by the following example:

Auftur londum for undann
Alvaldur fa er gaf fcaldum,
Hann feck gagn at gunne,
Gunntrör da flög mörgum,

Slydur-

Slydurtungur let flingra
Sverd leiks reigenn ferdar,
Sende grammur ad grundu
Gullwarpathi fnarpann.

Here it muft firft be obferved, that there is in every couplet a fyllable which governs the whole verfe, *rader quaedinni*, which is almoft always the firft word in the fecond hemiftich; and two words in the firft hemiftich muft begin with the fame letter, if it is a confonant; but when it is a vowel, one vowel may be put for another. Thus, for example, in the above ftanza the following words are thofe which govern each verfe, confifting of two lines or hemiftichs, *radar quedandi*, in the firft verfe, the word *alvadur*, becaufe it begins with a vowel, has, in the firft hemiftich of this verfe, the words *auftur* and *undann*; in the fecond verfe *gunhörda*, you find *gagn* and *gunne* in its firft half; in the third verfe *fverd*, whence in the firft hemiftich *flydurtungur* and *flingra*; in the fourth verfe, *gullvarpathi*, which requires *gramur* and *grundu* in its first half. Secondly, one finds in the first hemistich of each verse a *skotthending*, or two words, which have equal consonants with unequal vowels, such as are in the first verse, *löndum, undann*; in the second *hann, gunn*; in the third, *flydurtungur, flingra*; and in the fourth, *fende, grundu*. But in the second hemistich of each verse is an *adalhending*, where two words have both equal consonants and vowels, in the above-mentioned stanza: words of this kind are in the first verse *akvald, skaldumm*; in the second verse *gunhörda, mörgum*; in third verse *sverd, ferdar*; and in the fourth verse *gulvarpathi, snarpann*; consequently in a stanza, which, like the above, consists of thirty words, above one half of its peculiar properties are contained in the impossibility of changing one word for another, or transposing it, without making a great alteration in the whole verse. These assonances, or *hendingars*, are generally found in the first and last word of each line: sometimes however the one assonant word is placed in the middle

middle of the line, as in the inftance of the word *löndum* in the firft hemiftich of the firft verfe.

This confonance of founds muft be confidered as the neceffary ornament of a regular verfe by the ancient Skalds: the greater this uniformity is, the more the verfe approaches to perfection; it likewife ferves them as a guide in finging their verfes. We alfo find fomething of this fort in the Latin poets; Virgil fays,

—tales cafus Caffandra canebat.

And another poet,

Dum dubitat natura marem faceretve puellam,
Nates es o pulcher paene puella puer.

This has likewife been remarked by Boxhorn, who at the fame time quotes from Giraldus Cambrenfis, that this was alfo cuftomary among the ancient Cambrians, and in England : fo that it feems to have been the opinion of moft nations, that the elegance of poetry

poetry required this harmony of founds. For this reafon the Cambrians fay,

> Digawn Duw da y unie
> Wrth bob ctybwylh parawd.

And the Englifh,

> God is together gamman and wifdome.

David Rhaefus confirms this in his Grammatica Cambro-Brytannica, printed in folio, London 1592, and quotes feveral paffages from their verfes, which have a great deal of refemblance with the *hendingar* of the Icelanders.

I know not whether the agreement of the initial letters, cuftomary in the poetry of the Finlanders, might not likewife be mentioned here, as a proof of the fame cuftom being obferved there as in Iceland: I will therefore infert a paffage from Calamnii's Congratulation to the late king Adolphus Frederic, on his undertaking a voyage to Finland.

Kofla

Lofta kulki kuningamme
Adolph Fredric armollinen
Meidan maalla matkufteli,
Kaicki vereni venahti,
Kaicki lükahti lihani,
Eltae virteni viritin,
Kannoin minum kandeleni,
Ifaen iftuimen etehen,
Kaicki vallan kamarihin:
Iofta anvin andimia.

But this carries me too far from my fubject. Though we do not find any rhymes in our moft ancient poetry, it may, however, be faid with certainty that they are older than the introduction of the Chriftian religion. Skule Ejnarfon is therefore wrongfully accufed of having introduced the ufe of rhymes, which is now become fo general, that except England, which has preferved its blank verfe, no nation in Europe is pleafed with verfes that do not rhyme. The art of rhyming, which is by no means effential to poetry, and ftill lefs ufeful, as it only ferves to make it more difficult, was borrowed, it is not improbable, from the ancient northern íkalds, and has now spread itself beyond Europe; so that rhyming is become as universal as the complaint, that the number of versifiers increases in the same proportion as the number of poets decreases. Baretti relates, that he heard a Mosambique song in rhyme, from some Negroes at Madrid. Gages says the same of the Mexicans; and Nixbuhr mentions that the Arabs are great rhymers.

To conclude, I here present you with a specimen of an Icelandic poem which Rugman composed on the death of count Magnus de la Gardia. It was printed at Upsala; but is become so scarce, that I doubt whether any person in Sweden has a printed copy of it: it may at the same time serve to shew the nature of a *drottquade*, as the author has observed almost all the rules which constitute one.

    Aut er i seggia söti
    Saknar manns i ranui

Gret

Gret ylgur Ragnvald rytto
Rom-ſtamir haukar fromaſt
Kund Lodbrokar; kiendo
Kuillinda valir illra:
Kuóldrido klarar hreldoſt
Kueid ari már faſt reidar
Tijd fiello tar af giodi
Tafnlauſir æpto hrafnar.

Thuarr og vid theingils dauda
Thydur morg brád, i hijdi
Skreidaſt thui berſi ſkiædur
Skiott marti gráds, of otta:
Ox ódum falu faxa
Frar miog or leiptri tara
Huarma beckur ad hrockin
Hrant gron a baudar nauti.

Greto ſkinlaus agiætann
Gripdijr heidingia ſuipuls
Verdar of fædo fordum
Fleinthings allvakran kingia:
Og i oglodum huga
Undo ſier menn og hrundir
Seims kuado mundar foma
Sieirrhuor huit malar thuerri.

Heidingiar ef fua hedins
Harmadu kuanar barma
Stälir fier giordi ftala
Stijrir og Eida hiruft:
Thars i malmgufti giera
Grad thuarr og vod til brada
Varga kna vund oborgid
Vas, thaut rafn i afi.

Hvad bæri ofs er erum
Urdarbrunns tha alkunnir
Sira Jofurs thefs fara
Sueita dagliga neitum?
Og i hans erum faugru
Orda vidkuædi vordnir
Uppfræddir ad vier hreppa
Aftundum gledi háá?

Bæri ofs ey bliugum vera
Breifkleika holdfins veikan
Tijtt fyri fionir fettia
Synd flya, dygd i nijaft?
Hel med thui hroka ftoli
Hreikir fier a faul bleikum
Akuedr ymfra thioda
Andlat med quifti handar.

Hel

Hel vægir hauldum eigi
Hrijfur or theffo lijfi
Kejfara, Klerk og Räfir
Karlmenfko fulla Jarla:
Altignum amint fagnar
Og kot-af-röpa throti
Kurteifa kappa herfa
Kielling leggur ad velli.

Dæmi framm daglig koma
Drijir hel verk at nijo
Audlinga aburt leidir
Ofs dauggvar tara foffi:
Mannlunga mætfta fangar
Med fier hertekna hiedan
Færir og furdum ftorum
Fiaurleftir meingid befta.

Sidpridi, fæmd og heidur,
Somligur dygdar blomi,
Mangiæfka, vinfæl minning,
Metrda fremd ofgietin,
Frijdleikur, fegurd, audur,
Frækn, aft, og hyller dafto
Hel med fier dregur i duala
Deyr tho gott mannord eije.

Einn

Einn nu af æfi banni
Afgieck raud moens brecku
Mætur altygin ytum
Æ tregandi lægir;
Kurreis, vis, kiænn, til vurta
Kin-ftor lof dunga vinur
Haborin Jarl og Herra
Haukftandar malar grandi.

Dyr Magnus Delagardi
Dygdhår Odains bygde
Akurs vift af var rekin,
Er nara nift illfkiptin:
Mord hauxa fall hans færdi
Fridoftum brecko hlijda
Sorg ftora fua og morgum
Slædir lax hrundum fædo.

Thar fic ofs tho ad cyrir
Thad ann i gudi gladur
Als træd holds goto greida
Grand fyrtift vondra anda;
Hirdur i Gimlis gardi
Glatt fingur og famklingir
Utvauldum Eingla fueitum
Endalauft lof miuk raufto.

EPITA-

EPITAPHIUM.

COnditur hoc tumulo juvenili mortuus
    ævo
Magnus, de Magna Gardia gente fatus.
In multos canus dignus qui viveret annos,
    Hei mihi! quod juvenis concidit ante
    diem.
Hujus enim ingenium cepit non terra.
    Quid inde?
Tollite Cælicolæ, redditte Cælicolæ.
Dic tumulum fpectans oculo properante
    viator:
Magno Tuo Cineri fit pia terra levis.

Scripfit Upfaliae anno 1667,
die 14 Februarii.

                    JONAS RUGMAN.

LETTER XVIII.

To Profeſſor BERGMANN.

Of the Volcanos in Iceland.

Stockholm, Sept. 1, 1773.

HAVING received the collection I made in Iceland of the ſpecimens of the different ſubſtances of which their volcanos are compoſed, I take the liberty of ſending it to you; adding at the ſame time a ſhort account of theſe burning mountains, which is in part extracted from Icelandic writers, and partly founded on what I heard from the natives, as well as from my own obſervations; and which I do not think unworthy of your cloſer examination. Indeed it is much to be lamented, that ſince of late ſuch care and application have been beſtowed on the ſtudy of natural hiſtory, ſo little attention has been paid to the operation of Nature in this remarkable iſland; ·for

hitherto

hitherto a very fmall number of the many volcanos are yet fully known; but that we fhould be more ignorant in regard to the wonderful hot fpouting water-fprings with which the country abounds, is very extraordinary; not to mention many other uncommon appearances in Nature.

My time and attention have been too much confined and taken up to give you fo complete an account of the curiofities of Iceland as they deferve; but I flatter myfelf notwithftanding, that you will give a favourable reception to the few obfervations I fhall make, though they fhould not be fo important as might be expected. We may hope to fee this fubject treated upon more at large, when you have time and opportunity to compare the effects of fire in Iceland, with fimilar ones in other parts of the world.

I will not venture to determine how far the opinion of fome men of learning is founded on truth, that all mountains have taken their rife either from fire or water. How probable

probable foever this opinion may appear, of which we can find no traces in the moſt remote times, and the moſt ancient authors; yet it would be very difficult, nay almoſt impoſſible, to eſtabliſh it by experience: but be this as it may, I will venture to pronounce, that Iceland has been formed by eruptions of fire.

It is no uncommon event for iſlands to be produced in this manner; we have many examples of it; but the ſize and extent of Iceland, in compariſon to other iſlands, which owe their origin to the ſame cauſe, may raiſe ſome doubts againſt the reception of this hypotheſis. Nor can it be denied, that this, as well as ſeveral ſorts of ſtone which are to be found there, and which do not bear any diſtinct marks of the effects of fire, are likewiſe calculated to confirm thoſe doubts. Again, I ſee nothing to hinder me from conſidering Iceland as produced by fire, when I reflect that the ground in all parts of the iſland, and particularly near the ſea ſhore, conſiſts of *lava* or *tuffa*, which is frequently covered.

vered with other forts of ſtones, as at Lundō, and even with a hard kind of moor-ſtone *(ſaxum)* or with feveral ſtrata of different kinds of earth and ſtone, as at Laugarnœs, where the lava is fourteen feet in depth; when I find befides, that thofe rocks which have no traces of fire are compounded of fand mixed with fmall pieces of fpar, which may eafily be produced, in two or three thoufand years, fince the lava has laid the foundation; I am ſtill more inclined to fupport this opinion.

I am not however fo credulous as to believe, that the whole ifland was produced at once by fire; but I rather conjecture that it has been the work of fome centuries, by feveral cliffs and rocks having been produced at different times, whofe points have been connected by new eruptions, and which have formed the bafis of the whole ifland.

It is very difficult to determine, whether this fuppofition has any real foundation or not; however I think myfelf authorized to believe it, as well
from

from the arched figure into which the streams of lava have generally formed themselves, as from the probable connections of the sea and the volcanos there: I likewise believe, that from hence it may best be explained, why several islands have been swallowed up in great earthquakes, as a building may soonest be destroyed by tearing away the pillars on which it rests.

Thus I go further back with regard to the eruptions of fire in Iceland, than the common tradition among the vulgar people there, who believe that the first inhabitants of the country, whom they suppose to have been Christians and Irishmen, were so much oppressed by the Norwegian Colonists, that they were forced to leave the country, which they first set fire to, to revenge themselves. We cannot however determine, till after the arrival of the Norwegians, how often the eruptions of fire have happened. But this nation has preserved with great care whatever concerned their place of residence or habitation.

The

The first eruption of fire, mentioned by the antient records, is the *Ildborgar braun*, immediately after the arrival of the Norwegians on the west side of the island, in the ninth century. But it is not remarked as any thing extraordinary, only that the fire broke out near a farm belonging to Thore; and a stretch of lava, or a *braun*, of three miles in length, and two and a half in breadth, remains to this day as a monument of it. After this there are no eruptions mentioned till the year 1000, when the Christian religion was introduced there. At a time when the chiefs of the country were assembled, to consult about the reception of the Christian religion, information was brought that fire was thrown out at Plow. The Heathens considered this as a proof of the wrath of their gods, on which account they were resolved to refuse the new religion; but this resolution was overruled by Snorre Gode's asking them, " On whom did the gods display " their wrath, when those rocks on " which we now stand were on fire?"

The Icelandic Chronicles mention many instances of fiery eruptions observed in different places during the space of 800 years*; it is therefore difficult to conceive how Horrebow, who has been in the country himself, could affirm, that fire is emitted only from them very rarely, and in few places.

To be sensible of the dreadful effects of fire, the country itself need only be considered. The mountains are almost entirely composed of lava and *tuffa*, and the plains are crusted over with *hraun*, or tracts of lava, which are, however, in many places covered with earth or turf. The accounts which we have of certain eruptions of fire, also inform us, that they have always laid waste large tracts of land, either more or less.

I will not in this place mention the damages done to the inhabitants by the ashes thrown from the volcanos, which frequently covered the fields for

---

* The Chronicles give a list of 63 eruptions at Heckla and other places, from the year 1000 to 1766; of which twenty-three were eruptions of Mount Heckla only.

a fpace of twenty or thirty miles in length, and half a yard in height, and by which the cattle fuffered very much, as it caufed them to lofe their teeth, and frequently to drop down dead for want of food; and when they have been killed, pumice has fometimes been found in their liver and bowels. I will only name fome of the places fituate neareft to the volcanos, that have been utterly deftroyed by their effects. This has been partly done by violent earthquakes, which generally preceded the eruption; and partly by inundations of water from the ice melted by the fire; and laftly, by the quantity of glowing afhes and ftones thrown from the mouths of the volcanos, and the ftreams of burning matter which flowed down on all fides.

In 1311 eleven farms were confumed near Roidekamb, and as many more near Tolledyngr; and in 1366, 70 at Lillehered. Heckla deftroyed two in 1374; feven in 1390; and 18 in one day in 1436. In the fame manner fiive farms were laid wafte near Myrdals Jokul in 1660, and ftill more in 1693 near Heckla. In 1727, at leaft 600 fheep and 150 horfes were killed near Myrdals Jokul, by the flood and the pieces of ice which rufhed down with it. In 1728, many farms were deftroyed near Krafle, and a large lake called Myvatn, was entirely dried up, into which the ftreams of fire that rolled from the mountains, flowed during fome years, and formed a tract of lava of four miles in length, and one and a half in breadth. In 1755 Kattlegiaa laid wafte fix parifhes; and in the fame year the laft eruption of Heckla ravaged a tract many miles to the north-eaft.

It is not therefore to be doubted, but that the fire rages here with as much, and perhaps more violence than Vefuvius, Ætna, and other volcanos; notwithftanding which, I fee no foundation for the opinion of fome people, who affirm that there is a communication between the volcanos of Iceland and Italy; it might be maintained with as much foundation that Kattlegiaa and Teneriff,

Teneriff, or Krafle and Lima, communicate.

But before I quit this fubject I will mention a circumftance which is related both by Egbert Olafsen and Jacobfen. The laft time that Kattlegiaa emitted fire, a flafh of lightning, as it were, burft from the flame, and pierced through the cliffs which intercepted its way. The fame lightning in one place killed eleven horfes, three of which were in a ftable; a farmer was alfo killed by it near the door of his room; his upper cloaths, which were woollen, remained entirely unhurt, but his fhirt and waiftcoat, which were both of linen, were burnt; and when his cloaths were pulled off, it was found that the flefh and fkin on the right fide were confumed to the very bones. The maid-fervant, who wanted to affift him in faving the cattle, was likewife ftruck by the lightning, but did not die till feveral days after, during which time fhe fuffered inexpreffible torture. It is likewife faid, that when fhe put on her cloaths, they were finged by the glutinous fires, which

cleaved

cleaved to her body. At firſt, I heſitated to receive this as true, but when I read in your Coſmography, that Braccini had obſerved in 1631, that a column of ſmoak from Veſuvius extended over ſeveral miles of the country, from which deadly lightning proceeded; and that the ſame happened in 1767, when the iron rods erected in Naples became electric whenever Veſuvius emitted fire; I am the more inclined to believe that there is ſomething electrical in this kind of fire, as the ſame phenomena appear in thunder and lightning.

LETTER XIX.

To Professor Bergmann.

Of the Volcanos in Iceland.

Stockholm, Sept. 21, 1774.

IT scarcely ever happens that the mountains begin to throw out fire unexpectedly; for besides a loud rumbling noise, which is heard at a considerable distance, and for several days preceding any eruption, and a roaring and cracking in the part from whence the fire is going to burst forth, many fiery meteors are observed, but unattended in general with any violent concussion of the earth, though sometimes earthquakes, of which the history of the country affords several instances, have accompanied these dreadful conflagrations.

Among the traces left by these eruptions, are particularly the clefts which are frequently to be met with, the largest of which is Almennegiaa, near the water of Tingalla; it is very long,

long, and 105 feet in breadth. The direction of the chafm itfelf is from north to fouth: its weftern wall, from which the other has been perpendicularly divided, is 107 feet 6 inches in height, and confifts of many ftratas (each of which is about ten inches in height) of lava, grown cold at different times, as may eafily be difcovered by the apparent cruft, which is full of blifters, of a darker brown, and not fo much compreffed as the remaining part of the mafs of lava. The eaftern wall is only 45 feet 4 inches in height; and that part of it which is directly oppofite to the higheft part on the other fide, is no more than 36 feet five inches high.

It is likewife confidered as a fign of an impending eruption, when fmall lakes, rivulets, and ftreams dry up. Some perfons believe, that it does not contribute a little to haften the eruption, when the mountain is fo covered with ice, that the holes are ftopped up through which the exhalations, &c. often found a free paffage.

Though it is by no means my opinion, that this contributes much to it, it cannot be denied, that the fire is generally contained in thefe mountains covered with ice, or, as they are called in the country, *jokuls*.

The firft thing that is ufually obferved, before a new eruption of fire, is the burfting of the mafs of ice with a dreadful noife, whence it is called in Icelandic *Jókla-bliod* (Jokul's Sound) and *Jokla breftur*.

Flames then burft forth, and lightning and balls of fire iffue with the fmoak, which are feen feveral miles off. With the flames proceed a number of larger and fmaller ftones, which are fometimes thrown to an incredible diftance. I have feen a round ftone near Nafeirholt, about a mile from Heckla, which was an ell in diameter, and had been thrown there in the laft eruption of Heckla. Egbert Olafsen alfo relates, that at the laft eruption of Kattlegiaa, a ftone which weighed 290 pounds was thrown to the diftance of four miles.

A quantity of white pumice-ftone is alfo thrown up with the boiling waters; and it is believed, with great probability,

bability; that the latter proceeds from the sea, as a quantity of salt sufficient to load several horses has frequently been found after the mountain has discontinued burning.

Then follows generally brown or black pumice-stone, and lava, with sand and ashes.

The lava is seldom found near the opening, but rather *tuffa*, or loose ashes and grit; and indeed the greater part of the Icelandic mountains consists of this matter, which, when it is grown cold, generally takes an arched form, some admirable proofs of which may be seen in the cleft at Allmannagiaa: the upper crust frequently grows hard and solid, whilst the melted matter beneath it continues liquid; this forms great cavities, whose walls, bed, and roof are of lava, and where great quantities of stalactite of lava are found.

There are a great number of these caves in Iceland, some of which are very large, and are made use of by the inhabitants for sheltering their cattle.
I will

I will here only take notice of the cave of Surtheller, as the largeſt of all: it is between 34 and 36 feet in height; its breath is from 50 to 54 feet, and it is 5034 feet long.

It would be both tedious and difficult to claſs the different compoſitions of fire in theſe places, as it is not eaſily diſcovered to which they belong; for example, jaſper, of which great quantities of red and black are found incloſed in the lava, and mixed with it; I will therefore only name thoſe which have been evidently produced by the fire. Firſt, *tuffa*, a ſtone, feruminated aſhes and grit, which ſometimes is found mixed with lava, baſalt, and other ſorts of ſtones, and having been moiſtened by the ſpouting of water, grows hard by heat and length of time. Secondly, *lava*, is that kind of ſtone which has been melted by the violence of the fire, and varies according to the difference of the ſtate in which it ſerved as food to the fire. This lava is ſometimes found ſolid, and at others porous and full of

bladders

bladders and holes; in the infide it is filled up with opaque and brittle fquare cryftals of a dead white, or with green drops of glafs, which decay after they have been long expofed to the air. The colour of the lava is black, dark blue, purple, reddifh brown, or yellowifh, but ofteneft black or red. Where the fire has operated very ftrongly, it is, as it were, glazed, and looks like refin. In the frames or great tracts of lava it is fometimes obferved, that the cruft in growing cold has laid itfelf into folds; but generally it forms itfelf into a refemblance of a rope or cable, fometimes lengthways, and at others in the form of a circle, like unto a great cable rolled together; and generally fo, that its thicknefs continually augments from the center to the periphery. To this clafs I muft alfo count a black folid matter, which ftrikes fire againft fteel, and fometimes takes the forms of trees or branches: fome people have been inclined to think they are petrified trees, but I am rather

of

of opinion that it is a real jafper. Thirdly, pumice, black, red, and even white, which laft has moft probably been difcoloured by the boiling water. Fourthly, agate; I preferve the received name, though it is really nothing more than burned glafs. In fome few places is is found white, tranfparent, and almoft in the form of cryftal. The bluifh fort is alfo rare, but found in large pieces: the moft common is the black agate, which is found generally in ftratas, or in fmall nefts, and fometimes almoft in the fhape of cryftal, in oval, fquare, or pentagonal forms. The aftronomer, Mr. Ejnar Jonfon, has made ufe of this black glafs in his tubes, both in Copenhagen and Iceland, for the obfervation of the fun, and has found them greatly preferable to the darkened glafs. The green agate is found rather coarfer and more reddifh, like thick bottle glafs: it is called *braflinnubrodcon*.

Brimftone, which may be confidered as the proper fuel of the fire, is found

in

in great abundance, pure and mineralized: in the north, principally at Hufewick, and in the fouth, at Kryfewick, there are white brimftone mines which are called *Namas*. I fhall referve the bafalts for a particular letter.

LETTER XX.

To Profeſſor BERGMANN.

Of Mount Heckla.

Stockholm, Sept. 7, 1773.

THE cauſe of Heckla (or, as it is called in the country, *Hecklafiall*) having been more noticed than many other volcanos of as great extent, and no leſs wonderful and inſtructive, may partly be aſcribed to its having vomited fire ſo frequently, and partly to its ſituation, which expoſes it to the ſight of all the ſhips ſailing to Greenland and North America : as we conſidered it with greater attention than any other volcano on the iſland, I will give you a deſcription of the ſtate in which we found it on the 24th of September, 1772.

After we had ſeen many tracts of lava, among which Garde and Wvalupe Hraune were the moſt conſiderable,

able, we purſued our journey to the foot of the mountain. We had a tent pitched here, where we propoſed to paſs the night, to enable us to aſcend the mountain with greater ſpirits in the morning. The weather was extremely favourable, and we had the ſatisfaction of ſeeing whatever we wiſhed, the eruption only excepted.

The mountains is ſituated in the ſouthern part of the iſland, about four miles from the ſea-coaſt, and is divided into three points at the top, the higheſt of which is that in the middle, and is, according to an exact obſervation with Ramſden's barometer, 5000 feet higher than the ſea. We made uſe of our horſes, but were obliged to quit them at the firſt opening from which the fire had burſt. This was a place ſurrounded with lofty glazed walls, and filled with high glazed cliffs, which I cannot compare with any thing I ever ſaw before.

A little higher up we found a great quantity of grit and ſtones, and ſtill farther on another opening, which though not deep, however deſcended

lower

lower down than that of the higheft point. We thought we plainly obferved evident marks of hot boiling water in this place.

Not far from hence the mountains began to be covered with fnow, fome fmall fpots excepted, which were bare. We could not at firft difcern the caufe of this difference, but foon found that it proceeded from the vapour which arofe from the mountain. As we afcended higher, thefe fpots became larger; and about two hundred yards from the fummit we found a hole of about one yard and a half in diameter, from which fo hot a fteam exhaled, that it prevented us from afcertaining the degree of heat with the thermometer.

The cold now began to be very intenfe, as Fahrenheit's thermometer, which was at 54 at the foot of the mountain, fell to 24. The wind was alfo become fo violent, that we were fometimes obliged to lie down to avoid being thrown into the moft dreadful precipices by its fury.

We were now arrived at one of the highest summits, when our conductor, who did not take great pleasure in the walk, endeavoured to persuade us that this was the highest part of the mountains. We had just finished our obfervations, and found by them that Ramfden's barometer stood at 24-238, and the thermometer, fixed to it, at 27, when happily the clouds divided, and we discovered a still higher summit. We lost no time in deliberation, but immediately ascended it, and when at the top discovered a space of ground, about eight yards in breadth, and twenty in length, entirely free from snow; the sand was, however, quite wet, from its having lately melted away. Here we experienced at one and the same time, a high degree of heat and cold, for in the air Fahrenheit's thermometer was constantly at 24, and when we set it down on the ground, it rose to 153. The barometer was, here at 22-247, and the thermometer at 38.

We could not with safety remain here any longer, though we were very

much

much inclined to it; and defcended, after having confidered the laft opening there, one of the fides of which was entirely overturned, and the other quite covered with afhes and grit. In our return we obferved three confiderable openings, in one of which every thing looked as red as brick. From another the lava had flowed in a ftream of about 50 yards in breadth, which the Icelanders call *Stenaa*, or Stone Flood; and at fome diftance from thence the ftream divided into three broad arms. Further on we found a large circular opening, at the bottom of which we obferved a mountain in the form of a fugar-loaf, in throwing up of which the fire feemed to have exhaufted itfelf.

The laft eruption of mount Heckla happened in 1766; it began the 4th of April, and continued to the 7th of September following. Flames proceeded from it in December 1771, and in September 1772, but no flowing of lava, &c.

The mountain does not confift of lava, but chiefly of fand, grit, and afhes, ashes, which are thrown up with the stones, partly melted, and partly discoloured by the fire. We likewise found several sorts of pumice, and among them one piece with some sulphur in it. The pumice was sometimes so much burnt, that it was as light as tow ; their form and colour was sometimes very fine, but at the same time so soft, that it was difficult to remove them from one place to another : of the common lava we found both large pieces and small bits, as likewise a quantity of black jasper, burned at the extremities, and resembling trees and branches. Among the stones thrown out of the mountain we saw some slate of a strong red colour.

GEYSER.

LETTER XXI.

To Professor BERGMANN.

Of the hot spouting Water-springs in Iceland.

Stockholm, Oct. 3, 1774.

AMONG all the curiosities in Iceland, which nature presents to the eyes of an attentive spectator to raise his admiration, nothing can be compared to the hot spouting water-springs with which this country abounds. The hot springs at Aken, Carlsbad, Bath, and Switzerland, and several others which are found in Italy, are considered as very remarkable; but to my knowledge, except in the last-mentioned country, the water no where becomes so hot as to boil; nor is it any where known to be thrown so high as at the hot spouting water-springs in Iceland.

All thofe jets d'eau which have been contrived with fo much art, and at fo enormous an expenfe, cannot by any means be compared with thefe. The water-works at Herrenhaufen throw up a fingle column of water, of half a quarter of a yard in circumference, to the height of about 70 feet; thofe on the Winterkaften, at Caffel, throw it up, but in a much thinner column, 130 feet; and the jet d'eau at St. Cloud, which is thought the greateft amongft all the French water-works, cafts up a thin column 80 feet into the air: whilft fome fprings in Iceland pour forth colums of water, of feveral feet in thicknefs, to the height of many fathoms; and many affirm, of feveral hundred feet.

But, without relying upon what has been faid by others of thefe wonderful phænomena of nature, I think myfelf happy to have contemplated with mine own eyes the moft remarkable of thefe fprings, which has enabled me to give you an accurate account of it. I only beg leave to fay fomething of them in general, before

I treat

I treat of that which I saw in particular.

These springs are of unequal degrees of heat. From some the water flows gently as from other springs, and it is then called *laug*, a bath; from others, it spouts boiling water with a great noise, and is then called *hver* or *kittel* (*keſſel*). Though the degree of heat is unequal, yet I do not remember ever to have observed it under 188 of Fahrenheit's thermometer. At Laugarnas we found it at 188, 191, 193. At Geyser, Reykum, and Laugarvatn 212; and in the last place, in the ground, at a little hot vein of water, 213 degrees.

It is very common for some of the spouting springs to close up, and others to spring up in their stead; there are likewise frequent traces of former *hvers*, where at present not a single drop of water is to be seen. Many remember to have seen instances of this; and Egbert Olafsen relates, that in 1753 a new *hver* broke forth at Reikakio, seven fathoms in breadth, and three in depth, at the distance of 50 fathoms

fathoms from an old spring, which had been stopped up by a fall of earth. Frequent earthquakes and subterranean noises, heard at the time, caused great terror to the people who lived in the neighbourhood.

All these hot waters have an incrusting quality, so that we very commonly find the exterior surface from whence it bursts forth covered with a kind of rind, which almost resembles chaced work, which we at first took for lime; but we soon became dubious of this, as it did not ferment with acid; but we hope that you, Sir, will soon resolve us. This crust is in general very fine; but it is, however, most pure and clear at the spouting springs; for at the others, where the water flows, the parts precipitated by the water are sometimes mixed with earth, which makes the crust appear darker.

At the *hvers* it is very difficult, nay almost impossible, to examine within the opening the disposition of the passage which the water has formed, both by reason of the heat of the water, and

and the violence with which it is forced out. One may, however, with confidence judge of the great by the fmall; and it gave us the greater pleafure, as we had an opportunity at Laugarnas to examine the vein of water itfelf a confiderable way under the cruft.

The water had in this place taken its courfe through a bright grey clay, the furface of which was covered with a white rind; but was on the fide neareft the clay, quite fmooth, and crifped on the upper fide. The vein flowed a good way under this cruft, through a canal formed of a fimilar matter; and the whole canal was filled with cryftals, which had a very pleafing effect. I had not time to examine their nature and form on the fpot, as they were very fmall; but I expect a more particular account of this fubject from you, as you will find feveral fpecimen of them in the collection I fent you. We could not however, purfue the courfe of the water very far, as we were obliged to leave it to its fubterranean paffages, through which nature had feduced

ced it from its reservoirs, where heated by the warmth, and compressed by the exhalations, it at last bursts from its prison, by gushing forth at another place, in order to make way for its vapours.

The water in some places tastes of sulphur, and in others not; but when drank as soon as it is cold, tastes like common boiled water. The inhabitants use it, at particular times, for dying; and were they to adopt proper regulations, it might be of still greater use. Victuals may also be boiled in it, by putting it into a pot covered, and boiling it till a certain quantity is evaporated. Milk held over this water when boiling becomes sweet, owing, most probably, to its excessive heat; as the same effect is produced by boiling it a long time over the fire. They have begun to make salt, by boiling sea-water over it, which, when it is refined, is very fine and good. The cows which drink of it yield a great quantity of good milk. Egbert Olaffen informs us, that the water does not become troubled when alkali is
thrown

thrown into it, nor does it change colour from fyrup of violets. I do not know what degree of credit ought to be given to Horrebow, who afferts, that if you fill a bottle at one of the fpouting fprings, the water contained in the bottle will boil over two or three times during the time the fpring throws it forth, and if corked too foon the bottle will burft.

Though it cannot be denied that thefe fprings have fome communication with the Icelandic volcanos, yet they are feldom found very near them, but are difperfed throughout the whole country. For this reafon, hot fprings are found among the mountains, and even on the top of the ice mountains; as on Torfa Jockul, where a great number of hot fprings are to be met with; and among them two large *hvers*, which throw up the boiling water to a great height. There is likewife a lukewarm fpring near Haadegis Hnuk, on Gutlands Jokul, at the foot of the mountain, with many traces of former *hvers*. There are even in the fea hot fpouting fprings, which can only be

ap-

approached at low water; as at Reyka-fiord in Ifa-fiord, where four fprings may be obferved in the water by the afcending fteam, and one *hver* on the furface of the water. There are alfo two others in the Oddbiarnar fhoals, ftill more at Drapfkar, and a great number at Sando, Uurdholm, Reykey, and on the flat iflands. To give a better idea of the fituation of thefe fprings, I will give a lift of them, which I will endeavour to make as topographical as poffible.

In Borgarfiord's Syffel, near Leyraa, not far from the foot of the mountain of Skardfheides, we met with the firft *hver*, which is, however, not a very ftrong one; and not far from it there is a fmall bath. At Lunda Reykiadal there is a *hver* and a bath; and near a farm-yard, Varma-Lakiar-Mula, a warm fpring and a bath. A little farther to the north is the valley of Reykholts, which is two miles and a half in breadth, in the bottom of which hot baths are every where to be met with. This fpot may be difcovered at feveral miles diftance by the vapours

which

which exhale every where from the hot water, and unite in the air, refembling a prodigious fmoke arifing from fome volcano. The three principal *hvers* in this place are, Tunguhver, Aa-hver, and Scribla; the laft furnifhes water to Snorralaug, Snorre Sturlefon's bath, which is efteemed the beft in Iceland. From this place there is no hot fpring to be met with northward for a very large tract, till you come to Sneefield's Cape, where there is a lukewarm fpring near the farm called Lyfehol, in Stadefveit: at this place many remains of ancient *hvers* are to be feen. Still further to the north, in Dale Syffel, is a warm bath with fome fprings. In Soling's Valley, and further on, near the farm Reykaholer, in Reykianas, are many ftrong *hvers*; particularly three very large ones, the moft confiderable of which is Krablanda. From thence we came to the hot fprings of Flatdarna, Oddsbiarmarfkar, and Drapfkar, and afterwards vifited thofe at Talknc-fiord, Arnarfiord, and Ifa-fiord in Reyka-fiord, where there is a ftrong fpouting fpring.

After

After we had paſt Cape Nord, or the northern extremity of Iceland, we met with ſome warm ſprings at Reykar-fiord; others, together with a fine bath, at Biarnar-fiord, near Kaldadarna: at Hruta-fiorden there is a great *hver* called Reike-hver, and another as large at Midfiorden, called Reixalaug. When you go from hence ſouthward into the country, you will find a number of boiling ſprings at Hverevalle, three of which ſpout the water high into the air with a prodigious noiſe; ſtill further to the ſouth there is a *hver* near Geitland's Jokul.

If we turn again to the north, we find hot ſprings at Blanda, others near the haven at Skaga-Strand, and ſtill more at a little diſtance from thence at Skaga-fiorden; one of which falls from a rock thirty feet high. To the eaſt there are hot ſprings in many places of Vadle Syſſel, as at Olafs-fiordr, Langaland, Kriſtnas, and Hrafnegil; but in Thingo Syſſel there are ſprings of both ſorts (baths and *hvers*, in great number, and of conſiderable dimenſions. The *hvers* in Reykia Valley

Valley deserve to be particularly mentioned, amonst which Oxe and Badstofu are the largest.

On the east side of the country there are no considerable *hvers*, though warm springs are to be found in Selar, Laugarvalle, Rafukells, and Fliots valleys; and on the south, on Torfa Jokul. We then proceeded to Skallholt, where there are many springs; about a mile from thence the *hvers*, called Reikholt and Grafa, both which spout very high. The next *hver* is Geyser, which I shall afterwards mention more minutely. Not far from this last is Laugervatn, a small lake, round which a number of warm springs may be observed, and eight boiling ones. The road now leads us to the *hvers* at Oelves, which is thought to be the largest in all Iceland; the most remarkable of which are Geyser and Badstofu.

Here is also a dry *hver*, from which water formerly proceeded, but now emits only steam through its mouth; the heat of which however is so great, that
a pot

a pot of water placed over the opening boils in a very short time. We met with spouting springs at Krusevik in Gullbringe Syssel, the *hver* Eine, the *hvers* at Reikianas, and several at Langarnas in Kiofar Syssel.

From this list, which, however, is far from containing all the warm springs in Iceland, you may judge, Sir, of the prodigious number that we met with. Near most of them are warm baths, each of which merits a particular examination and description. Eggert Olafsen and Biarne Paulsen have made very curious observations on several of them; but I only beg leave to mention some which I made at Geyser, where is the largest of all the spouting-springs in Iceland, or perhaps in the known world. These observations were made the 21st of September 1772, from six o'clock in the morning till seven at night.

Among the hot springs in Iceland, several of which bear the name of *geyser*, there are none that can be compared with that which I am going to to defcribe, though the beft defcription will fall very fhort of it. It is about two days journey from Heckla, not far from Skallholt, near a farm called Haukadal. Here a poet would have an opportunity of painting a picture of whatever Nature has of beautiful and terrible united, by delineating one of its moft uncommon phænomena: it would be a fubject worthy the pen of a Thompfon to tranfport the reader, by poetical imagery, to the fpot which is here prefented to the eye. Reprefent to yourfelf a large field, where you fee on one fide, at a great diftance, high mountains covered with ice, whofe fummits are generally wrapped up in clouds, fo that their fharp unequal points become invifible. This lofs however is compenfated by a certain wind, which caufes the clouds to fink, and cover the mountain itfelf, when its fummit appears as it were to reft upon the clouds. On the other fide, Heckla is feen, with its three points covered with ice, rifing above the clouds, and with the fmoak which afcends from it, forming other clouds at

R fome

some distance from the real ones: and on another side is a ridge of high rocks, at the foot of which boiling water from time to time gushes forth ; and further on extends a marsh of about half a mile in circumference, where are forty or fifty boiling springs, from which a vapour ascends to a prodigious height.

In the midst of these is the greatest spring *geyser*, which deserves a more exact and particular account. In travelling to the place, about a quarter of a mile from the *hver*, from which the ridge of rocks near it still divided us, we heard a loud roaring noise, like the rushing of a torrent, precipitating itself from stupendous rocks. We asked our guide what it meant: He answered, it was *geyser* roaring ; and we soon saw with our naked eyes what before appeared almost incredible.

The depth of the opening or pipe from which the water gushes cannot well be determined ; for sometimes the water sunk down several fathoms, and some seconds passed before a stone which was thrown into the aperture
reached

reached the furface of the water. The opening itfelf was perfectly round, and nineteen feet in diameter; it ended above in a bafon which was fifty-nine feet in diameter; both the pipe and the bafon were covered with a rough ftalactic rind, which had been formed by the force of the water; the uttermoft border of the bafon is nine feet and an inch higher than the pipe itfelf.

The water here fpouted feveral times a day, but always by ftarts, and after certain intervals. The people who lived in the neighbourhood told us, that they rofe higher in cold and bad weather than at other times; and Eggert Olafsen and feveral others affirm, that it fpouted to the height of fixty fathoms. Moft probably they only gueffed by the eye, and on that account their calculation may be a little extravagant; and indeed I doubt that ever the water was thrown up fo high, though I am much inclined to believe, that it fometimes mounts higher than when we obferved it.

I will

I will here infert an account, how high the water was thrown the day that we were there, which I hope, will not be difagreeable to you. We obferved the height thus; every one in company wrote down at each time that the water fpouted, how high it appeared to him to be thrown, and we afterwards chofe the medium. The firft column marks the fpoutings of the water, in the order in which they follow one another; the fecond, the time when thefe effufions happened; the third, the height to which the water rofe; and the laft, how long each fpouting of water continued.

No.	Time.	Height.	Duration.	
1	At VI 42m.	30 feet	0 m	20 f.
2	- 51	- 6	- 0	20
3	VII 6	- 6	- 0	10
4	- 31	- 12	- 0	15
5	- 51	- 60	- 0	6
6	VIII 17	- 24	- 0	30
7	- 29	- 18	- 0	40
8	- 36	- 12	- 0	40

The

The pipe was now for the firſt time full of water, which ran ſlowly into the baſon.

No.	Time.		Height.	Duration.	
9	IX	25	48	1	10
10	X	16	24	1	00
	XII	35	\multicolumn{3}{l}{minutes we heard as it were three diſcharges of a gun under ground, which made it ſhake, the water immediately flowed over, but ſunk again inſtantly.}
	II	8	\multicolumn{3}{l}{the water flowed over the border of the baſon.}
	III	15	\multicolumn{3}{l}{we again heard ſeveral ſubterraneous noiſes, tho' not ſo ſtrong as before.}
	IV	43	\multicolumn{3}{l}{the water flowed over very ſtrongly during a whole minute.}
		49	\multicolumn{3}{l}{we again heard many loud ſubterraneous diſcharges, not only near the ſpring, but alſo from the neighbouring ridge of rocks, where the water ſpouted.}
11	VI	51	92	4	00

After

After this great effort, the water funk down very low into the pipe, and was entirely quiet during several minutes, but it foon began to bubble again; it was however not thrown up into the air, but only to the top of the pipe,

No.	Hours.	Min.	No.	Hours.	M'n.
1	5	7	18	5	42
2	5	9½	19	5	43½
3	5	10½	20	5	47
4	5	13½	21	5	48½
5	5	14¾	22	5	49
6	5	17	23	5	30½
7	5	18¾	24	5	51½
8	5	20⅛	25	5	54
9	5	21½	26	5	37½
10	5	23½	27	5	59
11	5	27¾	28	6	10
12	5	30¼	29	6	19
13	5	31¾	30	6	23
14	5	33½	31	6	26
15	5	35	32	6	29
16	5	36	33	6	30
17	5	38			

The force of the vapours which throw up this water is exceffive; it

not

not only prevents the ſtones which are thrown into the opening from ſinking, but even throws them up to a very great height, together with the water. I muſt not forget to mention a very curious circumſtance: when the baſon was full of water, we placed ourſelves before the ſun in ſuch a manner, that we could ſee our ſhadows in the water, every one obſerved round the ſhadow of his own head (though not round the heads of the others) a circle of almoſt the ſame colours which compoſe the rainbow, and round this another bright circle: this moſt probably proceeded from the vapours exhaling from the water. I remember to have ſeen ſomething ſimilar to it when travelling in the ſummer, particularly in the meadows, and it is ſooneſt obſerved when riding on horſeback, or in a carriage, when you have your ſhadow on one ſide.

Not far from this place, another ſpring at the foot of the neighbouring ridge of rocks ſpouted water to the height of one or two yards each time,

No.	Hours	Min.		No.	Hours	Min.
1	3	45	—	7	4	0
2	3	47½	—	8	4	3
3	0	50⅓	—	9	0	5¾
4	0	53½	—	10	0	8½
5	0	55	—	11	0	11¼
6	0	57¾	—	12	0	14

The opening through which this water issued was not so wide as the other; we imagined it possible to stop up the hole entirely by throwing large stones into it; and even flattered ourselves that our attempt had succeeded, but to our great astonishment the water gushed forth in a very violent manner, which shews how little the weak efforts of man avail, when they endeavour to proscribe bounds to the works of Nature. We hastened to the pipe, and found all the stones thrown aside, and the water playing freely through its former channel.

In these large springs the waters were hot in the highest degree, and tasted a little of sulphur, but in other respects were pure and clear. In the smaller springs in the neighbourhood the

the water was tainted; in fome it was as muddy as that of a clay-pit, in others as white as milk; and yet there are a few fprings where the water forces itfelf through a fire underneath as red as blood.

I have already obferved, that near moft of thefe fprings and *hvers* there are baths, which are frequently vifited by the natives: there are alfo in many places dry and fweating-baths. Eggert Olafsen mentions one of thefe baths at Huufevik, in North Iceland; and I had the curiofity of feeing one of them at Thibfaarhlot, not far from Skallholt, which confifted of a hut raifed of earth, into which hot fteams arofe from many holes. Fahrenheit's thermometer, which was at 57 degrees in the open air, rofe to 93 in the hut whilft it was open, and when it was placed in one of the little openings the fteam arofe to 135.

LETTER XXII.

To Professor BERGMANN.

Of the Pillars of Basalt.

Stockholm, June 6, 1773.

AMONG the effects of fire, some of which are extremely dreadful, and all of them very extraordinary and remarkable, none have in latter times attracted more attention than those large regular pillars known by the name of Basalts. There had formerly been hardly any places observed in Europe, where this kind of stone was found, the Giant's Causeway excepted; and the greater part of our mineralogists have, if I am not mistaken, considered them as a kind of chrystalization. Mr. Desmarets was the first who maintained in a dissertation presented to the French academy of sciences, that they were produced by fire, wherein he described some basalts found near St. Sandour in Auvergne.

This opinion at first appeared almost absurd to our natural historians, as it was not believed that volcanos had ever been in these places where basalt pillars were found.

This new discovery however occasioned a more exact enquiry concerning other places where these pillars are met with. All these enquiries only served to confirm Mr. Desmarets's opinion, by proving that these basalt pillars must have been produced by subterraneous fires.

There is no one surely will entertain the least doubt of a subterraneous fire having formerly existed where these pillars now stand, as at Stolpenstein in Meissen; near Lauban in Lusatia; in Bohemia; near Leignitz in Silesia; near Brandau in Hessia; in Sicily; near Bolsenna, Montebello and St. Forio in Italy; near St. Lucas in the district of St. Vicenza; near Monte Rosso in the Paduan district, and Monte Diavolo in the mountains of Verona; in Lower Languedoc; in Iceland, and in the western islands of Scotland; which you, Sir, have all

men-

mentioned in your Cosmography. Also in St. Giovanni, Monte Castello, Monte Nuovo, Monte Oliveto, near Cader Idris in Wales, in England, almost every where in Velay and Auvergne, where whole towns, as Chillac and St. Flour, are built upon these pillars. But as this matter has not yet been fully investigated, and it cannot be determined with certainty in what manner these pillars are formed, though they are known to be produced by fire, perhaps it will not be disagreeable to you, if I say something of the many basalt pillars in Iceland, as well as of those in the isle of Staffa, which you will readily acknowledge to be more singular than any thing Nature ever produced of this kind.

It is well known that these pillars are very common in Iceland, and some account is also given of them in the Physical Description published of the country. The lower sort of people imagine these pillars have been piled upon one another by the giants, who made use of supernatural force to effect it, it, whence they have obtained the name of the *Trolla-hlaud Trollkonugar-dur* in several places. They have generally from three to seven sides, and are from four to six feet in thickness, and from twelve to sixteen yards in length, without any horizontal divisions. But sometimes they are only from six inches to one foot in height, and they are then very regular, as those at Videy, which are made use of for windows and door-posts. In some places they only peep out of the mountains here and there among the lava, or still oftener among *tuffa*; in other places they are quite overthrown, and only pieces of broken pillars appear. Sometimes again they extend two or three miles in length without interruption. In the mountain called Glockenberg in Snefialdsnas, this kind of stone appears in a manner very different from any other place in Iceland; for on the top the pillars lie quite horizontally, in the middle they are sloping, and the lowest are perfectly perpendicular; in some places they are bent as a semicircle,

circle, which proves a very violent effect of the fire on the pillars already standing, as in most places, or at least in a great many, they are intirely perpendicular, and by their form and situation, that they have even been burnt in a perpendicular direction.

As to the matter of which the Icelandic basalts are composed, it is in some places similar to that of which the pillars at Staffa consist, though in others it is more porous, and inclines more to grey. And who knows, if an attentive and curious naturalist, who had both time and talents requisite for such an undertaking, might not easily trace all the gradations between the coarsest lava and the finest pillar of basalt? I myself saw some of this last sort at Videy, which were solid, of a blackish grey, and composed of several joints. And not far from thence, at Laugarnäs, near the sea-shore, I saw a porous glassy kind of stone, consequently lava, but was so indistinctly divided, that I was a long time undetermined, whether I should consider it as pillars or not;

but

but at length the reft of the company, as well as myfelf, were perfuaded that they really were fuch. But I will poft-pone the examination of the matter of which thefe pillars confift, and of the matter in which they are form-ed, till fuch time as I have given you the promifed defcription of the ifle of Staffa.

A piece of good fortune procured us the pleafure of being the firft who ever examined thefe wonders of Na-ture with an attentive eye. Among all thofe who have publifhed defcrip-tions of Scotland, there are none except Buchanan, whofe account, however, is very imperfect, that mentions a fingle fyllable of thefe pillars. Mr. Pen-nant, an indefatigable and experienced naturalift, in the fame year that we vifited this ifland, made a tour to Scotland to examine the natural pro-ductions of that country, but was pre-vented by a contrary wind from going to Staffa. Moft probably we fhould not have come there neither, if the ufual ebb and flood, which is very
ftrong

ſtrong between the weſtern iſlands of Scotland, had not forced us in our way to Iceland, on the twelfth of Auguſt in the night, to caſt anchor in the Sound, between the iſle of Mull and Morvern on the Continent, exactly oppoſite to Drumnen, the ſeat of Mr. Maclean. We were immediately invited to land, and breakfaſted there, with that hoſpitality which characteriſes the inhabitants of the Highlands of Scotland. Mr. Leach, another gueſt of Mr. Maclean, gave us many particulars of theſe pillars, which he had viſited a few days before. Mr. Banks's deſire of information could not reſiſt the offer of this gentleman to accompany us to Staffa; we therefore went on board our long-boat the ſame day, and arrived there at nine o'clock in the evening. It was impoſſible for our ſurprize to be increaſed, or our curioſity to be fuller gratified, than they were the next morning when we beheld the no leſs than beautiful ſpectacle which Nature preſented to our view.

If

If we even with admiration behold art, according to the rules prefcribed to it, obferving a certain kind of order, which not only ftrikes the eye, but alfo pleafes it; what muft be the effect produced upon us when we behold Nature difplaying as it were a regularity which far furpaffed every thing art ever produced! An attentive fpectator will find as much occafion for wonder and aftonifhment, when he obferves how infinitely fhort human wifdom appears, when we attempt to imitate Nature in this as well as in any other of her grand and awful productions. And though we acknowledge Nature to be the miftrefs of all the arts, and afcribe a greater degree of perfection to them, the nearer they approach and imitate it, yet we fometimes imagine that fhe might be improved, according to the rules of architecture.

How magnificent are the remains we have of the porticos of the antients! and with what admiration do we behold the colonnades which adorn the principal buildings of our times! and
yet

yet every one who compares them with Fingal's Cave, formed by Nature in the isle of Staffa, must readily acknowledge, that this piece of Nature's architecture far surpasses every thing that invention, luxury, and taste ever produced among the Greeks.

The island of * Staffa lies west of Mull, three miles N. E. of Jona or Columb-Kill, and is about a mile in length, and half a mile in breadth: it belongs to Mr. Lauchlan Mac-Quarie. On the west side of the island is a small cave, where there is a very convenient landing place, but where no regular basalt figures are to be met with. To the south of this cave are some narrow pillars, which, instead of standing upright, are all inclined, and look like so many pieces of an arch. Further on

---

* Mr. Bank's account of this island, as communicated by that intelligent gentleman to Mr. Pennant, and inserted in his Tour in Scotland, and Voyage to the Hebrides in 1772, is too curious to be omitted, as it is not only very interesting in itself, but is an undeniable proof of the accuracy and fidelity with which our author, Dr. Troil, has treated of the various subjects contained in this publication :———the Editor deems it therefore unnecessary to apologize for subjoining an extract of it to this letter.

you

you leave a small grotto on your right hand, which is not compoſed of pillars, tho' they appear more diſtinctly and larger above it, and in one place reſemble the interior timber-work of a ſhip. Directly oppoſite to it, only a few yards diſtant, is the peninſula of Bo-ſcha-la, which entirely conſiſts of regular though leſs pillars, that are all of a conical figure. Some of them lie horizontally, others incline as it were to the central point, as to the upper end, but the greater number are perfectly perpendicular. The iſland itſelf, oppoſite to Bo-ſcha-la, conſiſts of thick columns or pillars, which are not however very high, as they gradually decreaſe in approaching to the water, and extend into the ſea as far as the eye can reach. You may walk upon theſe with great eaſe, as from one ſtep of a ſtair-caſe to another, till you come to Fingal's, or more properly ſpeaking, to Fiuhn Mac Coul's grotto or cave, which enters into the mountain from N. E. to E.

This cave conſiſts of very regular pillars, which to a great extent on both

both sides, and in the most interior part, support an arched vault, composed of the obtuse points of pillars crouded close together. The bottom of the cave, which is filled with clear fresh water several feet in depth, is likewise covered with innumerable pieces of pillars, which compose its floor. The colour of the pillars is of a blackish grey; but between the joints there is a yellow stalactic quarry rind exhaled, which serves to make these divisions more distinct, and produces an agreeable effect to the eye, by the many different modulations of colour. It is so light within the cave, that one can distinguish the innermost range of pillars perfectly well from without. The air in it is very pure and good, as it is constantly changed by the rising and falling of the water during the tide. Very far into the cave there is a hole in the rock, somewhat lower than the surface of the water standing in it, which makes a pleasing kind of noise on every flux and reflux of the tides. One may walk in most parts of the

cave

cave on the broken points of some pillars rising above the surface of the water, but it is most convenient to go in a boat. We made the following measurements of the cave:

	F. I.	F. I.
The length, from the farthest of the basalt pillars, which from the shore formed a canal to the cave, — — 121 6	} 371	6
From the commencement of the vault to the end of the cave, 250		
The breadth of its entrance,	53	7
Of the interior end,	20	0
The height of the vault at the entrance of the cave,	117	6
Of ditto, at the interior end,	70	0
The height of the outermost pillar in one corner,	39	6
The height of another, in the north-west corner,	54	0
The depth of the water at entrance,	18	0
Of the inside end,	9	0

Above

Above the cave was a ſtratum of a ſtone mixed with pieces of baſalt. We made the following meaſurements:

	F.	I,
From the water to the foot of the pillars,	36	8
Height of the pillars,	32	6
Height of the arch or vault above the top of the pillars,	31	4
The ſtratum above this,	34	4

From hence, a little farther north-weſt, we met with the largeſt pillars which are to be found in the whole iſland. The place on which they ſtood was likewiſe quite free, ſo that we were enabled to examine it. The following was the reſult of our meaſurement:

The weſtern corner of Fingal's Cave:

	F.	I,
1. From the water to the foot of the pillars,	12	10
2. Height of the pillars,	37	3
3. The ſtratum above them,	66	9

Farther weſtward:

	F.	I,
1. The ſtratum beneath the pillars,	11	0
2. Height of the pillars,	54	0
3. The ſtratum above,	61	6

Still

Still more weftward :   F. I.
1. Stratum beneath the pillars,   17   1
2. Height of the pillars,   50   0
3. The ftratum above them,   51   1
Still more to the weft :
1. Stratum beneath the pillars,   19   8
2. Height of the pillars,   55   1
3. The ftratum above,   54   7

The ftratum beneath the pillars here mentioned, is evidently *tuffa*, which had been heated by fire, and feems to be interlarded, as it were, with fmall bits of bafalt; and the red or ftratum above the pillars, in which large pieces of pillars are fometimes found irregularly thrown together, and in uneaqual directions, is evidently nothing elfe but lava. Though a prodigious degree of fire muft formerly have been requifite to produce this upper ftratum, yet there are not the leaft traces in its exterior, the pillars having been removed by it, for the whole enormous mafs refts upon them.

When you move farther on, and pafs the northern fide of the ifland, you come to Corvorant's Cave, where the bed beneath the pillars is raised, and the pillars themselves decrease in height: they are, however, tolerably diſtinct, till you are paſt a bay which extends very far into the country, on the ſide of which the pillars entirely diſappear. The mountains here conſiſt of a dark brown ſtone, of which I cannot affirm with certainty whether it is lava or not, and where not the leaſt regularity is to be obſerved; but as ſoon as you paſs the ſouth-eaſt ſide of the iſland, the ſtones begin again to aſſume a regular figure, though ſo gradually, that it is ſcarcely perceptible at firſt, till at laſt, the regular and crooked pillars again appear with which I began my deſcription.

The pillars have from three to ſeven ſides, but the greater number have five or ſix, and ſo crouded together, that a heptagonal pillar is ſurrounded with ſeven others, which join cloſely to its ſeven ſides. In ſome places, however, there are little inſignificant openings, but they are filled up with *quarz*, which

which in one place had even made its way through a number of pillars, though without in the leaft deftroying their regularity. The pillars confift of many joints or pieces, of about a foot in height, which fo exactly fit upon one another, that it is difficult to introduce a knife between the interftices. The upper piece was generally concave, fometimes flat, and rarely convex; if the upper joint was flat, the loweft was fo likewife, but when it was excavated, the lower one was rounded and reverfed.

The fides of the pillars are not all equally broad. The following meafurements were taken of four pillars:
Nº I. with 4 fides.   F. I.
    1ft fide   Diameter   1   5
    2d   -   -   1   1
    3d   -   -   1   6
    4th   -   -   1   1
Nº II. with 5 fides.
    1ft fide   Diameter   1 10
    2d   -   -   1 10
    3d   -   -   1   5
    4th   -   -   1 $7\frac{1}{2}$
    5th   -   -   1   8

Nº III.

[282]

		F.	I.
N° III. with 6 sides.			
1st side	Diameter	0	10
2d	- -	2	2
3d	- -	2	2
4th	- -	1	11
5th	- -	2	2
6th	- -	2	9
N° IV. with 7 sides.			
1st side	Diameter	2	10
2d	- -	2	4
3d	- -	1	10
4th	- -	2	0
5th	- -	1	1
6th	- -	1	6
7th	- -	1	3

The pillars are all over as smooth, and as sharp cornered as those of the Giant's Causeway; their colours are generally black, though the external sides sometimes incline to yellow, as their surfaces are bleached by the weather. As to their grain and substance, they intirely resemble, and are most probably the same original substance as the Icelandic agate. As I have nothing remaining of it, I cannot examine

amine what effect borax and other alloys, or aqua-fortis, and the like, would have upon it: what is the nature of its proper gravity, and what polish it will admit of, it would, notwithstanding, be useful to be informed of in order to compare it with similar kinds of stone from other parts.

But in what manner have these regular pillars been produced? It is the received opinion that the fire has been accessary to it: you have yourself remarked, Sir, that it must either have been a matter which had been melted by fire, and burst afterwards, and that then a liquid, which we are yet unacquainted with, must have produced their regular crystaline figures; or else it must have been, as you have likewise observed, a kind of earth, which, after having been softened by the exhalations arising from a subterraneous fire, its whole mass was forced out of its situation, and assumed this regular form as it grew dry. I have noticed this distinct and regular appearance in dried clay, and even in starch when dried in a cup or bason.

For

For it may be demonstrated that they are not crystals formed by Nature, by their not being produced as all other cryftals are, by external appofition (per appofitionem) nor in any other matrix, as is common among cryftals.

It would be very difficult to determine whether the matter of which thefe prifmatic pillars confift, burft into thefe regular forms after it was melted, and was growing cold, or whilft it was drying, as you feem inclined to believe; I cannot deny that my eyes have prepoffeffed me in favour of the firft opinion, in all thofe places where I have feen any of thefe pillars; but as fo many objections may be offered againft this opinion, I am obliged to leave the matter undetermined. The following may, however, ferve as a proof, that I did not, without due foundation, believe them to be a kind of lava, which burft in growing cold and hard. Firft, you find both in the ifland of Staffa and many other places, that the pillars ftand on *lava* or *tuffa*, and are furrounded by this matter.

Secondly,

Secondly, at Staffa, there was a large ſtratum above the pillars, in which there were many pieces of theſe pillars irregularly thrown among one another, which leaves us to conjecture that they muſt have been more in number, and higher after an old eruption of fire, but that a ſubſequent eruption had overthrown them, and mixed them with the whole maſs. Thirdly, we found one of theſe pillars, on breaking it, full of drops, almoſt like a lactile or dripping ſtone; and none ſurely will pretend a baſalt to be of ſuch a compoſition. Fourthly, I have formerly ſaid, that the pillars in ſome places reſemble the inſide timber-work of a ſhip; that is to ſay, theſe pillars which moſt probably were quite ſtrait at firſt, in falling received this crooked inclination; nor were it alone the joints of the outermoſt or loweſt ſide which warped a little, but each ſtone was bent ſingly. Fifthly, we found on the ſhore at Hiſtra, near Skallholt, a piece of baſalt, with a piece of glaſs ſticking in it, in the ſame manner as granate formed cryſtals are found in the

baſalts

basalts at Bolsenna, which are like those that abound in the lava of Iceland and Italy. And lastly, a kind of stone near Langarnas in Iceland, which was much coarser, and more glassy than the common basalts, and evidently was lava burst into polyedrous and regular figures, tho' not quite so regular as the above-mentioned pillars.

What I have here said, might easily induce one to imagine that the basalt, after having been melted, and was grown again, had been burst into such pillars. But two objections, which you raise against this opinion, are difficult to be removed. First, this matter melts so easily, that it becomes glass without difficulty, before the blow-pipe for assaying, whence it seems that this mass must necessarily have been changed to glass, if it had been exposed to so great a fire as that of an eruption. But may one safely judge of an experiment made in miniature before the blow-pipe of the workings of Nature at large? Might not, perhaps, an addition we are unacquainted with, have prevented the mass mafs from becoming glafs, and caufe it to break into thefe regular figures, though we cannot now determine wherein this addition confifted? Secondly, we find that the trapp * in Weft-Gothland, which both in appearance and fubftance fo much refemble bafalts, though it does not form itfelf into pillars, ftands on flate; and how could this trapp have been formed by the fire, without, at the fame time, kindling the bed, which is of fo combuftible a nature? But fhould not, perhaps, the fire be able to form the trapp into pillars? Perhaps all bafalt pillars may have been a mafs of trapp in the infide of the earth, which, having been liquified during an eruption, was thrown up, and fplit into pillars? But, Sir, I fear to fatigue you with my conjectures and queftions; it would, however, be very agreeable to me and other naturalifts, if you would kindly communicate to us your thoughts on this fubject. This would no doubt, enable us to judge with more certainty

* A kind of ftone in Linn. Syft. Nat. Mineralogy.

of basalts, which at present engages the attention of the curious in general, and all naturalists in particular.

ACCOUNT of the Island of STAFFA,

COMMUNICATED

By JOSEPH BANKS, Esq.

IN the sound of Mull we came to anchor *(August 12, 1772)* on the Morvern side, opposite to a gentleman's house called Drumnen: the owner of it, Mr. Macleane, having found out who we were, very cordially asked us ashore : we accepted his invitation, and arrived at his house; where we met an English gentleman, Mr. Leach, who no sooner saw us, than he told us, that about nine leagues from us was an island, where he believed no one even in the highlands had been, on which were pillars like those of the Giant's Causeway : this was a great object to me who had wished to have seen the causeway itself, would time have allowed: I therefore resolved to proceed directly, especially as it was just in the way to the Columb-kill; accordingly having put up two days provisions, and my little tent, we put off in the boat about one o'clock for our intended voyage, having ordered the ship to wait for us in Tobir-more, a very fine harbour on the Mull side.

At nine o'clock, after a tedious passage having had not a breath of wind, we arrived, under the direction of Mr. Macleane's son and Mr. Leach. It was too dark to see any thing, so we carried our tent and baggage near the only house upon the island, and began to cook our suppers, in order to be prepared for the earliest dawn, to enjoy that which from the conversa-
tion

tion of the gentlemen we had now raised the highest expectations of.

The impatience which every body felt to see the wonders we had heard so largely described, prevented our morning's rest; every one was up and in motion before the break of day, and with the first light arrived at the S. W. part of the island, the seat of the most remarkable pillars; where we no sooner arrived, than we were struck with a scene of magnificence which exceeded our expectations, though formed, as we thought, upon the most sanguine foundations: the whole of that end of the island supported by ranges of natural pillars, mostly above fifty feet high, standing in natural colonades, according as the bays or points of land formed themselves: upon a firm basis of solid unformed rock, above these, the stratum, which reaches to the soil or surface of the island, varied in thickness, as the island itself formed into hills or vallies; each hill, which hung over the columns below, forming an ample pediment; some of these above sixty feet in thickness, from the base to the point, formed by the sloping of the hill on each side, almost into the shape of those used in architecture.

We proceeded along the shore, treading upon another Giant's Causeway, every stone being regularly formed into a certain number of sides and angles, till in a short time we arrived at the mouth of a cave, the most magnificent, I suppose, that has ever been described by travellers.

The mind can hardly form an idea more magnificent than such a space, supported on each side by ranges of columns; and roofed by the bottoms of those, which have been broke off in order to form it; between the angles of which a yellow stalagmitic matter has exuded, which serves to define the angles precisely, and at the same time vary the colour with a great deal of elegance; and to render it still more agreeable, the whole is lighted from without; so that the farthest extremity is very plainly seen from without, and the air within being agitated by the flux and reflux

reflux of the tides, is perfectly dry and wholesome, free entirely from the damp vapours with which natural caverns in general abound.

We asked the name of it; said our guide, The cave of Fiuhn: what is Fiuhn? said we. Fiuhn Mac Coul, whom the translator of Ossian's works has called Fingal. How fortunate that in this cave we should meet with the remembrance of that chief, whose existence, as well as that of the whole epic poem, is almost doub:ed in England!

Enough for the beauties of Staffa; I shall now proceed to describe it and its productions more philosophically.

The little island of Staffa lies on the west coast of Mull, about three leagues N. E. from Jona, or the Columb-Kill: its greatest length is about an English mile, and its breadth about half a one. On the west side of the island is a small bay, where boats generally land: a little to the southward of which the first appearance of pillars are to be observed; they are small, and instead of being placed upright, lie down on their sides, each forming a segment of a circle: from thence you pass a small cave, above which, the pillars now grown a little larger, are inclining in all directions: in one place in particular a small mass of them very much resemble the ribs of a ship: from hence having passed the cave, which if it is not low water, you must do in a boat, you come to the first ranges of pillars, which are still not above half as large as those a little beyond. Over against this place is a small island, called in Erse *Boo-sha-la*, separated from the main by a channel not many fathoms wide: this whole island is composed of pillars without any stratum above them; they are still small, but by much the neatest formed of any about the place.

The first division of the island, for at high water it is divided into two, makes a kind of a cone, the pillars converging together towards the centre: on the other, they are in general laid down flat; and in the front next the main, you see how beautifully
they

they are packed together; their ends coming out square with the bank, which they form: all thefe have their tranfverfe fections exact, and their furfaces fmooth, which is by no means the cafe with the large ones, which are cracked in all directions. I much queftion, however, if any one of this whole ifland of Boo-fha-la is two feet in diameter.

The main ifland oppofite to Boo-fha-la, and farther towards the N. W. is fupported by ranges of pillars pretty erect, and though not tall (as they are not uncovered to the bafe) of large diameters; and at their feet is an irregular pavement, made by the upper fides of fuch as have been broken off, which extends as far under water as the eye can reach. Here the forms of the pillars are apparent; thefe are of three, four, five, fix, and feven fides; but the numbers of five and fix are much the moft prevalent. The largeft I meafured was of feven; it was four feet five inches in diameter*. The furfaces of the large pillars in general are rough and uneven, full of cracks in all directions; the tranfverfe figures in the upright ones never fail to run in their true directions: the furfaces upon which we walked were often flat, having neither concavity nor convexity; the larger number however were concave, though fome were very evidently convex: in fome places the interftices within the perpendicular figures were filled up with a yellow fpar; in one place a vein paffed in among the mafs of pillars, carrying here and there fmall threads of fpar. Though they were broken, and cracked through and through in all directions, yet their perpendicular figures might eafily be traced: from whence it is eafy to infer, that whatever the accident might have been that caufed the diflocation, it happened after the formation of the pillars.

* As Mr. Bank's meafurement and dimenfions of thefe and other remarkable pillars, and of Fingal's Cave, agree even to a fingle figure with thofe given by our accurate Author in pages 277, 278, 279, 281, 282, of this work, the repetition of them would have been ufelefs; for which reafon they are omitted.

T 2   From

From hence, proceeding along shore, you arrive at Fingal's Cave, which runs into a rock in the direction o N. E. by E. by the compass.

Proceeding farther to the N. W. you meet with the highest range of pillars, the magnificent appearance of which is past all description: here they are bare to their very basis; and the stratum below them is also visible: in a short time it rises many feet above the water, and gives an opportunity of examining its quality. Its surface is rough, and has often large lumps of stone sticking to it, as if half immersed; itself, when broken, is composed of a thousand heterogeneous parts, which together have very much the appearance of a lava; and the more so, as many of the lumps appear to be of the very same stone of which the pillars are formed: this whole stratum lies in an inclined position, dipping gradually towards the S. E. Hereabouts is the situation of the highest pillars. The stratum above them is uniformly the same, consisting of numberless small pillars, bending and inclining in all directions, sometimes so irregularly, that the stones can only be said to have an inclination to assume a columnar form; in others more regular, but never breaking into, or disturbing the stratum of large pillars, whose tops every where keep an uniform and regular line.

Proceeding now along shore round the North end of the island, you arrive at *Oua na scarve*, or *The Cormorant's Cave;* here the stratum under the pillars is lifted up very high; the pillars above it are considerably less than those at the N. W. end of the island, but still very considerable. Beyond is a bay, which cuts deep into the island, rendering it in that place not more than a quarter of a mile over. On the sides of this bay, especially beyond a little valley, which almost cuts the island into two, are two stages of pillars, but small; however, having a stratum between them exactly the same as that above them, formed of innumerable little pillars, shaken out of their places, and leaning in all directions.

Having

Having paſſed this bay, the pillars totally ceaſe: the rock is of a dark-brown ſtone, and no ſigns of regularity occur till you have paſſed round the S. E. end of the iſland (a ſpace almoſt as large as that occupied by the pillars) which you meet again on the weſt ſide, beginning to form themſelves irregularly, as if the ſtratum had an inclination to that form, and ſoon arrive at the bending pillars where I began.

The ſtone of which the pillars are formed, is a coarſe kind of baſaltes, very much reſembling the Giant's Cauſeway in Ireland; though none of them are near ſo neat as the ſpecimens of the latter, which I have ſeen at the Britiſh Muſeum, owing chiefly to the colour, which in ours is a dirty brown, in the Iriſh a fine black: indeed the whole production ſeems very much to reſemble the Giant's Cauſeway with which I ſhould willingly compare it, had I any account of the former before me.

Thus much we have taken from Mr. Bank's account of the iſland of Staffa—which Mr. Pennant aſſures the public in a note to his tour in Scotland, (p. 269.) was copied from his Journal; concluding in theſe words: " I take the liberty of " ſaying (what by this time that gentleman, meaning Mr. " Banks, is well acquainted with) that Staffa is a genuine " maſs of baſaltes, or Giant's Cauſeway; but in moſt reſ- " pects ſuperior to the Iriſh in grandeur."

We think Mr. Pennant might have ſpared his reader this information, as Mr. Banks in his account informs us, that it is a Giant's Cauſeway formed of coarſe baſaltes.

LETTER XXIII.

From Chevalier IHRE to Dr. TROIL,

Concerning the Edda.

Upsala, Oct. 1, 1776.

SIR,

ACCORDING to your request, I send you an answer to the objections made by Mr. Schloczer against my opinion of the Edda, which, together with a translation of my letter to Mr. Lagerbring, on the subject of a manuscript of the Icelandic Edda, is, as you know, inserted in that gentleman's Icelandic history.

It gives me great pleasure to find that my thoughts on these subjects have been examined by men of learning in Germany, by which means a number of false nations which had been formed on the subject and design of this book have been removed; and I am very happy to receive any objections

objections which may tend to convince me that I have been miftaken.

Though I now refume the pen, it is not fo much with any immediate defign to refute thofe objections which have been made againft me, as to give thofe accounts and explanations which have been required of me, and which I think myfelf more ca,able of doing than any other perfon, as I can command the codex, whenever I think proper. Mr. Schloczer and I propofe the fame end to ourfelves, namely, the inveftigation of truth.

Mr. Schloczer's firft objection is, that I have not given a complete defcription of the manufcript, its fize, &c. He is perfectly right in this point, and I will briefly endeavour to repair this difficulty; but firft, I muft obferve a diplomatic defcription was not fo much required in that letter, as I had directed my attention more to the contents of the book than its external appearance.

I intended to fhew what was the view of the author of the Edda in compofing this work, what parts belonged to it, and which did not, wherein our manuscript differed from Resenius's edition, whence the book had obtained the name of Eddee, &c. &c. and its diplomatical descriptions would have afforded no information in any of these articles. This book was besides not addressed to any foreign man of learning, but to one of my learned countrymen, well versed in ancient literature, who had frequently had this manuscript in his own hands, and examined it, and was perhaps better acquainted with it than myself. It would have been very superfluous to tell him, it was written in ancient characters, in the Icelandic language, on parchment.

But to oblige Mr. Schloczer, and perhaps many others, I will inform them that this codex, as I said before, is written upon parchment, the colour of which is dark brown, which may proceed partly from its old age, and partly perhaps from its having been long kept and made use of in the Icelandic smokey rooms. It is in very good preservation, and in general legible. It is true, there are some

some round holes in the parchment, but these seem to have been there at first, as no part of the text is lost by them. The size is a small quarto, one finger in thickness, containing fifty-four leaves and a half, or one hundred and nine pages, besides a white leaf before, and one behind, on which there are, however, some bad figures, of which these on the first represent Gangleri, with Herjafuhar and Thridi, who resolve questions. The characters are old, and when compared with many others, seem to prove, that the copier lived about the beginning of the fourteenth century. But all this is of very little importance. Mr. Schloczer believes his subsequent questions may give more light in settling the principal point, as they tend to discover who was the author of the Edda, and what really belongs to it.

He is therefore more curious to know what is contained in this codex. Mr. Schloczer believes he has so much more reason for putting this question, as I myself have hinted, that besides Demisagor, Koeninggar, and Liodsgreinir, grienir, it contained a lift of Icelandic lagmen, and a *langfedgatal* or genealogy of Sturleson's ancestors. He therefore defires to know if this codex is not a magazine of all kinds of Icelandic works, which have been accidentally collected into one volume, and bound together? I anfwer to this, if the cafe were thus, Mr. Schloczer might have expected from a man who acted with candour and fome knowledge of the matter before him, that he would not have omitted this circumftance. I therefore now declare that there is nothing elfe in it, but what has already been mentioned; unlefs I add, that p. 92 and 93, after the author has defcribed the general rules of poetry, and the nature of letters, and the copier has left half a blank page before he writes the names of all the different forts of verfification ufed in the Icelandic poetry, another hand has patched in a fteganographical writing, of which I did not know what to make during a long time, and indeed I did not take great pains to decypher it.

I will

I will however give a specimen of it: *dfxifrb fcrkptprks bfnfdktb fkt pmnkbxs hprks*. As I was reading in Vanly's Bibliotheca Anglo Saxonica, I accidentally met with a similar collection of consonants, with a key affixed to it, which shewed that the whole secret consisted in placing, instead of each vowel, that consonant which in the alphabet followed next to it; also instead of *a, e, i, o, u, y*, the letters *b, f, k, p, x, z*, were put; and according to this rule the afore-mentioned riddle signified, Dextera scriptoris benedicta sit omnibus horis.

I afterwards found the same kind of steganography mentioned in a little work ascribed to Rhrabanus Maurus, under the title of De Inventione Litterarum, and which is so celebrated on account of the proof contained in it of the runes of the Marcomans. After letters became more universally known among the people, the subtle Monks however, desirous of knowing something which the vulgar were unacquainted with, invented various mysterious ways of writing in this man-

manner, which they not only make use of among themselves, but introduce in their public writings. This taste * with admirers among our ancestors in Sweden, and thence we find so many kinds of what are called *villrunes*, which were unintelligible to the vulgar. See in Bautil, Nº 25, 205, 331, 361, 539, 568, 571, 572, 581, 648, 748, 767, 817, 819, 822, 1001, 1088, and many more in Vormius. Perhaps what we call among us *helsinge runes*, have also no other origin, as the greater part of them only differ from the common runes, by having the staff taken away. It is however remarkable that our gravers of runes even made use of this cryptographys in monuments erected to the memory and honour of the deceased.

It is further asked, if there are any external or internal traces of the copier having considered all the above-mentioned pieces, or at least the three first parts as a connected work?

The answer to this may be found in the title of the book, which is at length
in

in the Goranfon edition, and runs thus:

Bok theffi heiter Edda. Henne hever fam fetta *Snorri Sturlo* f. epter theim hœlti, fem her er fhipat. En fyrft fra Afum ok ymi; tharnaeft fkalld fkapar mal ok heiti marga hluta. Sidaz hœttartal, er *Snorri* hever ort um *Hakon* k. ok *Skula* Hertuga; that is, This book is called Edda; and has been compofed by Snorre Sturlefon, in the manner it now ftands: viz. firft of the afes and ymi, afterwards the language of poetry, and its appellations of various things. Laftly, a differtation of the verfifications Snorre made upon king Hakan and duke Skule.

I mentioned in my letter to Mr. Lagerbring, that the Rubric was written in a later hand; which is right fo far as has been added after the Edda itfelf was begun, which may be feen by the narrow fpace left for it, fo that it has forced the copier to bring the laft line into that immediately preceding it. Befides, I clearly perceived that the manufcript

script was very old, and that no reasonable eye-witness could believe it was written in 1541, as Mr. Schloczer conjectures. But as it had been written with red ink, which had preserved its colour better than the black, I then believed the hand had been somewhat younger; but as I have now very minutely compared the writing in the Rubric with that of the Edda, I think I may safely affirm, that they are both written by one and the same hand. From hence it follows, that he who copied the Edda confidered the abovementioned articles, and no others, as effential parts of it.

I am come to the principal question, whether Sturleson is the author of the Edda? Here Mr. Schloczer seems to have taken most pains, to prevent me from deceiving the learned world in this point.

Because Mr. Schloczer has found that most antiquarians express themselves with a kind of circumspection when they speak of the Edda and its author, and instead of positively declaring

Sturlefon the author, as Arngrim and fome others have done; only fay, Creditur, exiftimatur auctor fuiffe: that is, he believes the matter to be at leaft dubious, if not totally groundlefs.

I will not infift upon it, that there is at leaft more affirmation than negation in thefe expreffions, efpecially as it is ufual, on mentioning an evidently falfe opinion, to add, falfo creditur, or fomething fimilar. For Mr. Schloczer himfelf remarks very judicioufly, that the opinion of thefe men is of very little importance, when they alledge no grounds for it. He therefore believes himfelf entitled to maintain with certainty, that Sturlefon has falfely been thought the author of the Edda. To fupport his opinion, he mentions three arguments in different places, which I muft now examine more clofely.

The firft argument is to be met with in p. 39, where Mr. Schloczer fubmits it to confideration, whether the ferious Snorre, overcharged with ftate affairs, could be fuppofed to have had time, and did not think it beneath his dignity

nity to write Aerarium poeticum, and become the predeceffor of Weinreich? Here I will only obferve, that Snorre was not conftantly lagman, and that he might have compiled this work before he obtained this dignity, or in the interval between the firft and fecond adminiftration of this confiderable charge; and laftly, even in its vacancies. Neither Mr. Schloczer nor I are able to determine how much time the management of a lagman's office requires. They hold feveral yearly court-days or affizes, after which I have always underftood that they are entirely free and difengaged; fo that I may fairly infer that the lagmen are not troubled with the examination of tedious records, or are employed in any extraordinary works. We find many Icelandic lagmen who have been poets laureats in Sweden and Norway, as Marcus Skaggafon, Sturle Thordarfon, and others. If Mr. Schloczer's argument was conclufive, he might go ftill farther, and prove, that Sturlefon could neither have written the Heimfkringla, or hiftory of the northern kings, which required ten times

more

more time, and more laborious difquifitions, than the Edda.

Mr. Schloczer founds his fecond argument on his believing it incredible, that any one in the golden age of poetry in Iceland fhould prefume to advance fuch abfurd things as I have done in my letter. He therefore believes the Edda to be a production of later times, when poetry was in its decline in Iceland.

To underftand the whole force of this argument, it muft be known, that Mr. Schloczer divides the Icelandic literature into three periods; the fimpler period, from the beginning to the introduction of Chriftianity; the golden period, from the introduction of Chriftianity to the clofe of the thirteenth century, when the black death or the great plague, as well as the fubjection of the Icelanders to the crown of Norway, checked the progrefs of poetry; and the laft, from that period to the prefent. I will not ftrictly examine this divifion, tho' I cannot comprehend that the

intro-

introduction of Christianity could contribute to the improvement of poetry; and still less, if the diger-death, which raged in the middle of the fourteenth century, produced the same effect on the surviving poets, as on the cultivation of the country and its population. But this I am clear of, that any one who would attempt to class the Icelandic poets with any degree of certainty, must be perfectly well acquainted with their language, and be able to weigh the faculties of their minds against each other.

It signifies very little under what particular dynasty the poetry of the Chinese most flourished, so long as we are able to understand their poems without the assistance of an interpreter.

As to the passages of Icelandic poets, which I have quoted in different places, they prove not a tittle of what Mr. Schloezer pretends they do. For Lopt Gutormsson's verses are not in the Edda; and though the other song is to be meet with in Resenius's edition of it, yet it
is

is not in the Upſala manuſcript. It is therefore not known to what period they belong; and they cannot by any means be made uſe of as proofs to ſhew, that Snorre was not the author of the Edda. It is highly proper to be well acquainted with a ſubject before one ventures to treat of it.

I will by no means preſume to defend all the phraſes I have made uſe of; though it is well known that cuſtom has introduced them into every language, which were they tranſlated into other languages, would not only loſe their original beauty, but appear aukward and graceleſs. For example, it would not be believed that to tread the ſtars under foot ſignified to be exalted and happy; nor would any one be underſtood who would, to expreſs a doubtful ſtate of mind, call it hanging water. And theſe phraſes, not to mention an infinity of others, were however in conſtant practice among the Latins.

But as to our ancient anceſtors in particular, who indubitably originated from the East, they no doubt brought their allegorical expressions from thence. And, in my opinion, the fondness of the ancients for riddles did not contribute a little to these metaphors in speech; for their merit frequently consisted in the most perverted expressions, which in process of time were revived and admired as beauties. We are not permitted the liberty to judge without distinction in mere matters of taste and genius, though they widely differ from what is practised in other nations.

Mr. Schloezer takes this third and last, and perhaps worst argument from the contradiction which I have observed between the Edda and Snorre's Heimskringla. I wanted to shew in my letter, that the ancients by their Asgard meant the town of Troy; and this I can prove, by the one having maintained the same things of Asgard as the other does of Troy. My opinion therefore is, that Troy and Asgard must necessarily signify one and the same place, unless we admit that Sturleson has contradicted himself.

It may eafily be apprehended, that what I have mentioned by no means implies that there was a contradiction between the Edda and Heimſkringla, but only that the above cited place had been called by two different names. Mr. Schloczer cannot poffibly be ignorant of the meaning of argumentationes ab abfurdo.

Hitherto I have mentioned the arguments with which Mr. Schloczer endeavours to ſhew, that Sturlefon is not the author of the Edda; but now to prove the contrary on my fide, I will content myfelf with one fingle argument, which is of fuch a nature as to make all others unneceffary. In the fuperfcription fubjoined to our Codex, the copier roundly affirms Sturlefon to be the author of this work; and his teftimony is fo much the more undeniable, as the nature of the copy itfelf proves, that it cannot be later than the 14th century; and that an Icelander had made it on the fpot, who certainly would not have thought it worth his attention and time to copy a work, if he had not known the author of it.

That this was the general opinion of the Icelanders, I think, may be proved thus; that though various conjectures are generally made concerning the author of an anonymous work, there are hardly any except Sturlefon mentioned as the author of the Edda.

I cannot on this occafion pafs over in filence what I have read in p. 326 of the Danifh Journal, which Mr. Lilie publifhed in 1756; namely, that the celebrated Arnas Magnaus, in a written account left us by Sumundr Trode, was of the fame opinion as Mr. Schloczer, that Sturlefon was not the author of the Edda.

The arguments which he makes ufe of feems to carry fome weight with them; that in the laft part of the Edda, called *Liödfgreinir* or *Skallda*, Sturlefon is not only quoted, but alfo recommended as a pattern to the poets; and that in this part mention is likewife made of the kings Hakan Hakanfon, Magnus, Erich, and Hakan Magnuffon, who all lived later than Snorre. This argument at firft fight feems to be decifive, but lofes its whole

whole force upon a nearer examination. The true state of the matter is this:

In the beginning of *Liodsgreinir* the author of the Edda says, that he has three different heads to treat upon; viz. the rules of poetry, its licences (licentia poetica), and its faults (vitia carminum), *settning*, *leif*, and *syrerbodning*. The two first of these subjects are perfectly discussed in the Liodsgreinir, but the last is wanting. A later writer has attempted to make up this deficiency, and has therefore made a supplement to Sturleson's Edda. It is not in the least extraordinary that he should have mentioned Sturleson, and given him his merited share of praise; but that this supplement does not belong to the genuine Edda, is proved by the Upsala manuscript, where it is entirely wanting.

In this manner it may be explained what is said of the late kings: they are never mentioned in the Edda; and I am much mistaken if Arnas Magnaus has not taken them from the *Sbaldetal*, or list of poets, where they are

are all taken notice of. This *Skaldetal* was no more than a supplement to the Edda, as I shall make appear presently. If therefore the learned Magnaus had ever seen our Codex, he certainly would not have entertained this opinion.

In regard to those appendixes, I am perfectly convinced that the catalogue of *Lagmen* and the *Langfedgetal*, or genealogy, are the works of Sturlefon himself. The subject contained in them refers entirely to Snorre, who was both Lagman and a descendant of the Sturlunga family. The *Aettartal*, or genealogical table, which from the beginning descends in a strait line from the fathers and mothers side to the sons, at Sturle extends to all the children, and daughters children; yet in some instances even there not to all these, but most probably to those only who were alive when this genealogical table was composed. The same is to be observed in the catalogue of the Lagmen, where it is very accurately mentioned how long every one of them possessed their place; but at the

the family of Snorre the catalogue ſtops without obſerving how long they maintained this charge the laſt time. It is therefore impoſſible that this genealogy ſhould have been compoſed before Snorre's time; nor is it leſs improbable that any one ſhould have omitted in later times to add the ſixteen years during which Snorre was Lagman the laſt time; or that he ſhould have forgot to mention this circumſtance of him in the whole liſt of Lagmen, who was the moſt conſiderable of them all.

I will in this place add, that it was very common, not only in the North, but even in other parts, to ſubjoin ſuch liſts, genealogical tables, and the like, to larger works, in order to reſcue them from oblivion, and prevent their being totally loſt to poſterity. In the ſame manner the copier of our Weſt Gothic law had added to it a *Konunga Längd*, or liſt of kings, as likewiſe a liſt of the biſhops of Skara and Lagmanner in Weſtgothland. Are Frode has in like manner affixed his genealogy to his

Schedis,

Schedis, or *Iſlandiga bok*, and ſeveral others.

It is more difficult to determine ſomething concluſive concerning the third appendix, or *Skaldetal*. I have always been of opinion, that it was begun by Snorre, as it commonly follows the Edda, and that it was afterwards augmented by one or more perſons: Vorinius did the ſame by a poem written by Saxo Hiærne, who obtained by that compoſition the regal dignity in Denmark, though as a Dane he was not properly intitled to be placed in the liſt of Icelandic poets.

That this catalogue was the work of ſeveral hands may in my opinion be perceived by more than one indication: immediately in the beginning it is ſaid, that Starkotter was the firſt of the Skalds, whoſe verſes the people had learned by heart; and in the end a certain *Ulfoer bin Oarge* is cited as the firſt, who, according to Mr. Schoning, lived in the ſecond century, and conſequently muſt have been ſeveral centuries older than the above-mentioned Starkotter. Theſe two accounts

counts can hardly be fuppofed to proceed from one and the fame author.

It is befides incontrovertible, that what is faid of the laſt Norwegian kings correfponds not with the time of Snorre. It would be of effential fervice if a man of Mr. Suhm's merit and abilities would critically examine this Skaldatal, and compare it with Vormius's lift of poets, which differs fo widely from it in feveral points.

This at leaſt may be perceived by every one, that the Skalds therein mentioned have not all lived in the thirteenth century; but that a great part of them exiſted in the tenth, eleventh, and twelfth centuries. The 230 Skalds, who, according to Mr. Schloczer's reckoning, lived in the thirteenth century, may be confiderably reduced in number, by one and the fame Skald being mentioned in three or four different places, as if he had been in the fervice of as many maſters. It is very remarkable that fome of thefe Skalds, as Oltar Svarte, Sigvatur Thordarfon, and others, have been received

received as poets laureats in all the three northern courts.

Nor is it lefs remarkable that fome of thefe Icelandic Skalds were taken into pay at the Englifh court, by kings Athelftan and Ethelred: this would require an examination to difcover how their *Skaldſkaparmal*, or poetical language, could be underftood in a foreign country, as both languages, without thefe poetical figures, differ fo widely from each other, as is evident from the remains of both.

It is laftly afked, if there are any internal or external marks, from which it might be guefled that the three parts of the Edda mentioned by me belong together, and form one work? But this queftion is anfwered by the title quoted above, wherein all the parts are clearly enumerated.

In regard to the third part, called *Liodfgreinir*, Mr. Schloczer defires to know how this title fuits to an ars poetica?

I have already in fome meafure anfwered this queftion in my letter to Mr.

Mr. Lagerbring, by citing the ſtrange titles the ancients ſometimes prefixed to their books. However, that a clearer idea may be formed of what relates to this appellation, it ſhould be obſerved, that Sturleſon immediately in the beginning divides all ſounds or tones into three kinds. The firſt he calls *vittlaus bliod*, or the ſound of inanimate things, as of thunder, waves, wind, and the like; to the ſecond he reckons the ſounds of irrational animals; and to the laſt, the articular ſounds of men, which are produced by means of the tongue, the palate, &c. He then ſpeaks of the ſound of the letters, how ſome are long, others ſhort; ſome conſonants, and others vowels and diphthongs: he then proceeds to the rules of proſody, and whatever elſe belongs to the Icelandic *ſkaldſkap* or poetry.

From hence it may be ſeen what has given riſe to this appellation; *Liodſgreinir* literally ſignifying no more than diſtinction of ſounds. Sturleſon has given as ſtrange a title to this

this Northern history, which he calls *heimſkringla*, and this from no other reaſon, but becauſe it was the firſt word with which the book began.

LETTER XXIV.

From Chevalier BACK to Dr. TROIL.

Of the Icelandic Scurvy.

Stockholm, June 12, 1776.
SIR,

THE accounts with which you have favoured us of the diseases which mostly abound in Iceland must be of universal service to the Swedes. When I had the pleasure and happiness of conversing with you on this subject, my attention was peculiarly raised by the information you gave me of the Icelandic scurvy, and of its dreadful consequences on those persons who were affected with it.

What Mr. Petersen calls the Icelandic scurvy, is the true elephantiasis, which is nearly related to the leprosy. Celsus has described it in the days of Augustus under the name of elephantiasis; and yet Arctæus has treated more fully upon it, in sect. 5, under the

same

same name. It is more terrible than any other disease, producing frequently a dreadful end: it gives a disgusting appearance to the patient, as the body by its colour, roughness, and scaly appearance, resembles the skin of an elephant. Whoever compares your description and Mr. Petersen's of this disease with that of the ancients, will not find it an easy matter to take the Icelandic scurvy for any thing else but the elephantiasis. In my opinion, both Ettmuller and Boerhaave, and his famous commentator baron van Swieten, would have done better not to call the elephantiasis the highest degree of the scurvy; or if they had not confounded those two diseases, so different in their beginning, progress, nature, and remedies.

Those among us who have written of the theory of diseases, have with more propriety given the name of scurvy where a gradual increasing languor takes place, together with a bleeding, stinking and putrid breath, and many coloured blackish-blue spots on the body,

body, particularly round the roots of the hair, and which principally proceeds from corrupted falt animal food, and the want of vegetables. The elephantiafis, on the other hand, which is alfo called *Lepra Arabum*, is rather an hereditary difeafe; the fkin becomes thick, unequal, gloffy, and lofes its fmoothnefs; the hair falls off, languor and want of feeling take place in the extremities: the face becomes difgufting and full of biles, and the patient gets a hoarfe nafal voice. In the real leprofy (impetigo, lepra Græcorum) the fkin becomes wrinkled and full of fcales, which feem to be ftrewed with bran, often burft, itch exceedingly, and are filled with a watery moifture.

Mr. Sauvage mentions feveral forts of elephantiafis; but it is a queftion whether they all differ or not, as he might have multiplied their number. I believe that the elephantiafis mentioned by Cleger in his Eph. Nat. Curiof. and Sauvage's javanefe elephantiafis are very like the Icelandic. At leaft it is certain that the elephantiafis

tiafis in Madeira, which Dr. Thomas Heberden defcribes in the firft volume of his Medical Tranfactions, almoft one hundred years after Cleger, is entirely the fame.

It is very remarkable that this difeafe has preferved its nature fo perfectly in the moft northern parts during more than a hundred years, and remained intirely fimilar to that in the hotteft climates. It appears the fame difeafe, at Martigues in Provence, has been defcribed by Dr. Johannes in the firft volume of the Medical Obfervations and Inquiries; and that it has been in the Ferro iflands, may be feen in the firft volume of Bartholin's Actis Hafn.

The difeafe obferved in Norway, which Mr. Anthony Rob. Martin defcribes in the Tranfactions of the Swedifh Royal Academy of Sciences, in the latter end of the year 1760, may likewife be reckoned amongft this clafs; as alfo that which appeared in feveral parts of Sweden, and of which Mr. Affeffor Odhelius gives an account in the third part of thefe Tranfactions

actions for the year 1774; all thefe may very properly be compared to Mr. Sauvage's Elephantiafis Legitima.

It was believed in the moft early times, that this difeafe had taken its rife in Egypt; but Lucretius pofitively fays, that it was firft difcovered on the Banks of the Nile. In Celfus's time it was not at all known in Italy; but Pliny relates, that it was firft brought into that country by the army of Pompey, from Egypt and Syria, but did not remain there long. In the twelfth century it was brought to Europe the fecond time by the Crufaders, and is frequently mentioned in the publications of the thirteenth, fourteenth, and fifteenth centuries: it was not however very violent in the fifteenth and fixteenth centuries; and in the feventeenth century it feems to have intirely difappeared in England, France, and Italy, when all the Lazar-houfes, which had been built on purpofe to receive patients infected with this difeafe, became ufelefs.

But how did this dreadful difeafe come from the South, where the dif-

cases connected with an eruption are most frequent, so far to the North? Could it not also have happened by means of the Crusades, our forefathers in the North having had likewise the honour to partake of them? nay, even the Icelanders were not excluded from a a share. The oldest Iceland writings give us examples of the elephantiasis in Norway, and other northern countries, as may be seen in the first volume of Olafsen's Voyage to Iceland, page 172. But it still remains a query, whether it was the true scurvy or not, which the learned author found mentioned for the first time, under the ancient Norway and Icelandic name of *skyrbjugur*, that appeared in the Norway fleet, in the year 1289, during the war of king Ehrick with Denmark. For according to Mr. Petersen's testimony, the word *skyrbjugur* is to this day frequently made use of to express the elephantiasis; though I must confess that the scurvy seems to be a common disease among the fleets in those days as well as in ours. However it would be useful for the hiftory of the difeafes common in the North, if the origin of them could be determined from thefe old accounts, efpecially as thefe accounts of the fcurvy are two hundred years older than any we have been yet able to difcover. We may moft probably expect this difcovery from our neighbours in Denmark and Norway, who elucidate the northern hiftory from ancient accounts with fo much zeal and happy fuccefs.

Mr. Anthony Rob. Martin relates, that in the above-mentioned place the number of perfons in Norway infected with this difeafe, in the year 1759, amounted to 150, for whom three hofpitals were erected; and Mr. Peterfon fixes the number of thofe who were ill of it in Iceland in the year 1762 at 280 perfons, for whom four hofpitals were eftablifhed,

You may afk, Sir, how this difeafe came to be fo firmly rooted in Iceland, as it has fo decreafed in the South, that it has almoft difappeared there?

I believe

I believe that this is not fo much owing to the climate as to the manner of life and diet. People whofe continual occupation is fifhing, are night and day expofed to wet and cold, frequently feed upon corrupted rotten fifh, fifh livers and roe, fat and train of whales, and fea-dogs; as likewife congealed and ftale four milk : they often wear wet cloaths, and are commonly expofed to all the hardfhips of poverty. The greater number of thefe are therefore to be met with in this clafs : on the contrary, where lefs fifh and four whey are eaten, and more Icelandic mofs (lichen Iflandicus) and other vegetables, this difeafe is not fo prevalent, according to an obfervation made by Mr. Peterfen in the above-mentioned Tranfactions.

We have a very remarkable inftance of the great effects of diet on the difeafes of a nation, in the inhabitants of the ifle of Ferro. Since fifhing has declined among them, and the inhabitants have cultivated corn, and live upon other food inftead of whale's flefh and bacon,

bacon, the elephantiafis has intirely ceafed among them, according to Mr. Peterfen's account. Things bore a very different afpect there ten years before this alteration: as a proof, I will quote Mr. Debe's own words from the firft volume of the Act. Hafn. pag. 98. Elephantiafis in infulis Ferröenfibus frequens ex victu et aëre, has habet notas; facies et artus hic fere ubique foedantur tumoribus plumbei coloris, qui exulcerantur foedum in modum. Rauci funt hoc morbo infecti, et per nares vocem emittentes. Vere et autumno invalefcens morbus plurimos enecat.

Experience likewife teaches us, that the greater number of perfons labouring under this diforder in our country refide near the fea-fhore, in the diftricts of Abo and Ocfterbottn, and in the ifles fcattered round the fhore, who in general get their livelihood by fifhing and catching fea-dogs: from what has been faid before it may be learnt what is proper to be done gradually to remove this deftructive difeafe. But I will referve for another occasion, whatever relates to this disease in Sweden.

About a hundred years ago plagues and pestilential fevers raged in Europe, as may be seen in the accounts of several physicians of the epidemical fevers which prevailed at certain times. But at present, when a better police has procured us more cleanliness in the streets and narrow lanes; and more neatness is observed in our apparel and habitations; as also since beer prepared with hops, wines, and other liquors are drank, which are very salutary, though they produce other diseases when made use of in excess; since fruits and vegetables, tea and sugar, are become fashionable; these and similar disorders are greatly diminished. Sir John Pringle proves the truth of these remarks, accompanied with several examples, particularly with respect to the diseases of England, in his Observations of the Diseases of an Army.

It is very probable that the elephantiasis, and many other great disorders in the skin, quitted the southern coun-

countries from similar causes; and have on the contrary maintained themselves towards the north, where a sufficient quantity of bread cannot be provided for the natives, and where the lower sort of people, who live entirely by fishing, do not eat any vegetable food, but only feed upon rancid oily victuals; and are besides unable to keep themselves clean and neat, being continually exposed to wet and cold on the sea-shore, &c.

I should repeat the observations which have been made upon this disease in Iceland, as they might perhaps serve to make our countrymen better acquainted with the disorder itself, and the manner of curing it. But you, Sir, might perhaps tell me, that this is a more proper subject for a physical book than for letters concerning Iceland; for which reason I will be as concise as possible.

Mr. Anthony Rob. Martin has given so exact an account of this disease, that I need not here enumerate its symptoms. Whoever compares

it

it with Mr. Peterfen's little differtation, will become perfectly acquainted with the elephantiafis, its beginning, progrefs, and greateft height; and will readily allow, that the Icelandic name of *liktraa* is given it with great propriety, which fignifies, that thofe who are infected with this difeafe in its higheft degree, refemble a putrefying corpfe more than a living man.

The elephantiafis is either inherited from the father or mother, who are afflicted with it, or it is not inherited. In the firft cafe, the difeafe frequently appears before the child is two years old, and always before the age of 25, fo that fuch perfons feldom live to fee thirty years. The fooner the difeafe makes its appearance, the fooner the patient becomes a prey to death. But thofe who have not inherited the elephantiafis, but have brought it upon themfelves, by their mode of living and other caufes, may drag on a wretched exiftence during twelve or fourteen years, and fometimes longer. The elephantiafis is of the fame nature in the South.

Before

Before this difeafe breaks out on any perfon, his breath is difagreeable and ftinking for three, and fometimes fix years preceding: he has a great appetite to eat four, half-rotten, and unwholfome food; is always thirfty, and drinks very much: fome are flothful and fleep, and when afleep are with great difficulty awakened; are fhort-breathed when the complaint afcends upwards; they fpit very much, and complain of wearinefs in their knees. They fhiver violently when they come out of a cold room into the open air; the eyes and lips become of a brown and blue colour: they have a weak fmell; with fome the feeling is likewife numbed; others have weak fight; and fome lofe it entirely, when their foreheads begin to fwell in the beginning of the difeafe. They have frequently thin hair, particularly on the eye-brows; the beard likewife grows very thin on both fides of the chin, and the fkin becomes gloffy, as if it had been rubbed over with greafe.

This

This disease is not found to be particularly infectious in Iceland: as a husband afflicted with it does not infect his wife, nor a diseased wife her husband. The children may likewise be brought up without danger in the house of their diseased parents. But it has been found by experience, that when one of the parents is infected with it, some one or other of the children always catch it. It is the same thing in Madeira, as Dr. Heberden observes. Dr. Johannes informs us that at Martigues in Provence, when one of the parents has the disease, one of the children or grand-children, or a descendant in the third degree, is certainly infected with it; but in the fourth degree it again disappears, and only shews itself in a bad breath, hollow teeth, swelled throat, and a darker colour than usual.

The more ancient writers who have treated of this disease, frequently relate, that people were even afraid of being infected by conversing with those who were troubled with it. The disease must therefore either have been

more

more violent in the beginning, and in the fouthern countries, as the venereal difeafes were formerly in the beginning of the infection; or the difeafe having but lately made its appearance, caufed more apprehenfions. It is, however, always advifeable to be cautious in converfing with fuch patients, and neither to wear their fhoes or cloaths, when they have been rendered wet with fweating. When the difeafe is arrived at fo high a pitch that the matter which flows from the fkin is corrofive, and eats into the flefh, it can no longer be denied, but that it then becomes infectious, and even dangerous to converfe too near with the patient.

As the elephantiafis, when it has attained its greateft height, is incurable, according to the teftimony of ancient and modern phyficians; it is fo much the more neceffary to notice the beginning of the difeafe, and the time preceding it, in order to prevent the danger.

A patient who finds himfelf in thefe circumftances, or lives in a place where the

the disease is rife, or has any other cause to believe that he has the least vestige of it existing in his body, either by inheritance, or through his own fault, should, both in his diet and in his whole manner of life, avoid whatever is likely to contribute to it, or render his body more liable to receive the infection, with the utmost caution. He must keep himself extremely clean; immediately put on dry cloaths, whenever those on his back become wet; eat no other food but what is easily digested, and abstain from all oily rancid whale's flesh, and the like. He must eat no half-rotten fish; nor their intestines and livers, especially if they are in a putrid state; on the contrary, he must confine himself to bread, roots, green herbs, cabbages, turnips, and salad of gentiana, campestris, sorrel (rumex acetosa, L.) rumex crispus, &c. &c. He must eat soups, boiled fresh meat, with scurvy-grass, sedum acre, and the like. He must make use of baths of the decoction of juniper, dry baths of juniper, &c. &c. In the same manner antimonial remedies would be very useful;

useful; and even Swieten's mineral mixtures, pills of an extract of hemlock (pilulae alterantes Plumiris), and ledum paluftre. I have likewife obferved with pleafure, that a girl in the parifh of Wefter Hannings was cured of a commencing elephantiafis in the year 1774, by making ufe, during a long time, of Huxham's antimonial effence, with a decoction of antifcorbutic herbs.

But every one will eafily apprehend, that poor wretched people, who are naturally moft expofed to thefe and the like difeafes, are likewife entirely incapable of averting them by obferving a proper diet and manner of life, which are, however, almoft the only remedies. Befides, thefe kind of people are generally carelefs of any illnefs fo long as they are able to ftir; they likewife feldom confult a phyfician, and when they do, it is out of their power to follow his prefcriptions exactly. Some perfons attacked with it have, however, been freed of it, after having had the fmall-pox. It might, therefore, be conjectured, that patients
afflicted

afflicted with the elephantiasis, if they had not had the small-pox, would be benefited by inoculation.

Some who have had this dreadful disease have gone from Iceland to Copenhagen, where they have happily experienced a cure. I will likewise mention, in justice to Dr. Thomas Heberden, that he is the only physician known to have cured the elephantiasis, after it had attained a very high degree. His manner of cure is this: he first mixes an ounce and an half of powder of bark, with half an ounce of sassafras root, and then adds as much simple syrup as is necessary to make the whole into an electuary; of which he gives the patient two portions a day, of the size of a nutmeg: he causes the hands and feet to be rubbed morning and evening with a mixture, consisting of eight ounces of brandy, an ounce of lye of tartar, and two ounces of spirit of sal armoniack. He lastly causes blisters to be constantly laid between the shoulders. This method regularly pursued succeeded in the course of five months,

after

after he had before made use of antimony, mercury, and the like, during the full period of seven years, without any lasting amendment. But I have already said too much of this loathsome disease.

Sed quænam medela excogitari peterit, quæ elephantem tam ingens malum expugnare digna sit? *Aretæus.*

LETTER XXV.

From Professor BERGMANN to Dr. TROIL.

Of the Effects of Fire, both at the Volcanos and the hot Springs; and also of the Basalts.

Stockholm, June 12, 1776.

SIR,

YOU have been so kind as to communicate to me your observations on Staffa and Iceland, and to desire my opinion of their natural curiosities. It would be very ungrateful if I hesitated to comply with this request, as you presented me with the intire collections you made there, that I might chemically examine the nature of each. Mere observations, without the assistance of an exact knowledge of the substances, in respect to their original matter and composition, instead of affording any sufficient lights whereby to enable us to to determine with certainty of them, would only lead us to draw very erroneous conclufions. Though the form, grain, colour, hardnefs, pofition, and external appearances may affift us in our conjectures of the true nature of minerals, and fometimes of the manner in which they are produced, yet we muft neverthelefs remain in uncertainty, till proper experiments guide us to a more clear decifion.

Forgive me for mentioning the conclufions, which, in my opinion, might be drawn from your obfervations, regarding the internal nature of thefe fubftances, fo far as I have been able to difcover them from actual experiments. But you muft by no means expect a folution of all the difficulties that arife on this intricate bufinefs. I will cautioufly endeavour to feparate what is certain, from what has been hitherto confidered precarious and doubtful; a due regard to truth will always prevent me from offering mere conjectures, or even credible opinions, with a peremptory decifion, decision, as incontrovertible arguments. Experience has taught us that we ought to judge of the works of nature with the utmost diffidence; and we do not want examples, even from the remotest times, of persons who have pretended to explain, with the most positive certainty, not only how our earth, but even how the whole world received its present form, and even its very origin. To determine the contrivance of so vast a machine over a writing-desk, is indeed one of the most daring enterprizes which the proud reason of man ever proposed to itself; and, more than any other attempt, shews his weakness and arrogance. All these imaginary systems have been by little and little overturned, though the greatest pains were exerted to compare them with nature, and examine their existence. Their arguments were then discovered to be founded on a few insufficient observations, or, what is still worse, on uncertain, and sometimes evidently false principles.

You,

You, Sir, will therefore readily excuse my timidity; for inſtead of endeavouring to diſcover all at once, as it were à priori, though without any certainty, the manner in which nature works, and forms things in ſecret, I prefer the more laborious method of diſcovering it gradually with certainty, by experiments founded on due obſervations; and ſhall not heſitate to confeſs my ignorance, wherever theſe guides in the ſtudy of nature ceaſe their inſtructions. I do not, however, reject all conjectures and propoſed opinions, whenever they lead to new reſearches, provided they are offered as mere conjectures, and not obtruded on us as certain truths, or determined opinions.

From what I have hitherto ſaid, you will, I believe, conceive my method; therefore I ſhall enter upon the ſubject, and briefly treat of it under ſeparate heads, in the following manner.

Of the Hot Springs.

YOUR defcription of the Icelandic fprings, the moft extraordinary which have hitherto been difcovered in the known world, was extremely agreeable to me, partly on account of the furprizing force of them, and partly on account of the great light obtained in mineralogy by the cruftated ftones formed in them. How thefe fprings may be accounted for, I hope I have fufficiently explained in another place*; I fhall, therefore, entirely pafs it over here. But now I will communicate to you what I could not then underftand, namely, the true nature of thefe depofitions.

You have prefented me with the following fubftances from the Geyfer:

1. The fubftance of which the water has prepared itfelf a bafon to run from.——It confifts of a hard, rough, greyifh, and irregular flaty, and generally martial cruftated ftone, over which a covering of fmall cryftalli-

* In my Phyfika befkrifning om Jordkloter, ult. edin.

zations

zations has formed itself, that resembles the lichen fruticulosus, or rather the Stahlsteindruse found in the Westerfilverberg; that is called the flos ferri or Eisen bluthe. These precipitations are opaque, without of a whitish grey, blacker within, and plainly shew the formation of several crusts on one another. Each of these flos ferri, as well as the crustated stone, has the hardness of a flint; however they are not so compact or strong as to strike fire with the steel.

The strongest acids, the fluor acid not excepted, are not sufficient with a boiling heat to dissolve this substance. It dissolves very little if at all by the blow-pipe with the fusible alcali, a little more with borax, and makes a strong effervescence with sal sodæ. These effects are peculiar only to a siliceous earth, and therefore there remains no doubt concerning the real nature of this crustated stone. Nevertheless I have melted it in the crucible; first, by weight, with half as much alcaline salt, and likewise with three times as much; and

and have obtained in the firſt caſe a fixed glaſs, and in the ſecond one, which, in diſſolving, yielded a common liquor ſilicum. The glaſs of the cruſtated ſtone is of a more yellowiſh brown than that of the cryſtallizations; and this difference is cauſed by the greater quantity of irony particles.

2. The porous cruſtated ſtone or ſinter, which is found in the moor ſurrounding the border of the baſon, is light, whitiſh, and here and there ſpotted with a ruſt colour: it is evidently an incruſtation upon moſs and ſimilar ſubſtances, which have been decayed by length of time, and left thoſe cavities. In regard to its compoſition, it is of a ſiliceous nature as the preceding, and alſo perfectly ſimilar in reſpect to fire and diſſolvents.

I have already mentioned the ſolution of the flint in ſal ſodæ with the blow-pipe; and as I ſhall hereafter have frequent occaſion to refer to it, I will in this place relate the whole proceſs. The late director of the mines (*bergmaſtare*) Mr. Cronſtedt, makes mention of this ſalt

salt in his Mineralogy, but it is very seldom; and he confiders it as less proper for ufing with the blow-pipe, becaufe it is too foon imbibed by the coals. It certainly does not afford a very good folution upon coals, and I therefore made ufe of a filver fpoon, made on purpofe; by which method I have been able to make good ufe of the fal fodæ, which in his examinations of the different kinds of earth in this manner, is very ferviceable, and even indifpenfably neceffary, as I fhall hereafter prove more at large, in a little differtation on the blow-pipe, and its proper ufe.

I have frequently inferted a fuppofition in my printed works, that though the filiceous earth cannot be diffolved in the ufual manner in water, yet it might with the help of a great degree of heat: and that this really happened at the Geyfer, is evidently proved by the above defcribed cruftated ftone. The hot water forms of itfelf the large filiceous bafon from which it iffues out of the fubftance, that is in a diffolved

diffolved ftate at the firft, but quickly precipitates on account of the heat decreafing in the open air. The heat of the water was not examined with the thermometer, till fuch time that the bafon was filled, when it was neverthelefs found at a hundred degrees, according to the Swedifh meafure. It is in all probability much greater under the earth; for its running through cooler channels, and its fpouting afterwards into the air to a great height, muft neceffarily very much diminifh the heat on account of the great difperfion.

This quick difpofition produces both the opacity and irregular form of this ftone, and prevents the particles from being fo clofely united, as might have been expected from the degree of the hardnefs of each, fuppofing the folvent power had diminifhed more gradually.

Mr. Scheele has difcovered the formation of the flint; and I myfelf have found out, within thefe two years, a method of obtaining, with the help of of some fluor acid, thirteen precipitated cryftals of the fize of fmall peas. This artificial pebble in all experiments, both in the wet and dry method, and even in the focus of a burning-glafs, in a piece that I fent to Mr. Macquer, difcovered exactly to him the fame qualities as the natural one.

All thefe circumftances, therefore, prove, that the pebble is a faline earth, which is compofed of fluor acid, and an original fubftance exifting in the watery exhalations. It is not quite fimple; but however, I have not been able to confider it as any other than an elementary earth: indeed my judgment is, that it cannot be compounded from any other principle.

I do not in this place mean a finer or coarfer powder, by the denomination of earth, as is generally underftood under this appellation; but I take the word in a chemical fenfe, to exprefs a fixed principle, which is obtained in analyfing any fubftance, and that cannot be diffolved in boiling

ing water, after the nicest mechanical division. It is well known that the dissolubility of any substance may be lessened by certain compositions; and that a solvent can better attack the substance, according to the extent of surface; and that lastly, water in an open vessel will not admit of any greater degree of heat than one hundred degrees, according to the Swedish thermometer. A substance may, by this rule, be dissoluble by itself, after having gone through a preparatory cleansing, or a chemical separation, or with the assistance of a greater degree of heat, though it might be indissoluble without any preparation, or with the usual method of boiling; and it is with a view to this circumstance that I call the flint a kind of salt earth.

I have likewise examined the substances you collected in the morass near the Geyser, and have found them to be the following:

3. A dark-red bole, which became darker in the fire, but was afterwards a little attracted by the magnet. It crum-

crumbles into pieces in the water, and is fine and tough to the touch.

4. A bluish-grey clay, which contains green vitriol of decayed pyritæ.

5. A brighter grey fort, which did not feem to contain any vitriol.

6. A white or yellowifh clay, with ruft-fpots.

All thefe forts become very hard in the fire, and take a good deal of time before they liquefy. The laft, when it foftens, is harfh and more fandy to the touch than the preceding forts.

The different forts of ftone collected at Laugarnas are of another nature: nor does the water here fpout out of a bafon, but through many fmall openings in the earth.

7. A whitifh irregular plated cruft, which often grows on the outfide into fmall globular blunt points. This in acids gives a fudden fermentation, that immediately ceafes without its being any otherwife attacked. It diffolves with borax by the blow-pipe with great difficulty, and without motion, but with a loud effervefcence

with

with fal fodæ. It is confequently a filiceous mafs outwardly covered with lime, and has fixed itfelf on the following fubftance.

8. A folid irregular plated and broken cruft, of a dark colour, but in many places tinged with bright blue fpots. It becomes quite fmooth in cutting, almoft like ftone marle, but does not crumble in water, nor does it become foft in it; with acid it fhews an effervefcence which foon ceafes; with the blow-pipe it grows hard, fcarcely melts at the thinneft edges, and is attacked with fome motion both by borax and fufible urinous falt and fal fodæ, but is not entirely diffolved by any of them.

9. The fubftance found at the bottom of the brook, which carries off the water that gufhes out, is brown, fpongy, and compofed of pretty hard flakes and threads, that are covered with fine glaffy cryftallizations. Thefe are clear only in fome few places; but lofe their brown colour, both in fire and marine acid, and become quite clear.

The

The small crystals puff up very much under the blow-pipe, almost like borax; they float in bubbles on the surface, and are dissolved with great difficulty by borax; they are attacked by sal sodæ with a strong ebullition: it is the same with the more solid flakes, but they do not puff up so strongly as the crystallization. These several qualities here mentioned evidently shew, that this crustated stone consists of zeolite.

10. From Reykum you sent me calcareous spar in lumps, that are externally rounded, as if they had been tossed backwards and forwards by the water, and rubbed against hard bodies. In them there are small greyish green crystallizations, that dissolve by the blow-pipe to a black slag; the sal sodæ causes some effervescence in them, but does not dissolve them; they are likewise attacked with some emotion by fusible urinous salt.

11. A loose, tubulose, whitish crustated stone, or an incrustation cavernous, and with impressions of leaves,

leaves, stalks, and the like. As to its nature it is filiceous; but seems at the same time to contain a different substance, as it dissolves more slowly with fal sodæ.

The spring which here bursts forth in a very sloping direction towards the horizon, according to your account, deposites a kind of sulphureous grease by its hot steam, on the cavities of the upper side; but I have found no specimen of this in the collection you communicated to me.

From what I have hitherto said, we may gather, that the Icelandic hot springs contain very different substances from what are to be met with in other places of the same sort, especially filiceous earth.

There is no lime at all near the Geyser; but at Laugarnas there are some faint traces of it, partly as an external covering, and partly as constituent parts in the zeolite, of which more will be said hereafter. The balls of lime found at Reykum are most probably thrown out by the spring;

spring, and have been rounded on the surface by the friction.

Of the Eruptions of Fire.

I HAVE in another * place treated pretty extensively of the dreadful devastations caused by subterraneous fires on the surface of the earth in many parts of the world, both in regard to their causes and effects; I have therefore not any thing to add in this place but what particularly relates to Iceland, and what may serve to explain the eruptions which have happened there from time to time.

Whether Iceland is to be considered as entirely produced by volcanos, is a question which most probably will remain unresolved many years. It is true, Sir, that according to the accounts you have collected there, the volcanos have raged in a great many places, and that the whole country is in a manner covered with traces of their destructive effects:

* Verlds beskrifn, § 149.

we alfo learn from undeniable facts, that new iflands have been produced by volcanos in many places. But all this proves not any thing more than that the moft dreadful effects have been produced by fiery eruptions in Iceland.

To determine this queftion, it would be indifpenfably neceffary, that a naturalift fhould thoroughly examine all Iceland. If a granite, or any other ftone or berg-art, was found in folid rocks, and not feparate or in loofe fragments, which may have been brought thither from diftant parts, I fhould entirely diffent from your opinion. But before thefe and the like difcoveries were made, I believe no conclufions could be drawn.

I may venture to maintain with more certainty, that your collection confirms what I before concluded from other reafons, viz. that in all volcanos pyrites are found, which on decompofing produce heat and fire; and likewife flate that, penetrated with bitumen, ferves to feed the fire.

12. The

12. The flate which you have brought from Iceland fplits into th n plates, which difcover many forts of impreffions, particularly of leaves; the colour is black, and it is exactly of the fame nature as the common aluminous flate.

13. The two pieces of furturbrand, or foffil wood, which you brought with you, bear evident marks of a vegetable compofition; and I may almoft affirm, with perfect certainty, that the largeft is a kind of pinus abies; on the outfide are barks and branches, and in the infide all the rings of the fap appear: the leffer is a piece of rind without wood; both are black, quite foft, eafily take fire, and flame in burning. After the flame is extinguifhed, one hundred parts afford forty-two parts of coals, which after being only calcined yield two parts of yellowifh-brown earth, that is attracted by the magnet, and partly diffolves with acids: it makes fome effervefcence with borax and fufible urinous falt; the fal fodæ alfo

alſo cauſes a little ebullition at firſt, but does not entirely diſſolve it.

Your conjecture, Sir, concerning the manner in which the furturbrand is produced, does not ſeem improbable. I have already obſerved a long time with ſurprize, that fiſhes, othoceratites, lituites, wood, &c. &c. which are to be found in ſlate, have been compreſſed or flatted, whilſt they preſerve their entire form and roundneſs in lime.

This ſame circumſtance may be obſerved in the two pieces deſcribed above, eſpecially in the larger, which is only an inch and a half in thickneſs, though it is nineteen inches in length, and thirteen in breadth. The outſide of it has no marks of any roundneſs, but is quite flat. An exceeding great weight is required to preſs a ſtick to a flat plate; and I cannot conceive how the moſt immenſe beds, which muſt neceſſarily have been ſoft when ſpread over it, could ever produce this effect. The cauſe of this is yet undiſcovered, and will probably remain ſo a long a long time; however something may be found there which seems to shew, that the bituminous slate has been produced in the same manner, as it has not only penetrated the substance of the slate, but every thing else which has been laid upon it, for it may yet be obtained by means of distillation. But by what means has this been brought thither? How could it be imbibed by the clay, in case this was under water, which however seems to be undeniable, from the prodigious number of marine animals which are found buried? and how could the inclosed bodies have been pressed down horizontally? All these problems I cannot as yet answer satisfactorily, much less explain with any degree of certainty.

14. Very coarse, heavy, and hard lava, full of bladders, almost black, intermixed with white grains resembling quarz, which in some places have a figure not very unlike a square.

The black matter is not attracted by the magnet; but if a piece of it is
held

held against a compass, the needle visibly moves. When tried in the crucible, it yields from ten to twelve pounds of iron in every 100 weight: it does not dissolve in the least with sal sodæ, with great difficulty with borax, and hardly visible by fusible urinous salt. It seems to contain a great deal of clay earth in its composition, which may be extracted by all solvents of acids.

It is well known that this earth, when it is entirely free from any other mixture, may by means of heat and drying be brought to that degree of hardness, as to give fire with a steel, which proceeds from the parts being brought closer together, and contracted in a space only half as large. By being thus contracted, it obtains a solidity and hardness; and besides, the surface is so much diminished, in proportion to the whole mass, that the water cannot penetrate any farther to soften it.

We have almost daily opportunities in the study of chemistry of convincing

ing ourselves, that a substance with a small surface cannot be changed in any manner by liquid solvents; but may however be attacked by them, in proportion to the different degrees of pulverization; nay, even a substance which cannot be reduced by the finest mechanical division, may frequently be separated, as much as is necessary, by a chemical one; that is to say, by a preceding solution in another solvent. The attraction is here in proportion to the extent of the surface; and the larger this is, the stronger will be the attack: consequently I cannot believe that any clay, petrified by heat or slow drying, can have undergone any essential change, but only that its parts have so contracted themselves as to give it the hardness of a flint to prevent it from imbibing any visible quantity of water. But as soon as it has been dissolved by any acid whatever, and its parts have by this means been brought out of its former contraction, to the requisite degree of fineness and expansion, it becomes as soft as before, without the acid contributing any more to it than has been said, as all kinds of acids succeed equally well.

I have a very good assortment of the lava of Solfatera, by which it is very evident that the sulphureous acid, which had penetrated the black lava, deprived it gradually, partly of its combustible quality, and had also whitened it (to effect which other substances, particularly silk, are likewise exposed to sulphureous exhalations) and partly had reduced it by solution, either to a perfect allum, or at least to the common nature of any loose clay. I have likewise produced all these effects with aqua-fortis, or any other acid, in a lava which had not yet suffered any change.

The white, which possesses more or less of those transparent grains or rays with which the lava is chequered, do not seem to be of the nature of quarz, as they cannot be attacked by sal sodæ; they are however, with some difficulty, dissolved by borax and fusible urinous salt.

These

These effects are perfectly similar to those produced upon the diamond, ruby, saphire, topaz, and hyacinth. The chrysolite, garnet, turmaline, and shirl, can neither be dissolved by sal sodæ, though they are somewhat attacked by it, when reduced to a fine powder; and upon the two last mentioned ones it produces a slight effervescence. On this account it is possible that the precious stones of mount Vesuvius, which are sold at Naples, are nearer related to the real precious stones than is generally imagined.

15. A finer kind of lava, quite porous within, and entirely burnt out, and considerably lighter on that account than the preceding ones. I have not found any such grains in it resembling quarz.

16. The so called Icelandic agate. This is of a black or blackish-brown colour, and a little transparent at the thin edges like glass, and gives fire with the steel.

It cannot easily be melted by itself, but becomes white, and flies in pieces. It can hardly be dissolved in the

the fire by fufible urinous falt; but it fucceeds a little better with borax, though with fome difficulty: with fal fodæ it diffolves very little, though in the firft moments fome ebullition is perceived, and the whole mafs is afterwards reduced to powder.

From hence it may be concluded, that the Icelandic agate has been produced by an exceffive fire out of the lava defcribed in N° 14. I have found no cryftals of this glafs in the collection. If any perfon has fuch in their poffeffion, they fhould be examined to fee if they are exactly of the fame nature and fubftance with the above defcribed agate, and if their form has not been produced accidentally by burfting afunder.

17. More or lefs light, fpongy, and burnt-out pumice-ftone, particularly black and reddifh-brown. Quarz cryftals are fometimes found in them; but oftener the rays and grains refembling quarz.

18. Stones thrown out of the volcano, grey or burnt brown, which feem to confift of a hardened clay mixed with

with siliceous earth. They are sprinkled with rays and grains resembling qurz, and some few flakes of mica. They fuse with great difficulty in the fire; with sal sodæ they shew some effervescence at first, but however it soon ceases: the parts resembling quarz do not produce any motion at all. From this we may conclude, that the lava mentioned in N° 14, principally originates from this mass.

The other loose stones which I have received from you, Sir, to all appearance have no absolute connection with the eruptions of fire, though some have been suspected of it. I will enumerate them here separately:

19. Red and green jasper, which, in some places where it is broken, is quite smooth and shining; this circumstance distinguishes it from the common jasper, which is dull and clay-like where it is broken. It has besides all the qualities of true jasper; strikes fire with the steel, does not melt in the most violent fire, but is dissolved by sal sodæ with an effervescence, &c. &c. As to the smooth-

smoothnefs of some parts, it cannot proceed from a commencing fusion, as it becomes black and dark in a weaker fire. We here only find a new link in the connected chain of nature, by which the jasper is united with the flint.

There is no black jasper in your collection; but the pieces, which to appearance come nearest to it, belong to the class of the trapp, and shall be described hereafter.

20. Grey, greenish slate, resembling jasper, that gives sparks with the steel, is attacked with a quick effervescence by sal sodæ, but not farther dissolved by it. In some places are grains resembling quarz, which are easily dissolved in fusible urinous salt, but do not shew the least effervescence in sal sodæ.

21. The small crystals, said to resemble cocks-combs; they are nothing but a different appearance or change of the heavy spar.

22. A chalcedon crust with smooth prominencies, like what they call hæmatites: this is dissolved with the utmost

moſt difficulty by fuſible urinous ſalt, with more eaſe by borax, and with a violent effervescence by ſal ſodæ, exactly as the flint.

23. Zeolite; two kinds: the one is ſolid, white, and internally, as it were, compoſed of globoſe parts, in which rays proceeding from the center appear that reſemble fine threads.

This ſort ſwells a little by the blowpipe, diſſolves perfectly with borax, ſeparates in ſal ſodæ with ſome effervescence, but ſoon ceaſes, and leaves ſome part undiſſolved.

The other ſort conſiſts of a plate, which in colour and break reſembles a carnelian: it has a quantity of ſmall prominencies in it, filled with irregular white cryſtals, and ſome of the cavities are filled with a looſe-grained and browniſh-red ſubſtance.

The ſubſtance reſembling a carnelian becomes white in the fire, bubbles up, and becomes fuſible.

The cryſtalline ſubſtance becomes more frothy in the fire than the carnelian, and has all the qualities of the zeolite.

The

The sandy substance hardly swells; is dissolved with difficulty by borax, and is attacked at first with a sudden effervescence by sal sodæ.

As it is not uncommon even in the professors of morality to pass from one wrong step to another, so are we not without examples of this kind in those who make nature their study. Ten years ago it was a general opinion that the surface of the earth, together with the mountains upon it, had been produced by moisture. It is true, some declared the fire to be the first original cause, but the greater number paid little attention to this opinion. Now, on the contrary, that a subterraneous fire had been the principal agent gains ground daily: every thing is supposed to have been melted even to the granite. My own sentiments with regard to it is this, that both the fire and water have contributed their share in this operation, though in such a proportion, 'that the force of the former extends much further than the latter; and, on

the

the contrary, that the fire has only worked in some parts of the surface of the earth.

It is not an easy matter to explain how the granite, which consists of clear quarz-cryftals, solid field-spar, and limmer *(mica)* with flat scales, has been able to support a fusion, without the quarz bursting, or becoming opaque.

This is yet less to be conceived of the field-spar, that becomes soft and liquid in a weak fire, and has a dull appearance. The glimmer splits its scales asunder in the fire, and frequently twists them together again in a very different manner from that in which they appear in the granite. Notwithstanding all this, if the granite is confidered as a production of the fire, it need not be wondered at, that the zeolite has likewise been comprehended in this supposition.

I will allow that cryftals may be produced by the dry method, and I know several ways of obtaining them, both by fusion and sublimation; but I can never be persuaded that the zeolite

has

has been produced by the affiftance of fire. It is true, that fometimes they are found in loofe ftones, and in fuch places where volcanos had formerly raged: it is likewife found in folid rocks that have never been expofed to thefe fires, as at Guftavenberg in Jemtland.

If more forts than one are alfo certainly free from all fufpicion of having been fubject to fufion, how is it poffible, without the cleareft proofs, to fuppofe that the whole genus has been fubject to it? If the Icelandic zeolite has been prepared by fire, we may juftly queftion how it can produce above five quarts in twenty-five of water in diftilling. This may likewife be applied to all the other forts, tho' they generally contain lefs water, and the red fort from Adelfors only one quart in twenty-five. This is evidently the water of cryftallization, in proportion to which each kind fwells more or lefs by the blow-pipe. The Icelandic and Feroe zeolites are moft fubject to this, almoft like borax; the Adelfors zeolite fwells much lefs, and that

from

from Upland, and several other sorts, so little, that it ceases in a moment; and even then produces so small an expansion of space, that it is scarcely perceivable to the eye.

Since therefore all zeolites contain this water of cryftallization, which is neither found nor expected in the productions of fire, it seems to me to be undeniable, that they have been produced in the way of moisture; besides, the zeolites do not consist of a simple particular kind of earth, but of three different sorts which are mixed together, and in a manner the one diffolved by the other, in consequence of which their connection cannot be confidered as an original earth. In all, the greatest part consists of filiceous earth, the next is argillaceous earth, and the least part is calcareous earth. The two last sorts may be diffolved by acids, and then precipitated by alkali volatile caufticum, by which the argillaceous earth, but not the calcareous earth, after being separated from the first by filtrating, may be precipitated by sal sodæ.

In this manner I have found that the zeolites described above, contain 48 in 100 of siliceous earth, 22 of pure argillaceous earth, and from 12 to 14 of calcareous earth. If these numbers are added together, and reckoned with what it contains of water, the produce is something more than 100. This surplus proceeds from the calcareous earth, that enters into the zeolite without fixed air, with which it is afterwards impregnated during the precipitation. Other zeolites contain exactly the same substances, only in different proportions.

Of those which I have hitherto examined, the Jemtland zeolite contains the greatest quantity of calcareous earth, that is to say, 16 parts in 100, and that from Feroe the least, namely, 8 in 100. The red zeolite from Adelfors contains the greatest quantity of siliceous earth, to wit 80 in 100, and the Icelandic the least, to wit, 48 in 100. The zeolite from Feroe contains most argillaceous earth, namely, about 25 in 100, and that from Adelfors the least, or about 9 in 100. When the original composition

fition of any kind of ftone is thus known, it is not difficult to determine its qualities.

The zeolites at firft froth and fwell in the fire, the canfe of which has been already explained.

They afterwards fufe more or lefs perfectly. The fwapparara may be reduced to a clear glafs, and the Upland red zeolite can hardly be brought to give any figns of vitrification on the furface.

It is well known that quarz, pure argillaceous earth and lime, cannot feparately be made to fufe, nor two and two mixed together in many cafes; but when all three are compounded, they are more or lefs inclined to fufion. One part of pure argillaceous earth, with one part of lime, and two and a half to three parts of quarz, afford a mixture, which is eafieft brought to fufe. If the compofition of the zeolites is compared with this mixture, they are found to be fufible in the fame meafure as the proportion of their conftituent parts approaches more or lefs to the above-mentioned compofition.

They are more strongly attacked by sal sodæ than by borax, or fusible urinous salt, because there is in all most siliceous earth, which is best dissolved by the solid alkaline salt in the dry way.

Lastly, several sorts have the quality of yielding jellies, that is to say, they change a proportionable quantity of acid to a semi-transparent congealed mass, which resembles a jelly.

These congelations may in general be produced in different ways; sometime the menstruum by length of time loses its power, when the dissolved part is attacked gradually, though imperfectly dissolved, so that in a manner it remains suspended half dissolved, and after some evaporation at last congeals to a tough coherent substance. This frequently happened in dissolving tin in marine acid, or aqua regia, when the inflammable substance decreases too much, and by that means weakens the connection between the metal and the solvent.

Sometimes a kind of gelatinous congelation is produced by an imperfect precipitation. For instance, when

when the liquor filicum is united with a certain quantity of acid, fo that the filiceous earth is not entirely feparated, but mains fufpended in the liquor. This much refembles a circumftance exhibited by fome zeolites, which I will now more fully explain.

As the red zeolite of Adelfors produces this effect more clearly than any other, it fhall ferve as an inftance of it. After this is feparated and freed as much as poffible from calcareous fpar, three or four tea fpoons full of it muft be thrown into a wine glafs half filled with common aqua-fortis; when after a fhort time the whole folution will be found in the form of a reddifh gelatinous fubftance, that nothing of it runs out if even the glafs is turned. To difcover the caufe of this, I have taken fome of the cleareft jelly, and diffolved it with boiling water in a glafs mortar, and left it to dry on a filtering paper after a perfect filtration, by which means the place which it occupied was incredibly diminifhed. I then tried this fubftance with acids, but it was not at all attacked,

tacked, and did not melt in the strongest fire alone. The fusible urinous salt hardly attacked it; borax dissolved it, though with difficulty ; but sal sodæ dissolved it perfectly with a strong effervesence. In consequence of this the gelatinous substance chiefly consists of siliceous earth expanded in the highest degree. But by what means has this indissoluble substance been introduced into a solvent?

We have before observed, that the Adelfors zeolite contains eighty parts in a hundred of siliceous earth, nine and a half of argillaceous earth, and six and a half of calcareous earth free from fixed air; all which substances are united as close as possible. If therefore the powder is thrown into an acid, and remains there during some time, the argillaceous and calcareous earth are immediately attacked by it; but these are internally connected with the siliceous earth, and consequently take a considerable part of it half dissolved into the spungy and swollen state, which all substances generally exhibit in the moment of precipita-

precipitation. The fame thing happens when a refinous gum is laid into fpirits of wine; part of the gum, together with the refin, is then immediately diffolved by the fpirit of wine on account of its connection, though the firft alone cannot be diffolved by it at all. If a fufficient quantity of water or acid is added before the liquor begins to congeal, no congelation enfues, but the filiceous earth falls in loofe flakes to the bottom, which evidently proves that the folvent, in regard to its quantity and ftrength, muft be confined within certain limits. An addition of fome chalk increafes its tendency to gelatinous congelations, partly becaufe the folution becomes more broken and folid, and partly by means of bubbles of fixed air, which attach themfelves to the fpungy filiceous powder, and make it lighter; whence the zeolite of Adelfors in this cafe feems to have an advantage over every other fort, on account of the lime-fpar naturally mixed with it; the principal part however no doubt depends on the

feveral

several parts which compose it. Some sorts afford only a gelatinous substance after a preparatory calcination; the cause of which most probably is this, that the calcareous earth has not before been enough united with the whole of it. It is well known that lime and quarz, when exposed to the operation of a fire, that has only caused them to bake together, nevertheless afterwards yield a gelatinous substance. Alcaline salt mixed with sand affords a similar demi-concretion, as when we calcine potashes; on which account the clearest solution a long while after precipitates siliceous powder, in the same proportion that the alcaline salt attracts fixed air, with which it preferably unites itself. This generally produces a gelatinous congelation, when the water is saturated with alcaline salt, and also is well charged with siliceous earth.

From the same cause, clay, spathose fluor, and other substances, hard to be dissolved in acids, may be brought to a gelatinous congelation, when they
have

have before by fufion been united with alcaline falt, borax, or calcareous earth: calcareous earth by itfelf never gives a gelatinous fubftance in acids, confequently it can fo much the lefs become a filiceous earth by this method, as has however been thought by fome, who would foon relinquifh their opinion if they would only make experiments themfelves; where there is no flint before, it cannot poffibly be produced by any other acid, but that which is obtained from fpathofe fluor.

But at prefent this is enough of the zeolite, of which I have treated more extenfively, as it is found in great abundance in Iceland, and is fuppofed by fome to be produced in the dry way; but I hope that this matter is at prefent entirely determined, not only by its feparation, but alfo by its production, which happens daily in the water. See N° II.

I have for feveral years paft endeavoured to difcover the number as well as the nature of the original kinds of earth. In the year 1758 Mr. Cronftedt counted nine; if he had lived longer

longer for the benefit of the sciences, he would no doubt have rectified this account. In consequence of my experiments I have discovered the following six sorts:

1. Calcareous earth, which after being saturated by acid of vitriol affords a kind of gypsum.

2. Terra ponderosa, which with acid of vitriol gives a ponderous spar, and in several respects is very different from the calcareous earth.

3. Magnesia, which, together with acid of vitriol, produces the English or Epsom salt.

These three kinds are generally found saturated with fixed air, and they are on that account subject to an effervescence with stronger acids.

4. Argillaceous earth, which, together with the vitriolic acid, produces allum.

The common argillaceous earth is always mixed with siliceous earth, but the sort here meant must be entirely pure.

5. Siliceous earth, which is not attacked by any acid yet known, the
fluor

fluor acid excepted. In the dry way it can be diffolved with a third part of its weight of fixed alkali to a tranfparent lafting glafs, which at firft is affected with a ftrong effervefcence.

6. Gemmeous earth, that is not attacked by any known acid, and clearly diftinguifhes itfelf from the preceding forts, by its being entirely indiffoluble, and being fubject to a weaker effervefcence in the fire with fixed alcali. It is found in all the gems or precious ftones.

I have in vain made ufe of various methods to feparate thefe earths into more fimple principles, and to all appearance others would have no better fuccefs than I have had: if they are really compounds, they are at leaft fimple in regard to the method known among us of feparating fubftances, and do not arife from one another. Whatever has therefore been objected to this opinion from prejudice, cannot fubfift after experiments have been made upon that fubject. We muft not pretend to improve nature according to our notions,

but

but endeavour to diftinguifh all kinds of fubftances, which have fufficient and lafting marks of diftinctions. No certain origin can be made unlefs the feparation and compofition of them, which may be relied on, has been made before. All the different forts of ftone and earth, hitherto known, are compofed of one or more of the fix principles forts before-mentioned, which fhall be proved more at large in another place, as foon as I am able to make fome experiments that require repetition.

Of the Bafalts.

OF all the mountains hitherto known, there are without doubt not any more remarkable than thofe that are compofed of angular pillars. A few years ago only one or two of this kind were known; but new ones are daily difcovered, which is a plain proof how much our attention requires being roufed to prevent

prevent it from flumbering, even on the moft important occafions.

It cannot much be doubted that there has been fome connections between thefe pillars, and the effects of a fubterraneous fire, as they are found in places where the figns of fire are yet vifible; and as they are even found mixed with lava, tophus, and other fubftances produced by fire.

The caufe of the regular form of thefe pillars is a problem which we have hitherto been unable to folve fatisfactorily. This difficulty has appeared fo infurmountable to fome, that they have thought it impoffible to be the effects of Nature, and have confidered them as works made by human hands: this idea betrays the utmoft ignorance in regard to the true nature of thefe mountains of pillars, and does not even deferve a refutation.

As far as we know, Nature makes ufe of three methods to produce regular forms in the mineral kingdom; namely, that of cryftallization or precipitation: 2dly, the crufting or fettling of the external furface of a liquid

liquid mass whilst it is cooling: and 3dly, the bursting of a moist substance whilst it is drying.

The first method is the most common, but to all appearance Nature has not made use of this in the present case. Crystals are seldom or never found in any considerable quantity running in the same direction, but either inclining from one another, or what is still more common, placed towards one another in several sloping directions. They are also generally separated a little from one another, when they are regular; the nature of the thing likewise requires this, because the several particles, of which the crystals are composed, must have the liberty of following that power which affects their regular disposition.

The basalt columns, on the contrary, whose height are frequently from thirty to forty feet, are placed parallel to one another in considerable numbers, and so close together that the point of a knife can hardly be introduced between them. Besides, in most places, each pillar is divided into several parts

parts or joints, which seem to be placed upon one another; and indeed it is not uncommon for cryſtals to be formed above one another in different layers, when the ſolvent has been viſibly diminiſhed at different times; but then the upper cryſtals never fit ſo exactly upon the lower ones as to produce connected priſms of the ſame length and depth as all the ſtrata taken together, but each ſtratum ſeparately forms its own cryſtals.

How then can the Giant's Cauſeway in the county of Antrim, Fingal's Cave at Staffa, and all other aſſemblages of pillars of the ſame kind, be conſidered as cryſtallizations? Precipitation, both in the wet and dry manner, requires that the particles ſhould be free enough to fix themſelves in a certain order; and as this is not practicable in a large melted maſs, no cryſtallizations appear in it, except on its ſurface, or in its cavities.

Add to this, that the baſalts in a freſh fracture, do not ſhew a plain ſmooth ſurface under the microſcope, but appear ſometimes like grains of different magnitude, and at other times

times resemble fine rays running in different directions, which does not correspond with the internal structure of the cryſtals, which I have endeavoured to examine in another place.

From what I have hitherto mentioned, the opinion that the baſalts have been produced by cryſtallization, becomes at leaſt leſs probable, whether we admit the wet or dry method. But I muſt not omit that the ſpars exhibit a kind of cryſtallization, which at firſt ſight reſembles a heap of baſalts, but upon a cloſer examination a very great difference is obſerved. The form of the ſpar is every where alike, but the baſalts differ from one another in point of ſize and number of ſides; the former when broken conſiſts of many ſmall unequal cubes, but the baſalt does not ſeparate in regular parts, &c. &c.

Nature's ſecond method to produce regular forms is that of cruſting the outer ſurface of a melted maſs. By a ſudden refrigeration Nature, to effect this purpoſe, makes uſe of polyedrous and irregular forms.

forms. If we suppose a considerable bed, which is become fluid by fire, and spread over a plain, it evidently appears that the surface must first of all lose the degree of heat requisite for melting, and begin to congeal; but the cold requisite for this purpose likewise contracts the uppermost congealed stratum into a narrower space, and consequently causes it to separate from the remaining liquid mass, as the side exposed to the air is already too stiff to give way. In this manner a stratum is produced running in a parallel direction with the whole mass, others still are produced by the same cause, in proportion as the refrigeration penetrates deeper.

Hence we may, in my opinion, very plainly see how a bed may be divided into strata. In the same manner the refrigeration advances on the sides, which consequently divides the strata into polyedrous pieces of pillars, which can hardly ever be exactly square, as the strongest refrigeration into the inner parts of the mass advances almost in a diagonal line from the corners. If we add to this, that a large mafs cannot be equal throughout its compofition, nor every where liquid in the fame degree, it will be eafy to difcover the caufe of feveral irregularities. If the depth of the bed is very confiderable, in proportion to its breadth, prifmatic pillars, without crofs-divifions, are produced, at leaft lengthways from the uppermoft furface downwards.

The third way is perfectly fimilar to the preceding in refpect to the effect, but is different from it by the mafs being foaked with water, and by the burfting of it afunder, being the effect of the contraction whilft it is drying. If we fuppofe fuch a bed to be fpread over a level fpace, the drying advances in the fame manner as the refrigeration in the former cafe.

This feparation into ftrata properly happens when a confiderable quantity of clay enters into the whole compofition, becaufe the clay decreafes more than any other kind of earth in drying.

We

We muft now examine which of thefe two ways may beft ferve to explain the manner in which the habits are produced, for it is hardly poffible that they fhould have been formed by cryftallization.

However well founded the opinion may appear of deducing them from a melted fubftance, feveral very confiderable objections however may be raifed againft it, which I fhall not forget to mention. It feems therefore more credible to me, that they have been produced out of their fubftance whilft it was yet foft, or at leaft not too hard to be foftened by exhalations. If we therefore fuppofe that a bed is fpread over a place where a volcano begins to work, it is evident that a great quantity of the water, always prefent on thefe occafions, is driven upwards in exhalations or vapours; thefe it is well known poffefs a penetrating foftening power, by means of which they alfo produce their firft effect; but when they are increafed to a fufficient quantity, they force this tough moift fubftance up-

upwards, which then gradually falls, and during this time burfts in the manner defcribed above.

My reafons for this opinion are thefe; firft, we do not find the internal grain of the bafalts melted or vitrified, which however foon happens by fufion, and for which purpofe only a very fmall degree of fire is requifite. It confequently is very hard to explain how this fubftance could have been fo fluid, that no traces of bubbles appear in it (at leaft I have not been able to difcover any after the niceft examination into the Scotch and Icelandic bafalts) and yet when broken appear dull and uneven. I know very well that lava is feldom vitrified within; but the great number of bubbles and pores which are found in the whole mafs, are more than fufficient proofs that it has not been perfectly melted to its fmalleft parts, but has only been brought to be near fluid.

Secondly, the bafalts fo much refemble the finer trapp, both in refpect to their grain and original compofition, sition, that they can hardly be distinguished in small fragments, as will be more plainly proved in the comparison which I will make hereafter. See N° 24.

But the trapp in all probability has never been melted, at least not in those parts where I have had opportunities of examining it.

Almost in all the West Gothic stratified mountains, the uppermost stratum is trapp; and it must be well observed that it always lies upon black allum slate. Is it therefore credible that this substance, which in many places extend above hundred yards, can have been perfectly melted, without causing the slate lying beneath it to lose some part of its blackness, even in those places where they touch one another, as this effect may be produced in a small culinary fire?

There is besides a finer kind of trapp, which is generally found in veins or loads, and frequently in very antient mountains, where not' the least traces of subterraneous fire are to be seen.

The basalt mountains seem to be very ancient, at least I do not know that the age of any one is ascertained. Should they then be so old, that the substance of the trapp was not yet perfectly hardened, when were they produced? Besides, we frequently find to this day clayey substances at a great depth, which are so soft that they may be scraped by the nail, but afterwards become very hard when exposed to the air.

There have without doubt been many eruptions of fire on the isle of Staffa, as the situation of the pillars and their being removed out of their places evidently prove.

You, Sir, have likewise brought a very clear proof of this from thence, which is a piece of basalt, that on the the exteriorly is full of hollows, and in a manner burnt.

A hard substance, when exposed to a degree of heat insufficient to melt the whole piece, may however be attacked by it in some parts of the surface most liable to become fluid.

The

The mixture of a large mafs is feldom every where fo uniform, that fome parts fhould not be more liable to melt than others.

Crooked pillars may be produced as well by the drying as the refrigeration of a liquid mafs; for this purpofe it is only neceffary that the furface fhould be bent, as the ftratum always runs in a parallel direction with it.

From what I have hitherto faid you will perceive it is my opinion, that the bafalts have been produced by the affiftance of a fubterraneous fire, but that it is not yet determined whether they have been rent afunder after the fufion, or by drying: this laft however appears more credible to me on account of the reafons I have mentioned. For to fpeak ftrictly, the fubftances inclofed in the bafalts, though they fhould even be volcanic, do not yet with certainty prove a preceding fufion, as a fubftance foftened by water may be as proper for it as one fufed by fire. I am however very far from being inclined to maintain my opinion any farther than it agrees with certain experiments and experience.

Truth will fooner or later be difcovered; and I know nothing more derogatory to the honour of a natural hiftorian, than having wilfully obftructed its paffage.

I will now give a more full defcription of the bafalts and different kinds of trapp which you have brought from Staffa and Iceland.

24. Bafalt from Staffa.—The piece prefented to me is a prifmatic hexagonal fragment, three fides of which are almoft of equal dimenfions, and are connected with one another; two others are larger, and are feparated from one another by the fixth and fmalleft; it is a little concave at the top, and convex at the bottom.

Trapp is generally found in fquare irregular cubes, whence it has moft probably obtained its denomination, on account of fome fimilarity with ftones made ufe of for ftair-cafes.

It

It is alfo found in prifmatic triangular forms, though rarely, as alfo in the form of immenfe pillars. Of this kind are thofe called Traeleftenar, oppofite Bragnum, at the foot of the Hanneberg, which have feparated themfelves from the remaining part of the bed; and in 1759, when I firft faw them, formed an angle of about eight degrees with the plumb-line.

The bafalt from Staffa, when newly broken, is of a blackifh grey, fhining, and fmall-fcaled; and I have difcovered with the microfcope fome fmall white particles fprinkled up and down.

The fineft trapp is perfectly fimilar when broken, only of a lighter colour, which proceeds from the greater quantity of white particles.

The furface decays to a grey-yellow loofe cruft, which lofes itfelf in the more folid mafs.

The fine trapp decays in the fame manner.

The bafalt when ftruck with the fteel hardly gives fire, though a fpark may

may now and then be obtained with difficulty.

This same circumstance may be observed of the trapp.

Its specific weight is about 3000, and that of the trapp about 2990.

It becomes very beautiful by cutting, polishing, and grinding.

Likewise the more fine kind of trapp.

It yields an ash-coloured powder.

The trapp yields rather a powder of a more light colour.

It soon melts to black glassy flags.

The trapp likewise.

The basalt is attacked by sal sodæ with an effervescence which soon ceases, and though some separation ensues, the greater part however remains undissolved. Borax perfectly solves it without effervescence, and gives a clear iron-coloured glass. It is solved with great difficulty by fusible urinous salt, and whilst cooling becomes of a whitish grey, and not transparent.

The same effects are produced by these acids upon the trapp.

One

One hundred parts of bafalt very finely powdered, and feveral times digefted with frefh aqua regia, and then well wafhed and dried, leave fixty-eight parts undiffolved.

The remainder of this fhews a little efferveſcence before it unites with the fal fodæ, and diffolves very little. It is diffolved with eafe by borax, and with difficulty by fufible urinous falt. It feems therefore to be a mixture of filiceous and gemmeous earth.

The folution gives by precipitation with lixivium fanguinis as much Pruffian blue as is equal to twenty-fix parts in 100 of iron; though the bafalt, by being tried in the ufual manner in the crucible, does not yield above ten in 100. This proves that lixivium fanguinis affords the moft exact method of affaying iron ore.

When at laft the folution is precipitated with cauftic volatile alkali, after the iron has been feparated by lixivium fanguinis, faturated with acid, pure argillaceous earth is obtained.

Some-

Sometimes a little calcareous earth appears after a preceding precipitation; when diffolved fal fodæ is added; but fometimes not the fmalleft traces of it can be difcovered, even with the acid of fugar, which is however the fafeft method hitherto known of difcovering it. The calcareous earth feems therefore to be accidental. This is however very certain, that the interftices between the pillars are fometimes found filled up with calcareous fpar.

The trapp is exactly of the fame nature, and contains nearly the fame allay, fo that the experiments differ only one or a half part in one hundred. The moft confiderable difference confifts in the calcareous earth appearing here more vifibly, fo that generally a flight effervefcence is obferved when an acid is poured on the powder.

25. Bafalt from Hvitara, near Skalholt, in Iceland.—The piece in my poffeffion is too fmall to difcover its form; only a part of the outfide can be diftinguifhed. When frefh broken it

it refembles the bafalt from Staffa, though fomething may be obferved in it which is very feldom difcovered in the laft. Thefe are fmall round cavities, not larger than pins heads, thinly fcattered in fome places, as likewife on the outfide. All thefe cavities are filled up with a white, green, or brown powder.

May not thefe perhaps have been fome particles of a fubftance, which eafily diffolving was become liquid, though the whole mafs had not a fufficient degree of heat to melt it?

But whence can thefe cavities be filled with this powder? In the midft of fo folid a mafs, no decay feems to be poffible.

The fubftance of the bafalt itfelf produces a little effervefcence with fal fodæ, and feparates without being vifibly diffolved. It diffolves in borax, as likewife in fufible urinous falt, although with more difficulty. By the common method of proving it in the crucible it yields ten parts in one hundred of iron. The fame circumftances may be be obferved in trying the powder that fills up the cavities; it only feems to melt a little eafier than the folid fubftance furrounding it.

26. The bafalt from Langarnas perfectly refembles coarfe trapp, though it has more white particles, and fometimes cryftallizations as large as a cherry-ftone; the dark-grey and white parts prove to be entirely of the fame nature by the blow-pipe, becomes fluid by itfelf, and produces a fudden effervefcence with fal fodæ, but without being quite diffolved by it: it is exactly as the preceding fort.

27. Black, folid gloffy trapp, knotty within, and refembling wood in its internal ftructure, being full of filaments. Many pieces are grown to a cruft of pumice on one fide or another, though their edges are quite frefh and fmooth; whence we may conclude, that they themfelves have not been melted, but have either been thrown into the lava, which was already burnt out, or that the lava has flowed over them: fome part of it however

feems

seems to have been more attacked by the fire.

The manner in which the fire and acids operate upon this trapp, is exactly the same as with the preceding basalt. There are likewise some grains scattered in it resembling quarz, which are not solved by sal sodæ, nor does it cause any effervesence; borax and fusible urinous salt entirely dissolves them, though slowly.

28. A compact dark-brown trapp from Vido, the surface of which is glassy and uneven, as if it had been made fluid by fire. It must also be observed, that crystallizations of fresh pyrites are frequently found in these glassy rough pieces. The glassy substance easily becomes fluid with some ebullition, almost like shirl; besides, it exhibits the same circumstances with acids as the preceding.

You will see, Sir, by this long letter, that in the eruptions in Iceland argillaceous and siliceous substances have been principally concerned, as has been the case in other parts. I know very well that Mr. Beaumé maintains, that filex might be made to afford allum with acid of vitriol after it has been diffolved in liquor filicum with fal fodæ. But when the fufions are made in veffels which contain no argillaceous earth, no allum can be obtained with acid of vitriol, which however may be obtained when the vegetable alkali is kept fluid during a confiderable time in a common crucible, becaufe the alkali diffolves fome part of the veffel itfelf. Pure filiceous earth is intirely indiffoluble by itfelf in acid of vitriol, let it be treated in any manner whatfover.

Let this account of thefe dreadful devaftations be fufficient.

Homo naturæ minifter et interpres, tantum facit et intelligit, quantum de naturæ ordine, re vel mente obfervaverit, nec amplius fcit aut poteft. *Baco.*

F.I N I S.

www.ingramcontent.com/pod-product-compliance
Lightning Source LLC
Chambersburg PA
CBHW051733300426
44115CB00007B/542